Getting to Church

Getting to Church

Exploring Narratives
of Gender and Joining

SALLY K. GALLAGHER

OXFORD
UNIVERSITY PRESS

OXFORD
UNIVERSITY PRESS

Oxford University Press is a department of the University of Oxford. It furthers
the University's objective of excellence in research, scholarship, and education
by publishing worldwide. Oxford is a registered trade mark of Oxford University
Press in the UK and certain other countries.

Published in the United States of America by Oxford University Press
198 Madison Avenue, New York, NY 10016, United States of America.

© Oxford University Press 2017

CIP data is on file at the Library of Congress
ISBN 978–0–19–023968–8 (pbk)
ISBN 978–0–19–023967–1 (hbk)

1 3 5 7 9 8 6 4 2

Paperback printed by WebCom, Inc., Canada
Hardback printed by Bridgeport National Bindery, Inc., United States of America

For Ed

Contents

Acknowledgments

THIS RESEARCH WAS supported by a Constant H. Jacquet Research Award from the Religious Research Association in 2002 and a grant from The Louisville Institute for the Study of American Religion in 2003–2004. Those, along with a URISC (Undergraduate Research, Innovation, Scholarship and Creativity) award (2005) and faculty development funds (2006–2008, and 2010) from Oregon State University, helped support a terrific set of students who were collaborators on different phases of this project. Sara Anable, Emily Ficker, Sabrina Wood, Brenda Chung, Megan Vandecoevering, Chelsea Newton, Meghan Neilson, Hilary Davidson, and Becky Rubenstrunk provided careful and resourceful interviewing, transcribing, coding, library research, and editing, in addition to hours of insightful conversation about the changing contours of religious faith and practice in the United States. Special thanks also to my colleague and friend, Mark Edwards, and to Ed Gallagher, Sabrina Alexander, Wendy Rudeen, Judy Greene, and Joan Seaman, who read chapters in draft form and helped me clarify and refine many of my ideas. Finally, I would like to extend my deep appreciation to the clergy, staff, members, and attenders who participated in this study for their good humor, generosity with their time, and insights on the meaning and practice of faith.

Getting to Church

I

Why Won't Religion Just Go Away?

WHY DO PEOPLE go to church? I have wondered about this question for many years. Growing up in the 1960s, in the days when little girls at the Presbyterian church wore white gloves and patent leather shoes that clicked on the linoleum in the hallway of the Sunday School wing, I wondered why I had to go to church. Despite the lovely clicking sound the shoes made, they were somewhat stiff, and I was expected to sit quietly, not wiggle, keep my skirt down, and listen to the story. It was fine for an hour, but shedding church clothes for play clothes held as great an attraction as the majesty of the organ and the rich, round sounds of the congregational singing. I wondered about it, too, as older friends faced the draft for the Vietnam War and considered whether or not their faith obligated them to go or not go to war. I debated with friends as the church itself debated whether and in what capacities women might lead the institution of which they were the majority of members. Most recently, as a professor teaching in a state reputed for being one of the "most unchurched" in the country, I have wondered about how to talk about religion and religious experience to students who have no experiences or vocabulary of their own, while not losing the other half of the class who identify themselves as evangelicals or Mormons, Catholics, Buddhists, or Baptists.

Why *do* people go to church? Why won't religion just go away? What are women's and men's connections and commitments to this institution? Surely people have other things to do—pressing responsibilities, sporting events, gardening, and child care, or simply sleeping longer—that are more important than spending an hour or three on the weekend at religious services. Surely health clubs and service clubs, cultural events, and hiking with the dog should be adequate to meet the social, personal, and contemplative needs people feel. Surely science can provide a more compelling and rational narrative around ultimate questions of why we are here, what our place in the cosmos is, and what it means to be human.

Or can they? Despite all the good reasons to expect otherwise, Americans are remarkably religious. The majority not only believe in God but identify themselves with congregations within one of the historic denominations and Judeo-Christian traditions that have long histories on the continent.[1] Affiliation with other traditions is also growing—whether American-born iterations of Christianity such as the Latter Day Saints, one of any number of entrepreneurial new religious movements, or one of the more ancient faiths now growing in America, such as Buddhism, Hinduism, or Islam[2]. Although there is some debate about the degree to which formal religious affiliation reflects either personal religious commitment or a connection to the specific history, beliefs, or requirements of one's faith, there remains ample evidence that the United States is pervasively religious across a diffuse spectrum of seekers, nominal seekers, irregular attenders, spiritual-but-not-religious individuals, committed believers, self-styled theologians, and institution builders.

Gender and the Formation of Religious Identity

Given the pervasiveness of religion in American life, it seems reasonable to ask what it is that men and women find compelling and attractive about their faith. What is it about specific traditions that draw new members? Is religious identity simply a residual of early socialization by parents, grandparents, or religious institutions that survives the process of adolescence?[3] Or is a sense of religious identity among adults part of a longer term process through which recent generations increasingly feel alienated from institutions of all sorts, and so think of religion as an individual private matter—if they remain religiously connected at all?[4] What are the processes by which women and men consider, approach, affiliate, and at times disaffiliate themselves from a particular congregation? Are these fundamentally different processes for women and men and, if so, why? These are the questions I seek to address in this book. It is my contention that if we look carefully at the process of religious affiliation and listen to the stories of women and men who have sought out communities of faith, we will learn much more about how religion works and why it matters. We will learn, as well, about the functioning of institutions whose mission is to meet men's and women's spiritual needs as well as provide a range of practical, intellectual, and aesthetic programs to their congregations.

Many scholars make the case that religious affiliation and participation are salient components of adult identity and well-being.[5] Within particular congregational cultures, women and men find opportunity to express and experience a sense of wholeness and religious moral vision or "religious goods" through the beliefs, practices, and buildings in which they worship.[6] Congregations not only provide a context for experiencing and recreating distinctive strands of religious tradition, but they are also sites for affirming and re-forming a sense of self with regard to culture and social class. Although the associations among religion, social class, and ethnicity are more complicated than is sometimes assumed,[7] the practices and theologies within religious traditions explicitly and implicitly reflect and reinforce a sense of class and culture simply because most congregations are relatively homogeneous in terms of membership.[8]

Congregations are also settings within which cultural ideals regarding gender are taught, enacted, struggled with, and recreated. So to understand adult experiences of faith, we must assess men's and women's distinctive experiences within congregations, including the particular ideas, programs, and perspectives that draw them toward affiliation, the ways and degree to which they become integrated into congregational life, and the articulation of these religiously gendered narratives with broader cultural ideals. We know, for example, quite a bit about the history and policies of religious institutions toward women being in positions of leadership.[9] Early in the United States' history, for example, theological emphases within revivalist Protestantism intersected with an emerging set of ideals around manhood and womanhood in the new Republic. During those decades known as the First Great Awakening, evangelical Calvinists in Congregationalist, Presbyterian, and Baptist communities throughout New England and the mid-Atlantic states preached a gospel of personal conversion in which women and men were equally called to repent and submit themselves to Christ. These evangelists also taught a model of wifely submission within marriage that paralleled themes of idealized womanhood and independent manhood.[10] Given the current pairing of conservative Protestantism, conservative politics, and conservative family values, it would be easy to read similar gender conservatism back into this earlier era. Yet analyses of personal correspondence and diaries from the time suggest that the experience of revival was quite different for women and men—and in both cases cut against the grain of prevailing gender ideals. Rather than echoing notions of womanly submission and masculine rationality and leadership, men wrote of their profound sense of being called to submit themselves to God and become more deeply connected to a community of faith. Women's revival narratives emphasized a powerful individual experience of grace and feeling challenged to follow Christ even at the risk of rejection by unsympathetic family and friends.[11]

Again in the eighteenth and early nineteenth centuries, New England experienced a second wave of revivalism in which gendered metaphors were again used to characterize the ideals of a Christian life. At a time when the theological backdrop was shifting from Calvinism toward a theology emphasizing free will, making a commitment of faith began to be described not as joining the "bride of Christ" (i.e., the church) but as a challenge to become a "soldier" in Christ's army. In the process, earlier emphases on the voluntary subordination of women to men, and of both to God, were replaced by the language of a more "muscular Christianity" in which new believers were urged to "grow up into the fullness and stature of manhood."[12]

Although the revivals of the eighteenth and nineteenth centuries temporarily increased men's church attendance, women had begun to outnumber men in US congregations as early as the mid-seventeenth century. Women continue to outnumber men in most US congregations, attend church more frequently, and report higher rates of religious commitment overall compared to men.[13] Women are also reported to be more religiously involved than men across the life course, to see themselves as more responsible for their children's religious upbringing, to be more involved in volunteering within religious organizations, and to describe church as a significant social outlet.[14] Women are described as joining congregations for the social network opportunities as well as a sense of being part of a community in which eternal security is assured, while men are described as being more willing to tolerate uncertainty about their salvation and have ample opportunities to network through other institutional affiliations and their employment. Some writers argue these differences are due to differences in biology and socialization that predispose women to be more risk averse than men.[15]

The problem with generalizing about gender differences in any religion or any other domain is that it often exaggerates the degree of difference and obscures the range of experience and beliefs among women and men.[16] For example, women's greater religiousness appears more among Christians than other religions, and it varies among Christians depending on the measure.[17] Even within American Protestantism, there is enormous variation in the degree to which men are expected to take responsibility for religious practices within families,[18] as well as for congregational leadership. Yet while a growing literature on personal or lived religion[19] has done much to inform our understanding of how religion shapes family life for women and men as parents and partners, we continue to know relatively little about how gender shapes the development of specific adult religious identities, or what women and men find good about particular types of worship, ministry, or programs.

Buildings and Believers

Religious identity also involves bodies—both the bodies of worshipers and the physical spaces in which people are drawn to worship. Yet the physicality of ordinary religious life and how that contributes to the development of religious identity and affiliation is something that has received very little attention among scholars. Much, of course, has been written about the meaning and motivations for religious affiliation. The religious markets paradigm posits personal connections, preserving and extending one's social capital, and appropriate programs and services, as explanations for if and where people worship.[20] Alternately, the religious subcultures approach[21] argues that religious affiliation is motivated by a drive for meaning and identity, and that religions thrive when they provide a distinctive and salient sense of belonging and connection. Neither of these perspectives does much analytical work at the level of religious experience as embodied in the ritual and practice of believers or the buildings in which they worship. In practice, post-Reformation Christianity has viewed many of the more physical dimensions of worship with suspicion and gradually, or with violent abruptness, stripped these away from both personal and corporate worship. No smells, bells, kneeling, statues, icons, candles, or even stained glass in some congregations, to distract from the preaching of the Word of God. Yet as persons, we breathe, feel, smell, tire, hear, see, and taste our way through the world. In a response to the sparseness of some iterations of Protestant worship, the past decade has seen a revitalization of interest in a host of physical dimensions of worship, ranging from dance and gardening among Unitarians, African Episcopalians or Jewish feminists,[22] to the eclectic use of icons, candles, incense, and fixed

hours of prayer among the avant garde of conservative Protestantism identified as the "emerging church,"[23] to the persistent salience of the material
"stuff" of religion in personal practices as well as building a sense of collective religious identity.[24]

Church buildings embody in their design the changing ideals of mission, culture, and purpose that distinguish various strands of tradition.[25]
The meanings and uses of religious space have primarily been explored
through analyses of church architecture. A substantial body of literature
argues that church buildings should and do reflect particular sets of theological doctrines.[26] Religious studies scholar Jeanne Kilde[27] broadens
that discussion by linking changes in architectural design with changing demographics, religious constituencies, and the subcultural religious
identity and mission of US evangelicalism. In her analysis, she argues
that the synthesis of evangelical revivalism and middle-class culture in
the nineteenth-century United States was the impetus behind the emer-
gence of the "theatre church"—churches characterized by a raised stage,
prominent music, open sight lines, and amphitheater seating. Whether
the megachurches of the late twentieth century, or the coffee house or
pub meeting of emerging postevangelical churches in the early twenty-
first century, the race, social class, generation, and theology of congregations continue to be embodied in the spaces in which people meet to
worship.

Seeking, Switching, Converting, and Belonging

What is it then that draws women and men into particular types of churches?
What is it about congregations and their theological narratives that create
a sense of belonging, contemplation, service, and spiritual well-being that
is not available elsewhere? Theories of religious growth and decline posit
multiple and somewhat contradictory theses about why people become
affiliated with particular traditions. Foundational sociologists from Weber
to Durkheim, DuBois, and Marx argued that religion played a significant
historic role in shaping culture and community, but it was destined to
fade in the face of the alternative modes of personal connection and pro-
duction associated with modern capitalism. Yet fifty years after sociologist Peter Berger[28] argued that modernity, science, and pluralism would
gradually erode the plausibility of religious absolutes, the United States
remains remarkably religious—whether measured in terms of growth of
conservative denominations or new religious movements. Moreover, the

privatization of religion anticipated in classic works of sociological cultural commentary, such as Robert Bellah's *Habits of the Heart*[29] or Wade Clark Roof's depiction of the baby boomers in *A Generation of Seekers*,[30] seems to be countered by the reemergence of conservative Protestantism as a social and political movement.[31] Increasing membership and consistent attendance in conservative churches,[32] a shift toward Roman Catholic and Orthodox traditions among former evangelicals,[33] and an increasing interest in non-Western and new religious movements[34] raise additional questions about the idea of religious privatization and decline.

From the perspective of rational choice theory, religions thrive when there is diversity among religious "providers," which compete for prospective members across a relatively stable level of demand.[35] In this model, religious consumers choose their affiliation based on their preferences for a particular religious aesthetic as well as their assessment of the costs and benefits of shifting from one social network to another should they affiliate elsewhere. Theories of religious subcultural strength,[36] on the other hand, argue that differences in growth and vitality across traditions are the product of subcultural boundaries between believers and "the world" that are clear enough to facilitate the formation of a distinctive religious identity, yet flexible enough to not alienate believers from the broader culture and community. From this perspective, religious subcultures attract and retain members because they offer a moral narrative that is religious enough to resonate with transcendent meaning and values, while not being overly demanding or rigorous.

Early work on changes in religious identity or affiliation focused on conversion as a process in which individuals move through a series of stages: feeling a tension or need for change; turning to religion as a viable mode for bringing about that change; becoming a seeker; some sort of turning point; building personal connections with people inside the new faith and weakening of connections to others; and intensive interaction.[37] These early studies concluded that the details of the conversion process may vary, but that relationships were consistently more important than mystical experiences in re-forming religious identity.

Given that just under half of Americans change religious affiliations at least once in their lifetimes,[38] and that most move within, rather than across, traditions, the majority of scholars now argue that the concept of "switching" or "reaffiliation" is more descriptive of the process of changing religious identity rather than the notion of conversion.[39] Switching is often related to marriage[40] or divorce[41], and it varies with age[42] and gender[43]—with younger adults and men being more likely to switch than are older adults and women. Although switching was associated with upward social mobility in the mid-twentieth century,[44] that association no longer appears to be the case.[45] Scholars also continue to debate the degree to which switching or reaffiliation involves a break from the past (an ideal that is consistent with conservative Protestant theology around fallen human nature and the need to move from being dead in sin to a new life in Christ through the experience of being born again[46]) or, within some traditions at lease, may be understood as a continuation and refining of one's core religious self.[47]

Believing, Belonging, and Becoming in Three Congregations

In this volume, I seek to bring together perspectives from analyses of congregational culture, theories of religious markets, and religious sub-cultural strength to assess gender differences in the experience of becoming affiliated with a particular church. Most broadly, I will make the case that religion matters and that it matters differently (not quantitatively, but qualitatively) in shaping the experience of women and men as they assess the people, programs, and messages offered within three diverse congregations. As we will see, congregations provide moral narratives, experiences, practices, and relationships that broaden the gender possibilities for women and men—opening areas of experience and framing relationships in ways that allow an expanded and more flexible gendered sense of self. Denomination, or theological tradition, also matters in ways that go beyond the parameters of rational choice notions of shifting religious markets and personal networks. Despite rhetoric suggesting that denominational specifics are fading or have faded away[48], men and women seek and see a varied range of religious values and ideals in the congregations to which they attach themselves, not simply as a means to extend personal relationships and appreciate particular styles of religious programs, but as a way to embed themselves in religious moral narratives that are deeply and personally formative.

To assess these questions, I draw on data that avoid some of the methodological limitations of recent studies by tracing men's and women's movement toward membership in congregations representative of the breadth of Christian tradition—Orthodox, conservative Protestant, and mainline Protestant traditions. By comparing movement into (and away from) both "high"- and "low"-cost traditions, we can assess the degree to which personal contacts and/or doctrinal and subcultural distinctives work differently for women and men, across different types of religious traditions. My central theoretical task is to place gender at the center of a comparison of the relative merits of current theories of religion as explanations for the process through which people consider, evaluate, join, or reject particular religious communities. To what extent do religious traditions attract men and women from a specific "market niche" who become drawn to a community through social ties and "rational" benefits?[49] And/ or to what extent are the distinctive subcultural substance and sense of religious identity and truth central to men and women becoming involved in a particular religious community?[50]

Between 2002 and 2009, I and a team of research assistants employed a number of different data collection methods in an effort to better understand congregational culture and the sets of ideals that draw women and men toward affiliation (for details, see the Appendix). Data were collected in three different faith communities: mainline Protestant (First Presbyterian Church), conservative Protestant (Valley Baptist Church), and Eastern Orthodox (St. Andrews Orthodox Church). These congregations represent diverse perspectives on sacraments, ritual, and practice, and are communities that stand in "high tension" and "low tension" with broader American culture. Of the three, Orthodoxy remains the least-studied tradition within the United States. Generally associated with specific immigrant communities, Orthodoxy has begun to attract members from other traditions and is growing not only through the addition of children of Orthodox parents, but through people transitioning from other Christian traditions, or none, as well.[51] Mainline and conservative Protestantism, on the other hand, are linked to much older immigrant communities in America—largely northern European—and remain less culturally and ethnically distinct from the Anglo-Protestant roots of American culture as a whole.[52] The specific congregations selected were located in the Pacific Northwest, allowing us to minimize some of the local, economic, and social variation that would add more layers of complexity to the analysis without significantly contributing to the project's central concerns. They also allowed us to assess concepts of conversion, switching, reaffiliation, and affiliation within traditions that offer different models of human nature, the church, salvation, and religious subcultural boundaries. We returned to the congregations again in 2016 to speak with clergy and staff about recent changes and to assess continuity in membership as well as overall membership growth or decline since the beginning of our research.

Outline of the Analysis

In the analysis that follows we take up these questions around congregational culture, the gendered narratives of those who are considering joining, core beliefs and experiences within types of congregations, and how people grow into deeper affiliation or end up moving away. In Chapter 2, we address the question of how local congregations embody and reflect particular sets of religious goods—both a distinctive sense of history, community, and theology—and how these are articulated through their buildings and practices. Chapter 3 explores how people become members at each of these congregations. We examine the process through which prospective members join, as well as clergy ideas around the appropriate content, format, and goals of the "new member" process. Chapter 4 shifts the focus and explores gender differences in the beliefs, practices, and ideas of community that draw women and men toward belonging. Chapter 5 moves on to examine the range of ideas members hold around the notion of spiritual growth—both how it is described by new and longer term members, and how women and men envision and experience the process of growth differently across congregations. Chapter 6 assesses gender differences in giving back—whether financially or as volunteers within these congregations' programs of service and outreach. In this chapter we also assess the ways in which women and men see their participation in these congregations shaping and reinforcing ideas about broader political and social involvement. Chapter 7 extends this focus to assess how membership reshapes a sense of self, relationships with family and friends, and, for some, experiences of change that eventually lead them to no longer attend. Chapter 8 draws these themes together by reflecting on gender, congregational culture, and the persistence of religion in the contemporary United States.

2

Buildings

A VISITOR AT each of these churches encounters dramatically different organizational, social, and visual experiences. From the architecture and the seating, to the format of worship, to the music and lighting, pastors' visions of a congregation—and specific things members appreciate about their congregation—embody and reflect distinctive streams of theological tradition and contemporary congregational culture.

Distinctive Histories and Mission
The Setting at First Presbyterian Church

The congregation of First Presbyterian Church meets in an historic stone building (affectionately called "the rock pile") in the center of the town's upper-middle-class historic district. The domed and semicircular sanctuary is lined with deep mahogany paneling. Enormous stained glass windows depicting Jesus' encounter with the rich man, or an angel and the women at an empty tomb, surround a sweep of wooden pews facing a raised choir section, grand piano, and massive pipe organ. Light filters into this quiet space, which reflects a sense of dignity, richness, and enduring history.

That history took an unexpected and uninvited turn in the mid-1980s, when membership decline caused the denomination to merge First Presbyterian Church with another historic Presbyterian church located only a block away. At the time, the congregational cultures were as different as the buildings in which they met. The more conservative and mostly working-class congregation met in a simple, white, wooden structure. The other, described as the "country club" church whose members were more theologically liberal, met in its castle-like sanctuary with a mid-twentieth-century wing of classrooms to the side. The merger caused some dissension among members of the smaller congregation whose building was eventually sold to an even smaller fundamentalist group. Yet, eventually, the success of the merged congregations in attracting young families, coupled with the slow passing of the older generations in both churches, has diminished the sense that the church houses two congregations meeting somewhat unhappily under the same roof.

Beginning in the late 1970s, First Presbyterian Church began experiencing the same graying of its membership that has characterized many other mainline congregations. In 1995, the church called a new husband-and-wife team as copastors and began to attract new, younger members with an active Sunday School, youth group, and adult education programs. Typical attendance now ranges from 150 to 250. The congregation includes a mix of middle- and upper-income families, older people and younger families, nearly all with ethnic roots that trace back to historic centers of Presbyterianism in Scotland, Ireland, Switzerland, and other nations in Northern Europe. On the whole, the congregation is well educated, with the preaching emphasizing the value of an intellectually respectable faith that is compassionate, generous, and tolerant of diverse interpretations and experiences. Printed sermons, bulletins, newsletters, and Sunday School materials advocate a healthy lifestyle, good stewardship, service opportunities, and events for elderly and youth, including volunteering for local Habitat for Humanity projects, food pantry, on-site preschool, and educational and social programs. Minimally focused on maintaining a distinctive Presbyterian identity, this particular congregation strives to balance long-standing programs and ministries with the needs of a congregation whose religious identity ranges from nominally religious civic leaders to committed social gospel, theological liberals, and to more theologically (and often socially conservative) evangelical Presbyterians.

A Sanctuary for Service and Stewardship

The architecture and appointment of the sanctuary at First Presbyterian Church embody the presentation of high culture (particularly in terms of music) that helped shape a new style of church building in the nineteenth century.[1] Centrally located in the sanctuary are a baptismal font, communion table, and pulpit echoing the sacraments of baptism and communion, as well as the centrality of preaching, that are historically core elements of Presbyterian identity. Abutting the main sanctuary is a suite of Sunday School rooms, which were built to accommodate the children of the baby boom. Downstairs are offices for the pastors and staff, and a preschool that serves the community during the week (income and expenses for the preschool constitute nearly half of the church's $600,000 annual budget).

A typical Sunday service lasts just over an hour. Printed bulletins provide an outline of the order of the service in which music is as prominent as the "preaching of the word." An organ prelude, classic hymns, and an occasional contemporary piece of music intersect readings from the Old and New Testaments, corporate prayers, greetings, and announcements. Although the pastoral team is responsible for preaching, and generally provides a welcome and closing blessing, it is common for other members to participate in the service as readers, provide special music, or lead the congregation in prayers of confession or affirmations of faith. Although women have been ordained as pastors and elders in this denomination since the 1970s, there are places where First Presbyterian Church appears fairly traditional in terms of gender. When the pastors had their second child, Reverend Patricia cut her preaching schedule in half and went to part time. The leaders of the youth programs have consistently been men, while the principal of the preschool and children's program leaders are women, as are all of the office staff and the volunteer leader of the congregation's home visitation program. The congregation provides a full slate of age- and gender-specific programs, including ones for young mothers, sewing groups, and separate women's and men's fellowship groups and topical Sunday School classes (in addition to occasional small group Bible/book studies and Sunday School classes for couples and young adults).

The Setting at Valley Baptist Church

As with First Presbyterian Church, Valley Baptist Church also has a long history in the community dating back to the mid-1800s. It is a conservative evangelical congregation, emphasizing the centrality of a personal relationship with Jesus Christ, contemporary music, practical Bible-centered preaching, and a plethora of programs for families and youth. Over the past decade, the church has worked to integrate women into a wider range of ministries, expanded leadership teams and small group Bible studies, and added a worship service in Spanish. Most important, in 1999, it hired a dynamic young pastor who proposed that he would move the graying congregation into a new period of growth and ministry if they would be willing to revamp their services, rethink their mission, and engage with the unchurched in their community. They agreed. Immediate changes included the institution of a praise band, use of Power Point slides on a big screen for contemporary praise song lyrics, announcements, and sermon notes (complete with video clips, fill-in-the-blank outlines, and "question of the day" icebreakers). In just a few years, regular attendance doubled to nearly four hundred, including a growing number of "unchurched" Pacific Northwesterners, recovering substance abusers, single parents, and young working-class families.

An Auditorium and an Audience for Jesus

Worshipers entering Valley Baptist Church arrive at a nondescript building that used to be the town's high school. Occupying an entire city block, this brick structure would be unidentifiable as a church building if it were not for signs posted at various locations around the building identifying it as a church and associated Christian school. With minimal space for parking in two small lots across the street, Sunday morning finds most visitors searching for parking along the side streets in this working-class neighborhood. Housing in this area consists mostly of small bungalows built in the 1920s, interspersed with older Victorians homes (most of which have been converted into apartments), and modest apartment complexes built on corner lots where older homes once stood. The worship center at Valley Baptist Church is located in the old school auditorium. With its sloping floor, high ceiling, and central stage area, a visitor enters "Sunday morning celebration" in a space reminiscent of a movie theater in lighter tones. The stage is set with amplifiers, microphones, and the instruments of the praise band. No pulpit, altar, communion table, or baptismal pool is visible. Apart from a plain wooden cross hanging on the wall to the left of the stage and large banners with scriptural themes along the side walls, there are no visible indicators that one is in a church rather than a theater. The enormous screen hanging center stage adds to the sense of anticipation of a show about to begin.

Preaching is done from center stage, with the congregation following an outline projected on the big screen. Explicitly religious language, symbolism, movement, and use of space are all minimal at Valley Baptist Church. Sermons, bulletins, and monthly newsletters focus on the practical application of biblical teaching, family-style events intended to build a sense of community, celebration of new believers' baptisms, teaching on how to have healthy families and work relationships, and "lives transformed by the Gospel."

Sunday services typically last for just over an hour and consist largely of congregational singing and a sermon. The pastor's wife greets the congregation at the beginning of the service, and then she and two or three others lead the congregation in three or four contemporary worship songs. Lyrics are projected on the big screen and people are free to sit, stand, or raise their hands during the singing. At the heart of the service is the "preaching of the word," the time when Pastor Mark explains passages from the Bible (mostly the New Testament) and illustrates how they provide practical guidance for how to live and grow as a Christian. Although there is an occasional guest speaker, preaching is nearly always the purview of the head pastor.

Although women are visible in weekly worship services and teach children's Sunday School, their administrative roles are limited to women's ministry coordinator, children's ministry director, Christian school principal, and office administrator. The lead pastor, associate pastor, worship director, men's ministry leader, high school and middle-school youth leaders, and all of the board of elders are men. Up until the arrival of Pastor Mark, adult Sunday School classes were also taught or supervised by men. In 2002, the church reinstated the office of deacon (after not having had deacons for many years) and allowed women to be selected for the office for the first time in its history.

As at First Presbyterian Church, Valley Baptist Church also offers a full slate of gender- and age-specific programs and ministries, including mornings for moms, marriage enrichment classes, youth groups and Sunday School classes, and retreats for women (featuring esteem-building sessions, crafts, and childrearing advice) and men (featuring sports, wood splitting, and building projects), in addition to six or seven small weekday groups hosted by lay leader couples and groups for older members.

The Setting at St. Andrews Orthodox Church

The congregation at St. Andrew's Orthodox Church represents a liturgical tradition that is both demographically smaller and less widely studied than is Roman Catholicism or Episcopalianism in the United States.

It is also one in which historic ethnic enclaves are being gradually transformed through integration into an American context and the absorption of a growing number of Christians switching from other denominations.

St. Andrews Orthodox Church was established as a mission congregation in 1990. Father Michael and his wife, Katherine, had both been to seminary and felt some responsibility for using that training. They were also keenly "interested in the richness of a full liturgical life" and didn't want to rear their children as "just Sunday Orthodox." The nearest church was far enough away that it made getting there for anything other than Sunday morning difficult. Plus they were "very interested in mission work," so they approached the bishop and asked that he consider founding a mission in their location. He told them that he would, if Father Michael (then not yet ordained) would be its priest. They talked it over and agreed that it seemed that was what God wanted them to do.

Unfolding Tradition in the Pacific Northwest

For several years the congregation consisted of only a handful of families who set up and dismantled an Orthodox altar with icons, paraphernalia for communion, and vestments, affectionately known as "the church in the trunk," that they transported each week to space borrowed from another congregation. Eventually the group bought a small house on the outside of town and transformed the living room into a sanctuary and the bedrooms into Sunday School classrooms for a growing number of families with children. In 2003, the congregation sold the ranch house and moved into a two-story historic building that had been renovated as meeting space and chapel. Although a small sign and Orthodox cross identify the structure as a church, it can easily be passed by as an unremarkable white wooden building perched behind some trees along a long stretch of rural road. Inside, the space is transformed. What was once a chapel rented for weddings is now an open space in which oriental carpets are spread over 1880s wooden floors. This area, in which all but the very old and very young stand for two to three hours of liturgy, is divided from the altar by an arched wooded screen of icons, the iconostasis. Doors on either end of this wall of icons open and shut periodically throughout the service as clergy and altar servers move between altar and sanctuary. Lighting is dim, the walls are lined with icons, and a four-foot-tall wooden Jesus hangs on a two-dimensional cross in one corner. Votive candles flicker in red glass holders along the iconostasis. Slender beeswax candles embedded in sand-filled brass candleholders are arrayed before icons of Jesus, the saints, and Mary (the *Theotokos* or Mother of God) with her infant son. The room glows with muted brilliance.

Between 2002 and 2009, attendance doubled and the church started offering regular children's programs, adult education classes, quarterly inquirer classes for those interested in exploring Orthodoxy, and service and outreach programs within the broader community. Still much smaller than the two Protestant congregations, weekly attendance is between seventy and eighty adults and thirty to forty children, including a diverse set of working-class and professional couples, representing both historically Orthodox regions (Greece, Russia, Eastern Europe, and the Middle East) and a substantial subset of Anglo-Americans and small number of ethnic minority families who have come to St. Andrew's from a variety of other church and nonchurch backgrounds. Nearly 80 percent of the congregation is from non-Orthodox backgrounds.

A typical Sunday service lasts two hours and follows a routine that has been established in its current form for hundreds of years, the core of which (the Liturgy of St. John Chrysostom) is said to have been formulated under Patriarch John of Constantinople around 400 C.E. Each service is organized around a particular intersection of annual, seasonal, and weekly cycles, and moves through a series of reading, chanting, and speaking that feels somewhat repetitive, unpredictable, and interminable to the newcomer. Sunday services are broken into two parts. The liturgy of the catechumens (initiates) centers on readings from the Psalms, the Beatitudes, the Epistles, and the Gospel, as well as a celebration of specific heroes of the faith or saints for a particular day. The reading of the Gospel and a short sermon on its content are the turning point in the service, after which begins the liturgy of the faithful (oriented toward those who are members). This second portion of the service moves toward the real center of the service—the celebration of the Eucharist or communion. Visitors and newcomers are welcome, but the centrality of communion (which is closed to non-Orthodox as well as Orthodox who are not prepared through confession, personal prayer, and fasting) means that Sunday morning is intended as a way for the faithful to "enter into the worship of heaven" rather than a time to introduce a generation of seekers to Christianity.

St. Andrew's is ostensibly the most patriarchal of the three congregations in that the ordination of priests and deacons, as well as the larger regional, national, and international leadership of bishops, metropolitans, and patriarchs, is reserved for men. Unlike the Roman Catholic Church, parish priests are married (unmarried priests are generally monks). Although women serve behind the altar in monasteries and have served at various times historically as nonliturgical "deacons," the jurisdiction of which St. Andrews is a part understands altar server and deacon as precursors to the priesthood; therefore, only men and boys who have the blessing of the local priest take on these responsibilities.

Explanations for why the priesthood is reserved for men vary, but in addition to the commonly heard explanation that Jesus commissioned his original twelve male disciples to be leaders of the church, Orthodoxy sees the priest's maleness as reflecting and preserving the history of Jesus as a real human man. Because there are moments in the drama of the liturgy where the priest stands in the place of Christ, that person ought also be a real physical man, as Jesus was a real physical man and not an abstracted God-person. Second, the reservation of the priesthood to men is understood by some as a way to balance the unique generative role of Mary in God's work of salvation. Unlike Western traditions, Orthodoxy considers salvation less as a judicial transaction in which Jesus died so that God would no longer hold sinners guilty, but that Jesus took a body into the grave so that real human bodies could experience resurrection, completeness of healing, and transformation into the image of God (*theosis*). Thus, rather than seeing Mary as "just the plumbing" for the incarnation, as several respondents described, she is as essential to salvation as is the Holy Spirit, because without her, Jesus would not have had a body and the resurrection and transformation of embodied human persons into new life would not be possible. Orthodoxy sees in gender some of the same mystery as in the Trinity where there is sameness of being and value, but also difference, and that both diversity and unity are foundational truths that human reason does best not to try and pin down.

The experience of women as readers, leaders, or servers seems as much a reflection of the culture of the foundational members of the congregation and the leanings of the local bishop as an explicit teaching of the broader church. Father Michael and his wife, Katherine, are careful to emphasize that the church honors both women and men, and that women are neither subordinate nor inferior. Women are spiritual mentors in the same way that men may be (whether sponsoring new members in congregations or leading monastic communities). They also teach, serve in leadership on the parish council, are readers and choir members (a position that is treated with the same degree of centrality to worship as is altar server or deacon), and are celebrated throughout the services of the church as teachers, heroes, witnesses, and martyrs. In describing their own division of labor within the congregation, Katherine explained:

> You know, some Protestant churches ordain women or even have husbands and wives both serving as clergy in the same church. In a slightly different way, that is what we have had at St. Andrews. We have a priest, our Khouri (Arabic for priest) or Presbyter (Greek), and the wife of the priest is Khouriyeh or Presbytera (priestess). When Father Michael was ordained, the Bishop said very clearly that although there aren't words of ordination for the wife of a priest, she is in fact ordained with him on some level. How can it be otherwise? The priest isn't an island. In fact, when St. Andrews was formed as a mission parish, we had no clergy. We were both lay leaders, with exactly the same responsibilities as each other. He was working full time in another job, and I served as the mission coordinator. Even after Father Michael was ordained, it continued to be my responsibility to work with him [to] catechize newcomers, answer questions, and respond to phone calls. So there was no difference in our authority in the early days before his ordination. In the Russian tradition, the priest is Batushka (father) and his wife is Matushka (mother) of the parish. I think that's unique to Orthodoxy and something people might not know about.

In short, St. Andrews is an American Orthodox congregation that is patriarchal, but oddly so. Clergy who serve at the altar are all men, but there are few other aspects of the congregation's life that are gender specific. Both men and women can be found in the kitchen washing dishes or sweeping the floors after each Sunday's potluck meal or preparing food for the annual ethnic festival; men teach small children in Sunday School, as do women; and fathers, brothers, or other-fathers exit with crying babies or hold toddlers during the services as frequently as do mothers, sisters, and other-mothers. Efforts to start a group specifically for women have fizzled numerous times and a men's group—intended as a safe place for men to talk about their personal lives—met successfully for several months, but it eventually lost momentum and ended.

Distinctive People and Practice

Into these different spaces, different types of people come to enact and embody core beliefs about God, themselves, and the church.

Clergy Vision and Local Culture
at First Presbyterian Church

As are many other Presbyterian churches, First Presbyterian Church is predominately upper-middle-class professional individuals and families. Approximately one-third is working class. The majority are engineers, doctors, lawyers, counselors, and other professionals who arrive for worship in an array of well-kept, late-model mini-vans, sport utility vehicles, and midsize family cars. The characterization of this congregation as the "country club" church is supported by a high proportion of members belonging to the country club, tennis club, and various civic and business associations. Although a growing number of younger members dress in jeans, tennis shoes, and t-shirts for worship, most members wear dresses, or suits and ties. As in the setting of the sanctuary itself, tasteful understated wealth is reflected in the demeanor of the congregation. Reverend Richard describes the congregation as follows:

> The church economically has some very affluent and successful people. There's a large cross-section of engineers, a couple of attorneys, a couple physicians, and a good set of schoolteachers. So a large professional class in the congregation here. At least one person in most households probably has a lot of postsecondary education. A degree or post-bachelor's, a master's degree as well. A lot of our parishioners are affiliated with the high-tech industry; and there are a handful of people affiliated with farming. Very Anglo, very white congregation. Theologically, I would say it is a pretty mainstream congregation, highly educated, and theologically mainstream.

Since the arrival of this young husband-and-wife pastoral team, the congregation has gone from aging and enervated to a more vibrant and generationally mixed fellowship. Personal connections and acceptance of theological diversity rather than identification with Presbyterianism or the reformed tradition itself are what Reverend Richard considers important to the congregation's sense of identity and growth.

My impression is that people don't come because we're Presbyterian; people here are similar to the people they've experienced in the Methodist church or the Lutheran Church. I think that relationships drive this church more than a set theology or belief structure. People aren't looking for doctrine; they're looking for people like them.

Although the pastors both emphasize how "a sense of community rather than a rigid belief structure" is central to congregational identity, and downplay the importance of a distinctly Presbyterian identity, social homogeneity, theological breadth, and social engagement are themselves very much characteristic of the denomination.

[In this church] there's a pretty high level of appreciation for not being rigid doctrinally. People like the diversity and the power of the different ideas that are an important part of the Presbyterian Church. People don't feel like they have to believe and say all the same things to be part of the congregation here. People who are real active civically are drawn to this church because we think we should connect our faith to what happens in the world ... not so much emphasis on getting to heaven. We think it's better for us to engage the world and bring our faith to intersect with the issues that are all around us both locally and globally.

At First Presbyterian Church, people may not identify with the Reformed theological tradition or be able to recite the Shorter Catechism, but they are nonetheless solidly within a stream of religious tradition in which diversity and theological inclusiveness are central elements of religious identity and congregations are predominately white, wealthy, and highly educated.

Shifting Models of Worship

Until recently, First Presbyterian Church worshiped as one group, with older parishioners sitting in the center and back and younger couples with children filling in the front, balcony, and sides. Worship services are a rich array of diverse elements—complex programs that begin with a pastor's greeting and move through nineteen different segments (reading, prayers, announcements, sermon, etc.) before concluding an hour and fifteen minutes later. Music in a diversity of styles is an important part of this congregation's identity. Services typically include an instrumental prelude (on the organ or grand piano, with an occasional instrumental quartet), an informal "gathering song," two hymns, a praise chorus, and a choral anthem. Lay readers lead the congregation from a central lectern, reading from the Psalms a call to worship, selections from the Old and New Testaments, leading a corporate prayer of confession and forgiveness, and directing the congregation to greet those seated around them (a "passing of the peace" in which either "peace of the Lord" or "good morning" suffices as a way to connect with other people). People spend the minutes before the service chatting with friends seated around them, making plans for later in the day, and passing information about an upcoming committee meeting or volunteer event. Much of the informal work of the church takes place during the half hour before and after the service as people exchange news, check in on who is sick and who is getting better, and organize volunteers, materials, and schedules for later in the week.

As with other mainline congregations,[2] First Presbyterian Church has been gradually adopting aspects of evangelical-style worship and programming in order to attract new members, while maintaining its commitment to a broad and intellectually respectable and historic faith. Several years after their arrival, Pastors Richard and Patricia added an early, contemporary worship service on Sunday mornings in which a big screen with projected lyrics and a sermon outline replaced paper bulletins, hymnals, and choral music. A group of four or five praise singers began to lead the congregation in hand-clapping choruses, many of which were also being sung across town at Valley Baptist Church. Most younger couples with children have shifted to this service, saying that they both appreciate the music and are glad to have more time in the afternoon because they get in and out of church sooner, especially when children are up early anyway. The exodus of these families from the traditional service was experienced as a loss by older members of the congregation, most of whom continued to attend the traditional service at 10:30. This and other changes, particularly regular difficulty finding volunteers for the children's and youth programs, have led to some families leaving the church. As Reverend Patricia explained:

> The church is younger than when we came, but we've started to gray a little bit again. We've lost a number of key families over the past couple of years. Some have gone because they're unhappy with the kids ministry (we have Sunday School during the traditional service

and some parents want their kids with them during that hour). A few left because they don't feel like they're part of the church as a whole since we've gone to two services. Not a lot ... they mostly just grumble about that! We're still trying to figure out what to do.

Being able to worship together with families and young children was seen as a sign of health, growth, and vitality for many, particularly older members who were there during years of decline.

Struggling to Connect

Now that the congregation is informally divided along generational lines between traditional and contemporary services, First Presbyterian Church is working to find ways to maintain the sense of community and family that had been developing during the pastors' first five years. As Reverend Patricia says, "being a family, only better than your family" has meant informal togetherness, acceptance, and emotional support that now seem somewhat diminished since switching to two services on Sunday mornings.

Finding ways to allow people to build deeper relationships has proved a challenge. Both finding time and identifying the kinds of activities or study topics that might bring people together on a longer term basis have been a source of ongoing frustration. Multiple small-group formats have been tried, but none have lasted longer than the specific task around which they were formed. In most cases, groups provided the opportunity for study and discussion of a Christian book on relationships or stewardship and an occasional meal, but they did not provide a platform for establishing deeper long term relationships. After each book or project was completed, there seemed to be little motivation for getting together. Although important to the leaders, members of the congregation don't appear that interested in ongoing small-group discussion or studies. As Reverend Richard described:

The emphasis on small-group ministry is right on the money because it creates deeper relationships between people. To me it's important, but to my congregation ... sometimes I wonder if they get it. I think that this church has struggled with making intimate commitments to one another. Just basic things like fellowship groups are what this church has struggled with, and so to me some of the relational pieces could be strengthened in this church a lot.

Although First Presbyterian Church identifies itself as being a family in which people care for each other, the level of personal connections remains somewhat superficial. People receive visits when they are sick, meals following a birth or a funeral, and other kinds of help through networks of loose ties, but the goal of building enduring commitments within small groups of friends has proved elusive. A core group of people are responsible and engaged volunteers, yet personal connections don't seem to move beyond the level of friendly and informal association. In part, the elusiveness of deeper commitments is itself related to the congregation's culture of breadth, flexibility, and acceptance. Lacking clear doctrinal commitments and with weak subcultural boundaries, people at the First Presbyterian Church find few distinctively religious motivations for building relationships within the congregation. As a result, commitments remain at the level of commitments in other social organizations: functional, enjoyable, but minimally involved or personalized. As one member put it, "a critical number of potlucks does not a community make!" An ongoing challenge at First Presbyterian Church, then, is to balance their identity as an accepting, nonjudgmental family in which all are welcome, with the expectation that people be committed to one thing specific: each other.

Clergy Vision and Local Culture at Valley Baptist Church

Apart from also being a predominantly white congregation, the people and practices of Valley Baptist Church are very different from those at First Presbyterian Church. This conservative Baptist congregation is located literally and figuratively on the wrong side of the tracks. The membership is mostly white working class—reflective of the town's economic base with a much smaller number of professionals, business owners, and engineers. The congregation also includes a small but growing number of recently homeless, recovering substance abusers, single mothers, and marginally employed. Not surprisingly, its budget is also smaller than that of the Presbyterian church, about $200,000 a year (not including the Christian school, whose finances are kept separate).

As with the First Presbyterian Church, Valley Baptist Church was also becoming a smaller, grayer congregation until the arrival of Pastor Mark. As Pastor Mark explains:

> This is a very old church that had experienced significant decline and a lot of liabilities: old constituency, old neighborhood, old facility,

bad reputation, significant flight out of the church in terms of young people. I knew that it was a tough situation that would require drastic turnaround and that brings with it a certain level of organizational trauma. So before we accepted the call, I told them we'd be making a lot of changes to the way they'd been doing things—the music would be totally changed, the service would be simplified, and ministries to unchurched people made [a] high priority.

The service itself has been transformed into a much more streamlined, simplified program in which music and preaching are central. Although not all older members welcomed the removal of the organ and installation of guitars, electric keyboard, and drums, few long-term members left the church. Pastor Mark credits the relative smoothness of the transition to the congregation's desire to see younger people in church again and their agreement ahead of time to significant changes in the look and feel of Sunday morning services. His wife Sara's active leadership in the children's ministry and women's small groups has also added to a sense of revitalized and relevant activities at the church.

Transforming Worship

Valley Baptist Church is thoroughly evangelical, with its Bible-centered, entertaining, pragmatic, and personal approach to what it means to be a Christian and a part of the church. A brief welcome, an offering (during which visitors are asked to "keep your wallet in your pocket; we're just glad you're here and hope you enjoy and receive from us this morning"), occasional testimony, and closing comment are similar to some of the same elements in the services at First Presbyterian Church. Yet the "worship celebration" at Valley Baptist Church feels less complex and much more informal than do the services at First Presbyterian Church. Most of the program is organized around the two dominant activities of singing and Bible teaching. For nearly half an hour, the congregation stands and sings contemporary worship music, the lyrics of which are projected on the big screen at the front of the sanctuary. Some worshipers periodically raise their hands, and most clap or tap their feet to the upbeat rhythms of the music. Songs are simple and encouraging, addressing God directly ("Jesus, we celebrate your victory, Jesus we revel in your love")[3] and emphasizing the hope, peace, and strength that are available through a personal relationship with Jesus Christ ("Your love is amazing, steady, and unchanging, your love is a mountain firm beneath my feet; Your love is a mystery, how you gently lift me, when I am surrounded your love carries me")[4]. A short set of announcements, followed by a humorous "question of the day" during which people are encouraged to chat with those around them, the offering, and a short prayer lead up to the main event: Pastor Mark's sermon. Practical, Bible-based teaching lasts about an hour and is what Pastor Mark considers his primary task. By all accounts, he does it remarkably and consistently well. After the service, over lunch, and even later in the week, people can be heard commenting on what a good teacher he is and how glad they are to have someone who can clearly and straightforwardly apply the Bible to everyday life.

For a church whose roots are in the inerrancy debates of the 1950s, interpreting and applying the Bible remains a central feature of church life. For Pastor Mark, however, good preaching is not enough. It is the authority of the text to inform everyday choices that is most important. Describing his approach as "calling the bluff between what people say about every word of the Bible being true, and the lack of putting into practice what the Bible teaches," he argues:

> My approach is to stick people's noses back in the book and ask, what does the Bible say we should be doing? Someone asked me, "How should we react to illegal aliens?" because we have this growing Hispanic ministry. So what do we do? We preach the Bible and see what it says about the alien and the stranger and the foreigner and how you treat them. What do we do about overcrowded jails? Well, what did Jesus say about people who are in prison and the way we respond to them? What do we do about those who are impoverished, what do we do about those cross-cultural events, the Bible talks to all these things. It can stand on its own two feet. With good interpretation, simply make it say what it's supposed to say in the cultural context of today.

Clear answers to personal questions are at the heart of his preaching ministry. Because the congregation is made up of people who are from unchurched backgrounds (for whom debates over infallibility and inerrancy have no meaning) and people who already believe the scripture is inspired and authoritative, his teaching rarely ranges into the territory of Higher Criticism or hermeneutics. Instead, in series of sermons on a topic that may span several months or more, Pastor Mark addresses questions about money and possessions (Jesus and your stuff), forgiveness (mending broken fences), how do you know you're a Christian (an exposition of

First, Second, and Third John), spiritual gifts, and who is Jesus (The Life, a two-year teaching series on the life of Christ).

Transforming Lives

Whereas First Presbyterian Church sees itself as an accepting family, Valley Baptist Church sees itself as a place where people are being transformed through personal encounters with Jesus Christ. Lowering the cultural and social barriers to church attendance, Valley Baptist Church seeks to engage unchurched and working-class members of the community through acts of "radical compassion" and a simple message that connects the Bible to everyday life, and people to each other. As Pastor Mark says:

> The church is a continuation of the ministry of Christ ... living lives of truth and grace expressed in acts of radical compassion so that people experience compassion in their lives, not as conversion prospects or giving units, but as whole people with joys and sorrows and hurts and victories. Relationships like that become bridges to express truth. We've spent far too much time telling people that Jesus loves them and not proving to them that we love them. And so that's been a big focus here. We're in an old neighborhood ... and the church has gone from thinking the location was a liability to thinking of it as an asset. We are closer to drug houses and poverty and to broken lives than anyone else in town, we are strategically located for ministry in people's lives. I think the church is being effective when lives are being changed more into the image of Christ. That's what we're shooting for. I don't mean religious conversion. I mean transformation that's faith based. So, people expressing faith in Christ and lives being changed by the power of Christ regardless of where they are in their spiritual journey. Not learning more details about the Bible, or increasing knowledge and understanding. Those are only tools to it. Anyone who comes here will figure out really quickly that we're very Bible based; you're going to study the Bible here. But, again, that is only a tool; it is not an outcome. I'm talking about change in life outcomes.

One of the challenges of leading a conservative Baptist congregation, Pastor Mark argues, is that members tend to shift an emphasis on knowing the Bible into an end in itself rather than trying to put what the Bible teaches into practice. Yet for him, the purpose of the church is less about knowing the right theology than it is about living the right kind of life. He talked at length about the importance of being relationally connected, compassionate, and humble as both a consequence of "a life being transformed by grace" and the means by which grace is extended to others. He described the congregation collecting "a mountain of canned goods and blankets and hundreds of plates of cookies" to distribute at Christmas time, his finding a couple of guys drinking beer on the church steps one evening and the next Sunday taking donuts to them at their apartment and inviting them to church, and visiting his friend John, who is homeless and sleeps under a bridge at the edge of town.

Low key, youth oriented, and user friendly, Valley Baptist Church is a rapidly growing congregation struggling to meet the needs of people who are economically and socially marginalized. The church supports eighty to one hundred elementary-age children attending Sunday School each week; a rapidly aging core of long-term members; an expanding Spanish-speaking worship service, ministry, and outreach; an aging building; and a K–8 Christian school.

Clergy Vision and Local Culture at St. Andrews Orthodox Church

St. Andrew's is a fairly occupationally and educationally diverse congregation. It is also a study in contrasts of old and new, ritual and change, corporate and personal experience, lifelong and newly Orthodox. Of the hundred or so families in the parish, only a handful have ethnic ties to places where Orthodoxy has been the primary expression of Christianity. These second- and third-generation Greek, Eastern European, and Palestinian immigrants and their children make up the "cradle Orthodox" minority at St. Andrew's. Quite unlike many ethnically homogeneous urban Orthodox churches, most parishioners at St. Andrew's have transitioned into Orthodoxy from a range of Protestant denominations (Episcopalian, Presbyterian, Methodist, Conservative Baptist, Christian and Missionary Alliance, Four Square, Assembly of God, Calvary Chapel, and Vineyard Christian Fellowship). Ethnically, these families are representative of an earlier wave of European immigrants, those Scots-Irish, German, Scandinavian, and Eastern Europeans who came to the Pacific Northwest in the nineteenth century or, more recently, as part of a migration of professionals from California or points "back East," following high-tech jobs to the Pacific Northwest. A small but growing number of members come from no specific religious background or other religious identification (people who previously identified as spiritual but not religious, agnostic, pagan, or Buddhist). Father Michael and his wife, Katherine, are themselves "cradle orthodox"—he from a family whose roots are in Eastern Europe, she from a first-generation family from the Middle East. Neither Father Michael nor Katherine ever imagined that they would be serving a congregation consisting largely of people who have transitioned from some other or no previous religion into the church.

Father Michael maintained his full-time job as an administrator within a large nonprofit organization for several years until the congregation became large enough to support a full-time priest and his growing family. It took several more years for the congregation to grow to the point where it no longer needed to borrow money from a fund initially set aside from the sale of their first building to balance their annual budget. The budget gradually increased from about $70,000 to just over $200,000 a year. With seven children, a diverse and growing congregation, and eventual responsibility for two additional "mission" churches spun off from the membership at St. Andrews, every moment of every day seems full. Still, Father Michael and Katherine maintain a steady stream of visitors and spend endless hours talking with people who have wandered into St. Andrews to inquire about Orthodoxy. Searching for truth, he argues, is what draws people to the church. Instructing them in the truths embodied in the services and the sacraments is his primary task.

> We have a very diverse congregation. You know, that's why in my mind it's clear what brings us together is this desire for the truth and for living the ancient Christian life. When you look at who we are; we have very young children, very old people, and everything in between. We have people who are very wealthy and we have people who are very poor, and ethnically we're from all over. Very few are from what you would consider traditional Orthodox backgrounds. My job is to make sure that the faithful who are going to receive the sacraments are properly instructed and prepared for their reception. As priest, I'm the guardian and minister of the sacraments, of the Holy Mysteries of the church, so that's my number-one job. Second is to actually be an instructor in the faith, a teacher, and that is by both word and example. And then I would say to provide spiritual guidance and direction to my congregation. But number

one, without a doubt, is the sacraments because there would be no church without the sacraments.

The sacraments, primarily weekly communion, stand at the center and focal point of Orthodox worship. Layered with meaning, the mystery of communion is understood as food for one's spiritual journey, medicine for healing and transformation, and movement forward into greater union with God and each other.

Teaching New People Old Truths

Intensely personal and corporate at the same time, participating in the services requires instruction, guidance, and practice. Providing that spiritual guidance to a congregation of new converts is no easy thing. Katherine describes the frustration she and Father Michael expressed in working with former Protestants who all too easily transform what is to her a flexible, personal, and vibrant faith into a list of rules that need to be observed. Truth and practice are important, but acquiring them is a process that takes a lifetime.

> I do think people come because they're searching for truth. What I've seen here (and in talking to people at other churches) is that people are searching for a deeper spirituality and truth. You have to be wanting something because Orthodoxy demands a lot! We don't have a ton of programs or things, just a Sunday School for the kids, so the only thing people can be attracted to is the searching for truth. But people, especially people who used to be Protestant, struggle with making it all legalistic instead of about a relationship. What they don't always get is that all these rules about fasting and everything else are supposed to help you become more like God. They are medicine we need to be spiritually healthy, not rules to follow.

In addition to struggles with "lingering fundamentalism," the congregation at St. Andrews struggled for many years with its ability to cultivate relationships among members outside of regular worship. Because the membership had been so small and spread across several towns, physical distances made it difficult for people to get together during the week, especially when there were generally already multiple opportunities each week to see each other at services. As the congregation has grown, however, the physical distances between parish families have become smaller, and play dates among those with small children, meal or ride sharing, and weekly small-group Bible studies have begun to be a regular facet of congregational life.

Because the Orthodox Church is liturgical and experiential rather than cognitive or pragmatic, weekly services focus on the ritualized movement, prayers, psalms, and rhythms of the liturgy. There are significantly lower expectations for extended or creative teaching. The gestures and substance of the liturgy, all pointing toward and leading up to the Eucharist is what is central. In fact, the notion that Father Michael could make worship relevant through his own creativity or innovation is contrary to Orthodoxy as living practiced ancient rite. As he explained, "Everything we do here has a purpose. Nothing is because someone just thought it would be good idea, or 'why don't we try this?' It all means something, everything we do, every detail. It all makes physical, because we're physical, the theology of the Church. Nothing is just because someone liked it."

Worship at St. Andrews is relevant not because it is in tune with contemporary cultural trends, but because, as Father Michael says, it draws participants outside of time "into heaven itself" and "enacts the whole narrative of the good news." In multiple layers, senses, and cycles, the stories of creation, fall, redemption, and renewal are told over and over again. Within these annual cycles, the active, routinized engagement of sight, hearing, voice, taste, and smell create a sacred space in which an individual encounters God.

Practicing To Be Perfect

People stand at St. Andrews. They stand for hours. Vespers Saturday evening is closely followed by Matins early Sunday morning. Worshipers arrive at what seem like random intervals, walking to the front of the church to light a candle, cross themselves, and pray before a favorite icon. Young children wander between parents and to the front, where they can see, and to the back, where they can sit and sing bits of the liturgy and observe what is going on. Parents occasionally leave and return with children who have needed to use the bathroom or have begun to cry, been offended by a sibling, or need a snack. With no pews in which to confine the congregation, these movements are less distracting than might be expected. Overall people appear to be doing the same thing and their own thing at the same time. This, coupled with the multitude of small variations in the services as the church winds through cycles of the liturgical year, makes for a sense of stability in an overall framework within which there is ample room for individual movement and variety.

Divine Liturgy follows seamlessly about an hour and a half later and moves through a seemingly endless series of requests for mercy; acknowledgment of the holiness of a triune God; a repetitive and somewhat cyclical series of anthems, choruses, and readings sung by a small choir; accolades for particular saints; psalms and gospel readings for the day; and prayers for innumerable archbishops, bishops, ministers, deacons, governors, travelers, the sick, the persecuted, the poor, and the faithful. Everyone is included. For someone for whom this is all relatively new (as was the case for me), the services not only seem to go on forever but appear to retrace the same ground multiple times. Yet during the months in which we visited St. Andrews, the repetitiveness and interminableness of the liturgy resolved into a still long, but much more reasonable practice in which I began to realize that my own mind was wandering at the moment Father Michael sang out, "Let us attend!" or that I had missed an entire section and just tuned back in during a second run-through of the same (or similar) material. Services are long, but nothing is missed (even for those who are not particularly good at attending).

Sacraments: Embodied, Collective, and Remembered
Sacrament as Food for the Body

At St. Andrews, the movement of the whole service is toward the Eucharist. It is the center and goal of all the morning's activities. Although Orthodoxy teaches that Christ's body and blood are really present in the Eucharist, it makes no effort to explain how or where that presence exists but accepts this mystery in the same way it accepts the mystery of the incarnation or the mystery of humanity's deification, with active gratitude and celebration. In these matters, Orthodoxy, as popular writer Frederica Mathews-Green points out,[5] is content to admire the butterfly without pinning its head to a board. The entire second half of the Divine Liturgy is devoted to the enactment and celebration of this doctrine, with members lining up toward the end of the service to receive communion from a long-handled golden spoon. Communion is open only to Orthodox Christians who have prepared through prayer, fasting (since the night before), and regular confession, although anyone may go forward for a blessing during this part of the service. There is something distinctly child-like in this model of communion: the combination of fasting since the night before and standing for hours makes physically palpable church doctrines about spiritual poverty, human fragility, and the need to be fed. At both the individual and corporate levels, the gift of this little morsel of food parallels the gift of Christ, symbolizing the unity of baptized believers to Christ and to each other. A potluck lunch that follows the conclusion of the service further underscores ideas about the church as both extended family and body.

The congregations of both First Presbyterian Church and Valley Baptist Church also regularly observe two sacraments: communion and baptism. But these are not nearly as central to weekly services nor are they understood as being as profoundly efficacious (as doing as much religious "work" or being a "means of grace") as they are within Orthodoxy, nor are they closed to anyone who is not part of that denomination or who has not prepared through some personal devotional ritual. Still, the sacraments at Valley Baptist Church and First Presbyterian Church point to their residual salience within Protestantism of the meaning and importance of visible signs in the lives of believers.

Sacrament as Collective Memorial

At First Presbyterian Church, communion is served on the first Sunday of every month, either by members coming forward to take a piece of bread from a small loaf and a tiny plastic communion cup of grape juice from pairs of elders stationed at several locations at the front of the sanctuary, or from trays of cracker fragments and thimbles of grape juice passed up and down the rows of seated parishioners. Both members and nonmembers who are Christians are invited to participate. Both Protestant congregations understand communion as a memorial and remembrance of Christ's crucifixion. Although "nobody wants to go back and split hairs over how we understand Christ being present in Communion," as Reverend Richard says, the sacrament is accompanied by more ritual speech at the First Presbyterian Church than at Valley Baptist Church. These movements convey a sense of mystery and dignity that in some way this simple bread and grape juice are not ordinary because they point, even if vaguely, to the importance of the body and sacrifice and remembering in much the same way as the sanctuary itself communicates memory, stability, and place. As Reverend Richard says:

Worship is the central, defining act that we do that says we are in community with others. There's opportunity for people to kind of

deepen knowledge of God through worship and I think that the
music is an incredibly important outlet for people to feel connected
to God.... The sacraments are really important symbols of our
being a community. That's why we like to have people come forward
to take communion ... receiving the elements from other people in
the church. There's that connection.

Not everyone feels the same way about what it means to receive communion from other people in the church (one long-term member talked
about how it "does nothing for me to receive communion from someone
I don't know that well. If I know them, it's fine, but if it's just Joe Schmo, it
doesn't do a thing for me. I lose interest."). As a result, the church alter-
nates between passing communion trays through the pews and asking
people to come forward and take the elements from pairs of individuals in
the front. Yet regardless of the manner in which the bread and tiny cups of
juice are distributed, the ministers recite the same words of institution as
they stand behind the communion table. Moving down several steps from
the lectern, Reverend Richard or Reverend Patricia stands at the same level
as the congregation and prays over the elements, holding high and tearing
in half a small loaf of sourdough bread while reciting words connecting
this action to Jesus' body on the cross. As quiet music plays, a reflective
congregation is asked to eat the bread when they receive it and hold the
cup so that all can drink together, enacting both individuality and community through the movements of communion.

Sacrament as Remembered Sacrifice

Valley Baptist Church also serves communion on the first Sunday of the
month, but it is more radically minimalist in its approach. Consistent with
the simplicity of the building and the outline of the services, the distribution of communion countermands any sense that the elements might be
something other than simple crackers and juice. In both words and signs,
the practice points to the wholly symbolic and memorial nature of the act.
Standing behind a table located front and center on level with the seating
rather than the stage, Pastor Mark speaks about what will happen later in
the service:

Later on, we're going to be serving communion. Just so you know,
we welcome anyone to take part who has put their trust in Christ.

Doesn't matter what church you're from or what you've done. If you've trusted in Jesus, this is for you. If you're new or haven't been around much before, we'll explain this all in a little more detail later. I just want you to know up front so that you won't be wondering what all this stuff is up here. There's nothing spooky about what we're going to do. It's just our way of remembering that Jesus gave himself for us; more on that later.

Highlighting both the symbolic and inclusive nature of communion, the pastor demystifies and deritualizes the practice by highlighting how it draws on ordinary things to remember an historic event. More momentous, to be sure, than birthdays and cake, but essentially the same notion of celebrating something with natural ingredients (the bread itself is so small one member described it "as so symbolic it's almost invisible, about half the size of a tic-tac!"). When the elements are passed (either on trays through the seated congregation or occasionally by elder husband-and-wife pairs at stations around the sanctuary), no words are spoken other than a paraphrasing of the New Testament text explaining that we "do this in remembrance of Him." At Valley Baptist Church, communion is nothing extraordinary or "spooky," but a ritual that invites believers to remember the sacrifice of Jesus as creating a way to bring broken people back into relationship with a loving God.

Conclusion: Tradition Embodied

Comparing the use of religious space, ritual, and pastors' visions for the mission of the church provides a way to explore the enduring influence of theological and tradition-based distinctives on congregational life and worship. As in studies of religious architecture, social class, and shifting emphases in the mission of the church,[6] we find buildings, demographics, and religious ritual intersecting in ways that provide a cohesive religious experience within these congregations. First and most obviously, the social class of the congregation is reflected in and by the buildings in which they worship. This is particularly true of the two Protestant churches in this analysis. The relative wealth, privilege, and position of many within the Presbyterian congregation are echoed in the depth of color, carved stone, and tapestries of the building's sanctuary. The place and the people who worship there are landmarks and pillars of the community. In contrast, the straightforwardness of the Baptist church's architecture—its simplicity, clean lines, auditorium-style seating, and big screen—invokes and reflects a less formal, working-class congregation. The differences between the two are distinctive and subtle, echoing the boundaries and ambiguities in taste and consumption that are associated with social class as well as theological worldview.

The theological distinctives of each tradition are also embodied and reflected in the buildings in which these congregations worship. A Reformed heritage is celebrated as the foundation of this contemporary Presbyterian congregation, and its significance is echoed in the solidity of the building itself. It is old, but modifiable. New technology is added for the contemporary service and "praise band," but pulpit, communion table, and baptismal font remain as physical reminders of the centrality of preaching and sacraments within Presbyterianism. The pastors' vision of the mission of the church, like the building, is also a blend of traditional and contemporary, offering an exegetical Bible study and a Jesus Seminar book in parallel Sunday School classes without endorsing either as the approved hermeneutic of the church, and emphasizing the rationality of faith in sermons intended to inspire generosity and kindness within an educated and prosperous congregation.

In a similar fashion, the minimalist visual appeal of the Baptist church focuses attention on core elements of evangelical theology and subculture. The simple wooden cross and the fill-in-the-blank sermon outline underscore the belief that faith itself is a straightforward, personal, and practical matter. The absence of Bibles and hymnals from the pews reinforces the idea that believers should own and study and bring their own Bibles, rather than reference a church copy on Sundays. Practical sermons appeal to the heart rather than the head, inviting attenders to "just sit back and relax and enjoy being with us this morning." At the same time, the baptismal tank, obscured by the big screen unless it is in use, underscores both the nonnegotiability of adult baptism for membership and the Bible-centric, personal confession of faith that are essential elements of conservative Baptist evangelical theology.

In both of these churches, the energy and action of worship move between auditorium and stage. Although attenders actively participate in singing and may move around the sanctuary during communion, for the most part, worship takes place in the front as a performance to be observed. In contrast, the worship of the congregation at St. Andrews appears to run in parallel with the priest in front, facing and moving about the altar, and the congregation standing and listening and occasionally singing along with the choir located in the back of the sanctuary. Rather than performance for the congregation, worship is performance with the congregation. During most of the service, everyone faces forward. The liturgy itself moves the congregation forward, drawing attenders from "this world" into participation in the next. The open doors of the iconostasis invite this movement, as does the music coming from behind, as sound flows toward the altar. Rather than worship happening between the priest and the congregation, the movement of the service is toward the front, draws attention toward the iconostasis, through the open doors flanked by icons of Jesus as an infant and Jesus the final Judge, into the altar and beyond to the kingdom of God. Somewhat ironically, in a sanctuary where a literal wall separates the congregation from the "holy place" and where an onslaught of sight, sound, and smell await, the whole combines to invite the worshiper not so much to sit back and receive, experience, or ponder, but to move inwardly beyond, further up and further in, to this story that is told week after week and year after year. Overall, the expectation that the worshiper adapt to all this, rather than the church respond to the tastes or individual needs of the worshiper, sets Orthodoxy theologically and experientially apart.

Although "denomination" itself may be declining as a marker of religious identity, the subcultural distinctives that are the foundations of that identity appear to be more enduring. They present themselves as threads of belief, practice, and a sense of community, embodied and reflected in the buildings themselves, that are the "stuff" of congregational culture. These distinctives may be muted or vitally celebrated. Regardless, they permeate the experience of worship and the character of congregational life. Whether the sacramentalism of Orthodoxy, the minimalism and drive for cultural relevance of evangelicalism, or the sense of history and respect for the individual within the Reformed tradition, these patterns of worship highlight the coherent and enduring values that are at the center of corporate religious experience. And, as we will see, these matter differently to the women and men who are considering becoming part of each of these very different congregations.

3

Becoming

ALL THREE CONGREGATIONS in this study are interested in growing. Each is keenly interested in providing a caring, supportive community to its members and being a meaningful presence in the wider community. Each also has its own distinctive process through which new members become integrated into the congregation.

The New-Member Process at First Presbyterian Church

New members become formally affiliated with First Presbyterian Church either through a letter of transfer indicating they have been a member at another Presbyterian church or a confession of faith. The former is efficient and straightforward—prospective members move into town, start visiting, decide to join, and request their former Presbyterian church send a letter indicating their intent to join and identification as Presbyterian. For people wishing to become members who are not Presbyterian or are unaffiliated, the process of joining begins with a quarterly dessert and introduction to Presbyterianism held at Pastors Richard and Patricia's home, followed by an invitation to participate in a set of seminars intended to engage new members in worship and service. Reverend Richard described their new-member process this way:

> We're moving away from a three-Sundays-in-a-row new membership class (something we patterned after Saddleback Presbyterian's [mega-church] model of 101, 102, 103) because we found it pushed people through too quickly. We're moving to a "purpose-driven" church model because I think of the church as a postmodern,

relational church. Building relationships is more important than a systematic program. Mormons do that very effectively—they build relationships, communicate "what we can do for you," and make it clear how they can help them improve their family life, etc. So we think building relationships should come first. Then, as people get in, they can join a class that has more about spiritual disciplines and later do more about spiritual gifts and ministries.

Whether in the older model of three, one-hour classes on consecutive Sunday mornings, or the newer model of a dessert at the pastors' home four times a year followed by evening seminars on spiritual growth and finding a ministry niche, the new-member process at First Presbyterian begins with a brief overview of what it means to be Presbyterian and the history of this specific congregation.

Introductions: Dessert with the Pastors

Arriving one October evening for a prospective member dessert at the pastors' home in a suburban subdivision, I joined a group of eleven others interested in getting to know more about First Presbyterian. One elderly couple in the group was a retired minister and wife, recently moved into a retirement community nearby. Another elderly woman came without her husband—they had also moved back into the area after living elsewhere for many years. Two other older women had grown up Presbyterian but hadn't been to church for years. Then a friend invited them to First Presbyterian, and they'd become regular visitors. A middle-aged woman who felt disaffected from the Methodist church she'd been visiting because the music was too loud, two younger couples (one in their late twenties, the other in their early forties), and a single man also in his twenties rounded out the group. Brad, the husband in the middle-aged couple, had met Reverend Richard playing golf and had had a friend also recommend the church. Brad had grown up in a Catholic household, but his wife, Mary, was Presbyterian and thought the Catholic Church was too big and impersonal. They were impressed that the church had a husband-and-wife pastoral team and so visited and liked the sermons. The structured services felt comfortable to Brad, and Mary liked the friendly atmosphere. As we chatted in the corner of the room before things got started, Mary commented on how she considers herself and her husband as low-maintenance church attenders: they only come on Sundays and don't see themselves ever being extensively involved in other activities during the week. The youngest couple at the meeting had recently moved—Rina into the area from out of state, and her boyfriend, Harry, into Rina's apartment shortly after she got settled. Rina was interested in finding a church and had been church shopping. She visited each place for several weeks in a row in order to get the flavor of the place and to see what felt comfortable. When she visited First Presbyterian, she knew it was where she wanted to be. She brought Harry to a Sunday service before coming to the new membership dessert. Harry told the group he was uncomfortable with church in general, having attended only a handful of times anywhere in the past, and said he really didn't know what to expect.

The evening began with Reverend Patricia inviting people to help themselves to some of the desserts she'd "worked all day to prepare"—and laughed, saying she'd picked them up at the local bakery on the way home. People helped themselves to dessert and settled into small group conversations scattered around the living room. Eventually Reverend Richard stood and suggested the group get started with introductions. He then talked briefly about the history of the local congregation and the current membership process. He joked about the Presbyterians being the "frozen chosen" with temperaments inclined toward valuing things that are decent and orderly—following the sober Scots who brought the denomination to the United States—but also as a tradition that values tolerance, living under a broad theological umbrella, education, respect for personal autonomy, and community-building. To underscore these points, he made it clear that while he thought it was worthwhile knowing how Presbyterians differ from other denominations, those differences don't make Presbyterians better than other churches. "It's not that we're better, we just want to accent how we're different from other churches." In closing the meeting, he talked about the process of becoming a member and what that implies about involvement.

> So now you know a little about us. In terms of process: if you want to become a member of the congregation or know more about the Presbyterian church or this particular Presbyterian church—where we've been and where we're going, or where we think we'll be going—we're offering a seminar Sunday evening next month from 4 to 8 p.m. Child care will be provided. It'll give us a chance to get to know each other a little better and to move from being an attender of worship (which you all have been at some level) to a deeper

sense of belonging ... maybe getting your kids plugged into the kids groups, or getting plugged into a small group experience in the church where you can go to a deeper level and develop some really meaningful relationships with people. I don't know about you, but Sunday coffee hour doesn't quite get very deep lots of times. So we hope that at the first seminar that you'll develop a deeper sense of belonging to our church.

Seminar One: Presbyterian Perspectives on Spiritual Growth

At the seminar on spiritual growth the following month, the composition of the group had changed slightly from those that attended the pastors' dessert. The single man had dropped out, but two new couples were in attendance—an engaged couple that been church shopping in the area, and a young couple with small children. The group met at the church and again began with a brief overview of the objectives of the seminar as a way to introduce people to each other and the church and to provide opportunity for people to consider the topics of spiritual growth and spiritual gifts.

If you attend these seminars, you are then eligible to join the church, but you are not obligated to join the church. You may have heard that we live in an era of believers but not belongers, so we're glad you're here and feel close enough to come tonight and check it out and learn a little more.

Reverend Richard and one of the lay ministry leaders distributed three-ring binders with worksheets and discussion questions on spiritual growth and spiritual gifts, along with a booklet, "About Being Presbyterian." As we went around the room and again introduced ourselves, it became clear that about one-third of those present had grown up Presbyterian and were moving (or renewing) membership; the other two-thirds were from other Protestant denominations or had grown up Roman Catholic.

After introductions, Reverend Richard provided a more detailed overview of the beginnings of Presbyterianism in the Reformation, its overall structure and organization, and its emphasis on being theologically open and continually reforming. He talked about growing up Lutheran and the difference between Lutheran and Presbyterian ideas around communion.

Lutherans believe in transubstantiation, which means that celebrating communion results in the bread and wine becoming the actual body and blood of Jesus. Presbyterians, on the other hand, believe that bringing Jesus' body "back for communion" would disregard his rising again and ascending into heaven. Bringing back Jesus' body in the form of communion doesn't make sense, so Presbyterians believe that communion brings Jesus spiritually to us. It isn't just symbolic, because Jesus' spirit is truly present when we remember his death and resurrection.

He went on to describe baptism as a sacrament, or "means of grace," in the Presbyterian Church, and why the church baptizes infants rather than just adults. "We're one of the early Reformation traditions, so we understand baptism as uniting a child to the church. It doesn't guarantee salvation, but symbolizes the child entering the family of God and the commitment of both the parents and the congregation to rear the child in a Christian atmosphere."

After a break, Reverend Richard moved on to talk more specifically about how their goal is to see people become connected to the church for the long haul—and how being a member means finding out what your gifts are and using them within the church.

Membership is not just for show; it means that you are working toward increasing your commitment. The longer membership process is designed to help people understand this and give them a chance to explore their gifts. We're not interested in putting people in slots. We want to put people where their gifts would be best used. We want people to be passionate about what they do.

He went on to talk about how it is important for people to feel connected and to bring whatever it is they have to serve one another. He and Patricia wanted the church to feel like a family—that everybody belongs and has something to offer.

The seminar then shifted to the study materials provided in notebooks—fill-in-the-blank pages working through scripture passages related to spiritual growth and spiritual gifts. The material outlined basic concepts around discipleship "to be a learner" and the importance of building habits of daily prayer and Bible reading, as well as habits around regular worship, giving, and service. The seminar ended with the opportunity for participants to sign a "covenant," committing to grow in these disciplines.

Seminar Two: Presbyterian Perspectives
on Spiritual Gifts and Ministry

The following month, prospective members were invited to a second seminar on finding your spiritual gifts. The purpose, Reverend Patricia explained, was to help people identify how God had uniquely shaped them for ministry. As Reverend Patricia explained, "At FPC, we want to focus on an individual approach to ministry rather than the institutional approach. Instead of beginning with the question, 'What does the church need?' we want to begin with the question, 'What do you need to enjoy fruitfulness and fulfillment?'" She and another presenter worked through the outline provided in class notebooks, detailing how each unique person was created for ministry, saved for ministry, and called into ministry. "Ministers aren't the people in front of the congregation— we're all gifted, authorized, and commanded to be ministers of Jesus Christ in the world. The body of Christ needs all of its members, and so the plan today is to begin to discover how God has shaped you uniquely for ministry."

During the morning sessions, participants worked through a number of Bible passages on the topic of spiritual gifts. The group then divided into smaller groups, which were given "ministry guides" with exercises to fill in that would help people identify areas in which they might be gifted. In one exercise, group members were asked to rate one hundred statements such as: "I can communicate scripture in ways that motivate others to study and want to learn more" or "I can visualize a coming event, anticipate potential problems, and develop backup plans." They then tallied up how many points they scored across items, with higher totals indicating their own personal profile of gifts. The groups then began a series of exercises intended to identify people's "heart" or "passion" with questions such as "If I could snap my fingers and know I wouldn't fail, what would I do?" and "At the end of my life I'd like to look back and see I'd done something about … (fill in the blank)" and were given the opportunity to consider and list key achievements and why those felt important. The morning session wrapped up with additional workbook exercises "linking gifts and heart" in which Reverend Patricia gave examples of how specific passions paired with specific spiritual gifts might suggest aptitude for particular types of ministry and service.

After a break, participants began two personality assessments provided in the workbooks. Questions asked about introversion/extroversion, task versus people orientation, and personal style. Putting these together on an XY chart helped identify a personality profile that was intended to help people refine their sense of where they might be both passionate and successful in serving within the church—whether people are leaders, work better in groups or alone, and are people or task focused. At the end of the seminar, Reverend Patricia asked participants to consider signing the "ministry covenant" included in the binder indicating their commitment to discovering their unique heart and gifts for ministry, and willingness to serve where needed and in cooperation with others for the good of the whole body.

> We want to encourage you to commit to the ministry covenant and be sure to complete your self-evaluation, if you haven't already, so that you can schedule an interview with one of our ministry guides. They'll work with you to select two or three ministry opportunities that best match your gifts and interests. It is then your responsibility to connect with the people leading those ministries—hopefully within two weeks so your ideas are fresh in your mind. Then start serving with joy in what God has called you to do. Connecting with other classes or small-group ministries is also a good idea so that you can strengthen your faith within our church family.

The Affirmation of Faith: Becoming Presbyterian

Once prospective members have completed these two weekend seminars, they are ready to be received into the church. Four times a year, during a regular Sunday morning service, Reverend Patricia or Reverend Richard asks new members to come stand in the front of the sanctuary. After brief introductions, one of the elders reads from the Book of Common Worship,[1] saying "On behalf of Session [of elders] I present (name) and (name), who have been received into the membership of this congregation by transfer from (name of the previous) congregation" or "by reaffirmation of faith" (if previously baptized but not currently a member elsewhere).[2] The service continues with affirmations of faith in Christ and commitment to being a faithful disciple and member of the congregation. The congregation as a whole stands to read aloud with the new members the Apostles' creed and a prayer of commitment. After the passing of the peace, the service moves back to the regular order of Sunday morning worship with a hymn, scripture reading, and sermon.

If a prospective member has not already been baptized, that sacrament is incorporated into the new member service. Adults and minor children alike are sprinkled on the head with water poured ceremoniously into a basin by Reverend Patricia as she reads the words of the baptismal service from the Book of Common Worship, asking the candidates to affirm their intention to be baptized, leading them and the congregation in prayer and reciting the Apostles' creed, asking the Holy Spirit to bless the water so that it will be water of redemption to equip the candidate and the church for faithful service. She then calls forward each person to be baptized and sprinkles handfuls of water over each head in turn saying, "I baptize you in the name of the Father, and of the Son, and of the Holy Spirit. Amen!" with a great smile and humor at the orderly, but somewhat messy, process of baptizing adults in their Sunday best. "You are a child of God, sealed by the Holy Spirit in baptism, and marked as Christ's own forever."

The New-Member Process at Valley Baptist Church

Relationships are the primary means through which people first hear about and visit Valley Baptist Church. As Pastor Mark described during a conversation in his office one afternoon:

> While "Joe church person" will come up to me after worship some day and say "Hi, I'm Billy Joe and this is my wife Suzie and our kids. We just moved into town and want to join your church," most people come because they're thinking maybe they have a need for something, but don't even know what, and someone they know tells them about the church. They come and sit in the back and bolt as soon as the service is over. Then eventually, maybe four weeks, maybe six months later, once they've had a chance to check things out and have decided that they can trust me a little bit, they'll come up with a question or ask to talk to me about something that's going on in their life.

People come not only by personal invitation but also as referrals by people who might themselves be members elsewhere, but know a neighbor or coworker who is looking for a church or might enjoy the informal, seeker church environment at Valley Baptist. After Pastor Mark's arrival, the church cleared its rolls of inactive members (cutting the on-paper membership in half, from about four hundred to two hundred members). Since his arrival, the number of regular attendees has dramatically increased from less than one hundred to nearly four hundred people per week. Most of this growth has come through attracting two very different constituencies: the "unchurched" and "disciple-makers"—an emphasis that is typical in evangelical seeker churches.

> We are an open-door church. Which means that we consider our prime customer to be someone who doesn't go to church, hasn't been in church a long time. We have other people that don't fit that criteria, but that is our number-one customer; no one is more important to us than that person. So the kinds of people who will be comfortable here are either people who are early on the faith curve, people that are checking it out, have just kind of crossed the line of faith, are new in their faith and people who like to help people like that. People in the middle, who would not call themselves beginners or are not passionate about being a part of a place that helps beginners will be dissatisfied in a church like this.

Posters throughout the building, and many of the church's printed notices, reiterate the congregation's identity as an informal, personal, seeker-friendly place made up of "ordinary people growing closer to God and helping others along the way."

Kicking the Tires at a Saturday Seminar

The membership process at Valley Baptist begins with a Saturday morning breakfast at which prospective members are invited to "kick the tires" and discover what the church is all about. Joining a set of mostly younger couples and ministry leaders in the basement meeting room at one of these quarterly seminars, I'm presented with a name tag, coffee, donuts, and a folder stuffed with brochures on children's ministry, student ministries, morning for moms, community groups, Christian preschool, elementary school and child care center, and the recent stewardship campaign, along with a list of Sunday School classes and their locations, older member special events, typed pages detailing the church's corporate values (authenticity, diversity, cultural relevance, excellence, creativity, compassion, anointed teaching, small groups, spiritual gifts, and interpersonal evangelism), ministry activities, an organizational chart, global ministries (missionary) partners, facilities map, a listing of lay leadership team members, short bios of the pastors and staff, a thirty-page constitution of the congregation, a survey of attenders' contact information and interest in taking the next step toward membership and/or interest in specific church ministries, and finally an outline of the topics for the morning's events. It is a thick folder and a lot to digest.

The seminar proves to be three hours of fast-paced, entertaining, and informative presentations on the church's programs and core beliefs. On the surface, Valley Baptist appears to be a rather un-Baptist place. There's little mention of distinctively Baptist history or beliefs, and speaker after speaker presents the church as a place where diverse people are accepted and loved and helped to grow in their faith no matter where they are or where they've come from. On this particular Saturday morning, I joined a group of about fifty prospective members seated at tables for eight spread throughout the room. After an introduction in which Pastor Mark explained, "We're not here to sell you on anything or give you a pitch. I truly believe that there may be someone in this room that God is leading somewhere else for some reason in terms of your makeup and what you're looking for. We want you to find the place God has for you. So this is not a pitch, but a blueprint for where God has us going . . . because putting down roots is a big decision."

The first thirty or forty minutes of the morning are all introductions. There's Mary who grew up in a small town nearby and had visited three times this past month. She has a two-year-old and loves the pagers the nursery staff gives to parents when they drop kids off before church. Having a pager lets her relax and enjoy the service, knowing if there's a problem she'll get a call rather than find a child "melted down" after the service. She explained that her husband couldn't make it, but he loves the church, too. Mary was seated at the same table as two friends who had been visiting with her. After introducing themselves, they went on to describe how on their first visit they "loved hearing Pastor Mark play the piano and sing before preaching" and decided to keep coming back. A middle-aged couple at the same table said they were currently splitting their time between two churches—Valley Baptist, which they "love," and another where they're long-time members and "feel married to." They have twin twelve-year-olds who talk about the sermons they hear at Valley Baptist more than they talk about what was said at their other church, and so the parents are rethinking where they think they should be longer term—or at least while the kids are still living at home. At the next table, one of the elders introduces himself and his wife as long-term residents and members who are delighted with the sound Bible teaching and new energy they've seen since Pastor Mark's arrival. Another man, John, is attending with his wife and describes how they had been church shopping since moving from California six months ago and love the music, the preaching, and the kids' programs at Valley Baptist. They have been regular attenders for several months and recently enrolled their children in the preschool, and "they just love it." After telling the story of how they ended up at Valley Baptist, John tuned to his wife to give her opportunity to comment. She replied, simply "ditto," and passed the introductions on to the next couple at the table. That couple told a similar story of moving to town, church shopping, and feeling they'd landed on the right spot when they visited Valley Baptist. After them, Anne, a young woman in her mid-twenties, described having attended for about eight months. She moved to the area for graduate school and appreciated the positive messages. "Most churches are gloom and doom," she said. "Everyone's going to hell, etc. But here I don't feel like that. I feel energized." Her friend, Zoe, had joined her a couple of weeks ago. Zoe was driving nearly forty minutes to get to church, but said it was worth it to be somewhere "real": "I was raised in church and kind of dropped out when I was in college. It was hard to find time and a place that felt genuine instead of formal or phony. It seems like folks here are not like that at all. There's a realness. And like everyone else is saying, I love the music and think it's overall a very uplifting place."

Over and over again, as the introductions moved around the room, similar stories were told of people moving into the area, visiting a number of churches, and finding the young energy and practical Bible-based sermons at Valley Baptist compelling. Scattered around the tables were eight or nine lay leaders—men who were elders, Sunday School teachers, and the principal of the Christian school, as well as three women who work in the office, teach in the school, or help coordinate the moms' ministry. Most of them spoke about the church recovering from depressed attendance and shrinking ministries in the 1970s and how God has used Pastor Mark to really turn things around. "We're an independent church," one of them explained. "There's no outside agency that dictates what we do. We're a conservative Baptist church in the sense that we're conservative on the Bible as the perfect word of God and final authority for how we live and what we do, but other than that we will do just about anything to reach someone for Jesus Christ. We're not out to make Baptists, but are passionate about making disciples who magnify him." During the remainder of the morning, each of the leaders present spent a few minutes describing some aspect of the church's history, organization, beliefs, ministries, and next steps toward making a "family connection" by becoming a member.

At the conclusion of each Saturday Seminar (each of which follows a similar pattern, with similar people and stories as those just described), prospective members are invited to fill in a short questionnaire about their experience that morning and to indicate whether or not they would like to talk with the pastor or one of the elders in person about anything, including membership. As at the Presbyterian church, people who are currently members at a conservative Baptist church may join Valley Baptist by transfer of letter. Others join through a process of meeting with an elder, who asks about their experience of being born again and explains that the church requires adults to be baptized by immersion before they can participate in congregational meetings or become involved in leading any of the church's ministries. Although the leadership presents the church as not interested in splitting hairs over minor points of doctrine, in this regard Valley Baptist is a very Baptist place.

Baptism: Celebrating Membership and New Life

In keeping with the desire to minimize things that sound and feel "weird" or "spooky" to newcomers, and to make Sunday morning worship easily accessible and user friendly, baptisms are held once every three months during a special evening service. The baptistery itself is hidden from view backstage and is only revealed at these "new life celebrations"—appearing as a picture window high in the wall otherwise obscured by the projection screen. Candidates receive instructions on what to wear ahead of time and to bring a set of clothes to change into afterward. Pastor Mark meets again with those joining by baptism to hear their story, review the questions that will be asked during baptism, and review the process.

About one hundred people attend these evening services celebrating "new life." The service begins with twenty minutes of singing three or four praise choruses, and then Pastor Mark steps down into the tank, visible through a big window in the wall above the stage, and says:

> I want to welcome you to what is an exciting evening here. We want everything we do here tonight to give praise and glory and honor

to God because he is alive and well and changing the lives of ordinary people today. Just in case you've never been to something like
this before, I just want to make it clear that no one's becoming a
Christian here tonight. Nobody's going into the tank at one end and
coming out the other a Christian. All these people are Christians
already. They're here in obedience to God, to give testimony to what
God has done in their lives.

Pastor Mark then introduces the pastor of the Latino group that meets in
the building who interviews and baptizes a young man in his twenties,
and a twelve-year-old girl, asking each in turn, why they are there tonight,
what Jesus has done for them, and if they intend to follow Jesus. Pastor
Mark then steps back down into the tank and is joined by the youth pastor
to assist in baptizing three teenagers, asking the same general questions.
There's Sarah, a freshman at the local high school who lost her grandmother this past year and during her grief was invited to Valley Baptist.
"I found peace in church, with people here and in Jesus." "Tell me what
Jesus has done for you," Pastor Mark says. "He died for me and taught
me how to follow him and helped my family . . . to believe that Christ died
on the cross and rose so we could follow him." "And is it your intention
to live for Jesus from here on out?" "Yes." Sarah crosses her arms over
her chest and, flanked by the two men, is dipped over backward under
the water, as Pastor Mark says, "Then it is my privilege, Sarah, to baptize
you in the name of the Father and the Son and the Holy Spirit" (she goes
under the water). "Buried with him in the likeness of his death, raised
with him to newness of life." The congregation bursts into applause as
they help her stand back upright. Sarah and the pastors exchange a hug
and then Pastor Mark gives her a hand as she climbs the steps and exits
the tank stage left.

Stories from these adolescents highlight an experience or decision in
which faith becomes real in response to a crisis or loss. Others said it was
time to make the faith they had known since childhood their own and that
baptism was a way to "make known to others and in my heart that I want
to follow God and be obedient to him." Adult stories reflected many of the
same themes. Greg, who had been attending Valley Baptist for six months,
talked about how "Jesus changed my life 180 degrees, making me a better
dad, partner, and son." Donna, who was approached by the youth pastor
on the street one day when a team was out canvassing the neighborhood
asking people what they'd like to hear as the topic of a Sunday sermon,

said she'd like to hear a sermon on why Christians are such hypocrites. A week later she received a copy of a postcard the church had mailed to households in the neighborhood and saw that the title of the first sermon in an upcoming sermon series was on why Christians are such hypocrites. She went to hear it and had been attending ever since. Taylor, who "grew up in a loving Christian family," described himself as knowing God for a long time, then went on to say his spiritual life took off when he started attending Valley Baptist, and he had decided now was the time to make a public declaration of faith in Jesus Christ. Connie explained that "the devil is not striking me down anymore or causing me any downfalls since I gave myself to the Lord on July 19th at 10 pm," and that she had "lived a different life since then." And April, who was being baptized the day after the church threw her a birthday party, clarified the finer points of her story with the help of Pastor Mark's gentle prompting.

PASTOR MARK: Tonight you're here, so it has been a big week for you!

APRIL: Yes, before I wasn't big on going to church at all, but he's shown me that not all churches are the same, that I can live a good life.

PASTOR MARK: That's right; you can have a new life in Christ.

APRIL: I'm starting over in life.

PASTOR MARK: And what did Jesus do for you?

APRIL: He died and rose for me so that I could be forgiven.

PASTOR MARK: And is it your intent to follow Jesus from now on to the best of your ability?

APRIL: You bet it is.

PASTOR MARK: Then it is my privilege to baptize you . . .

The dialogue continued, with Pastor Mark dipping her backward into the water, helping her stand, and giving her a hug and a hand as she exited, dripping and smiling from the pool.

After the baptisms are completed, Pastor Mark turns to the congregation and says, "I tell you, there's a lot of things that go on around here but that's the best. It's not about water, but about how God changes lives. If you're here and you haven't experienced new life in Jesus, I want you to know it is for you, too. God offers it to you freely. It's just up to you to take it. And you can do that tonight." It's a subtle invitation—not an altar call, but an offer for anyone who realizes this is the moment for them to stand up, confess their faith, and be baptized as well. This particular evening there were no takers, and after Pastor Mark exits the baptismal pool the youth pastor (now changed and dry) takes up his guitar and leads the congregation in singing two more praise choruses. As they end, Mark reappears—also changed and dry—and begins a short sermon on how the grace of God can transform ordinary lives. A final song closes out the hour-long service.

The New-Member Process at St. Andrews

Among these congregations, St. Andrews' membership process is by far the simplest for those who are already Orthodox—anyone who has been baptized and chrismated in a canonical Orthodox jurisdiction elsewhere (whether Greek, Antiochian, Russian, Serbian, Romanian, Albanian, or any other iteration of those national churches now present in the United States) may become a member of a particular parish by simply beginning to attend. Adult members in good standing (defined by the national church as those having received the sacraments of confession and communion at least once in the past year, and making some financial contribution, pledge or tithe) may vote at the annual meeting and be elected to serve on parish council or as lay delegates at the regional and national meetings that shape policy and make recommendations for regional and national leadership.

Becoming an Inquirer

For people from non-Orthodox backgrounds, the process is more lengthy and involved. It begins with a weekly inquirers' class that Father Michael offers two or three times a year, followed by several months to more than a year of reading, participation, and regular meetings with the priest in preparation for being received into the church. When I asked Father Michael about whether or not visitors found this process a bit daunting, he laughed and said:

Well, it is my responsibility to make sure people are ready and that takes time. It is the Holy Spirit that calls people into the Church. Most of the time people come because they're searching. Often they've done some reading about the Orthodox faith and decide at some point to check it out in person. How do people join? Well, they have to start coming! (Laughs) And then, once they attend, then they need to start reading or visiting with me so I can guide them as to how to learn more about the faith. I have inquirers' classes a couple of times a year at this point. So they can come to those, and they need to participate as best they can in the worship services and the daily life of the Parish community, so it is a progression of involvement. And then, after a year's time, if they are still interested, then we would begin a more one-on-one kind of counseling session with the catechumen—the person wanting to be received into the Orthodox Church. And then they would be received into the Church through the Holy Mysteries of either Baptism (triple immersion to show their dying and rising with Christ to newness of life) and/or Chrismation (sealing with holy oil or chrism consecrated by the Bishop) that is the gift of the Holy Spirit ... depending again on whether they were Christian or what kind of Christian before coming into the Orthodox Church.

Inquirers' classes typically meet on a weeknight for six to eight weeks and are attended by ten to fifteen people from an eclectic array of backgrounds: a woman in her fifties was looking for a smaller and more intimate congregation than the Episcopalian church she currently attended; a disaffiliated Roman Catholic saw an ad the church was running in the local paper and decided to learn more; and a woman who described herself as "getting into trouble asking too many questions in Catholic School" and her husband (a former mainline Christian who currently identified as Buddhist). They had attended a church festival, came for vespers afterward, and had been attending ever since. Rounding out this particular class was a young couple who were attending a large evangelical church, but whose parents were members and were urging them to consider Orthodoxy; a member of a local Mennonite church who described himself as wanting to learn more about Orthodoxy after starting to read about church history; a teacher who had been given a book on the early church and had been invited to come by a coworker who had joined the previous year; a retired counselor who had attended a Bible college in the Midwest; a couple who identified as pagan and had been invited by a friend from their neighborhood home-schooling group; and two students who had become interested in Orthodoxy through reading material for a class on world religions.

Joining the group's first meeting, I found myself seated around a rectangular table with fifteen others in a somewhat chilly church hall. Father Michael began by introducing himself and passing out a list of books and topics that he would be covering in the weeks ahead. He explained that

it would be good for people to bring their Bibles because he'd be talking about specific passages, in addition to going over the history of how
the Bible came to include some texts and not others. The substance of
the first discussion covered Orthodox perspectives on how the teachings of the New Testament church are preserved in their fullness in the
Orthodox Church and how other traditions, even those that are not specifically Christian, may contain partial but incomplete truths about God's
nature and redemptive work in the world. "The Orthodox Church," Father
Michael said, "while not a perfect institution, is the historic extension of
the New Testament church; the institution through which God's story of
redemption and grace are most fully communicated to the world." The
claims of simultaneous exclusiveness and openness appeared to surprise
a few of the people sitting around the table, and one (currently evangelical)
young man raised an eyebrow and said under his breath, "Whoa, I don't
get it." So Father Michael went on to explain:

> Now that's my bias. Does the historic New Testament church exist?
> We're going to discover that it is existing. Is there a church that con-
> tinues the faith and practices of that Christian church? It is impor-
> tant for everyone to draw their own conclusions, but it'll come as
> no surprise, because I'm an Orthodox priest (smiles), that through
> study we will find that the faith and practice of the New Testament
> church has been preserved in its entirety in the Orthodox church.
> Depending on what your faith background is, especially if you're
> Christian, you'll find some similarities as well as differences. When
> most people first come to an Orthodox church, it is quite a shock
> even if they've read something about it ahead of time. So it is clear
> that, compared to other churches, the Orthodox church is different,
> even to some of our Roman Catholic friends, and our Anglican and
> Episcopalian friends who also use liturgy, because these as we will
> see . . . and again this is my bias, my conclusion . . . differ from what
> we find as the practice of the Orthodox church that has preserved
> the fullness of the teaching and practice of the apostles. Now wher-
> ever God is working there is grace—that may be outside the church.
> We say, "We know where the church is, we do not know where it
> is not." I would never say I know whether someone is saved or a
> Christian or is going to heaven even if they're Orthodox. The church
> is a mystical body that has an historic structure and presence that
> is the Orthodox church. It is a mystical body that has institutions; it
> is not an institution with mysteries. That is important! To be saved

is to receive the life of Christ and be united and part of that mystical body. So someone may be saved who doesn't appear to be in the institution, but who *is* in the mystical body of Christ. And certainly there are those in the institution who are not part of the mystical body of Christ. Only God knows.

Over the next two months of weekly meetings, Father Michael provided an overview and introduction to the theology and practices of the church. After introductions at the first meeting, he launched into a discussion of how contemporary Orthodox belief and practice developed through oral tradition, consensus, and the authority of regional leaders appointed by the apostles; how those leaders met to affirm "what was believed everywhere and by all" when challenged by alternate understandings of core doctrines; and how these councils established the texts of the New Testament based on those gospels or letters that were most widely received, practiced, and doctrinally coherent. At subsequent meetings, Father Michael talked at length about the evolution of the creed and its centrality in specifying the doctrine of the trinity, the incarnation, and the church. At the same time, he made the case that there is room for change in the music and detail of the liturgy, as well as appropriate cultural expressions of faith outside of the current liturgical forms—giving examples of drumming in African Orthodox services after the conclusion of liturgy, or the efforts of Orthodox youth to write folk or rock or punk music with Orthodox content.

> There's nothing wrong with contemporary Christian music; it just doesn't get you all the way to where you want to go. The basic idea is that the Holy Spirit has preserved in the practice of the Church those things that are most useful for our sanctification. It is the lyrics, not the melody, that matter. When we modify lyrics, we often do so for our own tastes and entertainment and don't get as much benefit as a result.

During these classes, Father Michael spent much of his time answering questions about the distinctions between Orthodoxy and the Roman Catholic tradition—how, for example, the Orthodox understanding is that for the first thousand years of church history the Bishop of Rome was considered the first among equals but did not hold distinctive authority; or how the bread and wine are not changed into the body and blood of Christ but are two things at once—both bread and wine and the body and blood of Christ—during the Eucharist. He also spent a great deal of time answering questions about the differences between Orthodoxy and Protestantism: clarifying how kissing an icon is not idol worship, but that "reverence given to the image is carried to the prototype" in the same way a person can kiss a picture of a beloved relative or friend who has died or moved away, and that the presence of icons is consistent with the idea that the church is a "great cloud of witnesses" outside of time and reaffirms the notion that something can be two things at once—both fully God and fully human, both bread and wine and the body and blood of Christ, both painted wood and the presence of a real historic hero of faith. Classes also focused on a number of other doctrinal distinctives. For example, the idea that sin is whatever takes you off the narrow path to eternal life, and death, rather than sin, as an indelible part of human nature and of nature itself after the fall; the idea that salvation is a process of life change and not simply a decision to "accept Jesus as your personal savior"; the understanding that the crucifixion was not as much a judicial payment for sin as it was God taking a body through death so that those who have united themselves with Christ may also experience the resurrection of the body; or the affirmation by various historic church councils that Mary is appropriately called "*Theotokos*" (God bearer) because the name underlined the idea that Jesus was fully God and fully human—having two natures and two wills rather than one. Little was said about the church's programs or staffing or ministry opportunities. Most people took a lot of notes.

I wondered numerous times during these meetings about how complicated and academic and abstract the discussions were. Surely there was too much specific doctrine to be affirmed or practices to participate in; surely most people would eventually decide to go elsewhere. That did turn out to be the case, as half those participating in both series of inquirers classes that I attended eventually dropped out. One young woman who had been received into the church a few months before said this was typical of both the inquirer classes as well as regular adult Sunday School classes. Yet from her perspective, the complexity of the content didn't seem to put people off. They might miss some of the detail, but there was always something to which they could connect. "People don't have to get all of it, or agree with all of it," she said. "There are some ideas that are nonnegotiable, like the incarnation and the trinity, but there's also a lot of teaching that is seen as useful and good but not essential. That's one of the weird things about Orthodoxy—it is unambiguous about some doctrines and basic practices, but also really personal and flexible in terms of allowing people to begin with what they're able to do and go on from there."

Disciplines, Sacraments, and Entering the Church

After completing one of these classes, Father Michael would begin to meet individually with people to talk through any remaining questions or reservations and to encourage them to start living as though they were Orthodox as they moved closer to membership. Most of the time Father Michael advised catechumens (those formally on the path to being received into the Church) to keep a simple "prayer rule" at home and to pray with the congregation as often as possible at Saturday evening vigil, Sunday morning liturgies, and any additional weekday feast days or special services. Catechumens are also encouraged to begin participating in the fast periods prescribed by the church—typically abstaining from meat, eggs, dairy, and alcohol on Wednesdays, Fridays, and other weekdays during major fasts, including Lent (the forty days prior to Palm Sunday) and Holy Week (the week between Palm Sunday and Easter). Taken together, these periods of fasting comprise nearly half of the calendar year. The spiritual disciplines of Orthodoxy—fasting in particular—are the subject of much discussion among prospective and newer members who often struggle with Orthodoxy's ostensible legalism. As Father Michael's wife, Katherine, described as we talked one afternoon:

> Fasting is important, but you know, without prayer, fasting is just a diet. Anyone can abstain from food. The devil fasts all the time (she laughs), so not eating meat or dairy or not having wine or something is not that big a deal. Praying, loving your neighbor as yourself? That's hard. People often get stuck on all this, but it isn't legalism—it is discipline. We do these things not because we have to, but because they are means through which God can begin to slowly make us more like Christ. To curb the passions that make us spiritually and physically sick.

As prospective members continue to meet with Father Michael, they pick up more of these practices, and eventually, with his blessing, are received into the Church—most often on Pascha (Orthodox Easter, the date of which is typically several days to a month before or after Easter is celebrated in the West), at Christmas, or the parish feast day in July. The catechumen begins his or her formal entry into the Church by doing a "lifetime confession" the Saturday before, as evening vigil comes to an end. In the same manner as parishioners over the age of seven regularly participate in confession, the catechumen stands beside the priest before an icon of Christ and there confesses to Christ, with the priest as a witness who occasionally gives counsel. During this process, parishioners who are not staying for confession talk quietly as they exit the back of the church, while a member reads from the book of Psalms until all the confessions have been completed. At the conclusion, candles are blown out, lights dimmed, and the remaining congregants trickle out to their cars for the drive home.

In the morning, half the congregation will have returned, earlier than usual, for baptisms that take place either in a horse trough on the church porch or, weather permitting, in a pond nearby. Father Michael reads through the words sanctifying the water, blowing on it, and pouring in a dribble of blessed oil in the shape of a cross. Incense fills the air as the catechumens stand by shivering in t-shirts and shorts. One by one, they step into the water and kneel. Father Michael places his hand on the catechumen's head and says, "in the name of the Father" and dunks the person once, "the Son" and dunks the person again, "and the Holy Spirit" and dunks the person a third time. The porch is crowded with people pressing in to see, standing on benches along the edge, lifting children, taking pictures with cell phones, leaning over the railing to get a better view. The newly baptized, shivering and drenched, are wrapped in a towel and hustled into the church to dry off and change into a white baptismal robe.

The second part of the service, anointing with oil or Chrismation, is held inside the church and is intended to enact a "personal Pentecost" in the same way that baptism enacts participation in the crucifixion and resurrection of Christ. Newly baptized individuals, as well as anyone joining the Church who was previously baptized, meet Father Michael in the doorway to the chapel, where they and their sponsors pause for prayers, to renounce the devil and the errors of the religious tradition (if any) that they are leaving, affirm their intent to be united to the Orthodox faith, and read the Nicene Creed. They then proceed together into the church, holding onto the edge of Father Michael's stole, and circle three times around a small table in the center laden with the paraphernalia of Chrismation, while the choir sings "as many as have been baptized into Christ have put on Christ." Chrismation follows. Father Michael dips a small brush in a vial of fragrant oil blessed by the Bishop and brushes it on the newly baptized person's eyelids, ears, neck, hands, and feet, saying as he anoints each part, "The seal of the gift of the Holy Spirit." The congregation responds by saying, "Amen." After bowing to kiss the cross and kneeling to be prayed over and receive absolution for sin, Father Michael wipes off what remains of the oil with a tiny sponge, saying, "You are baptized, you are illumined, you are anointed with Holy oil, you are cleansed, in the name of the Father, and of the Son and of the Holy Spirit, amen." The "newly illumined" members receive a large, lit candle from their sponsors, which they hold for the remainder of the service as a reminder to be a light for Christ in the world. Father Michael says some words of encouragement about the struggle ahead, and the congregation, after a brief intermission to offer congratulations to the newly received members, shifts into a normal Sunday hour-and-a-half liturgy.

Conclusion: Rituals of Scope and Time

Each of these congregations sets aside specific times and rituals through which prospective new members are introduced to the teachings and ministries of the church and are invited to become members. The amount of time it takes to move through this process varies enormously. Half a Saturday morning, followed by a brief meeting to give testimony about being born again, a letter of membership transfer, and either baptism and/ or affirmation of faith at a Sunday service introduces visitors to the beliefs and programs at Valley Baptist and makes someone a member. Three or four seminars on denominational history and the importance of spiritual gifts and growth, followed by presentation to the congregation on a Sunday morning where new members read together an affirmation of faith and promise to be faithful members of the congregation, are the core of the membership process at First Presbyterian. St Andrews requires no transfer of letter or public ceremony for those who are already Orthodox, but months of study and practice for those moving into the church for the first time.

The duration of the process fits the depth of doctrine, teaching, and practice that clergy ask new members to embrace and in which they hope all members will continue to grow. We return to the question of spiritual growth in Chapter 5. Before that, however, we take up the question of how women and men experience the process of joining—what attracts them, what do they find valuable and worth their time any given Sunday morning—within and across these three diverse congregations.

4

Belonging

WHAT DO PEOPLE think when they are moving through this process? What makes sense or seems odd? Are there places where gender matters and, if so, how? To answer those questions, we tracked groups of individuals who were visiting or considering joining each congregation. We interviewed most of them several times as they worked through their own process of considering greater commitment to the congregation, beginning with questions about how their perspectives on faith and practice have changed over time. In this section, we focus on three aspects of that process—the personal and religious history of prospective members, motivations for attending, and the substance that attracted women and men to these congregations.

Beginning to Belong at First Presbyterian Church

Just over half of the women and men we interviewed who had attended an introductory dessert or new member seminar at First Presbyterian had grown up going to a Presbyterian church. Some dropped out during their early adult years but found themselves rethinking their involvement when they married, moved, or had a child, and had come to consider being Presbyterian a part of their adult identity. Another quarter either were now or had at some time been affiliated with other older denominations (Methodist, Lutheran, or United Church of Christ) and found the Presbyterian tradition close enough to their beliefs that it seemed a reasonable fit. Most of the remainder were compromise joiners—families in which one person had some background in a Presbyterian or Lutheran or Methodist church and the other had grown up Catholic or evangelical or nothing, and First Presbyterian seemed to be a place where they could settle and both be more or less content. A small number of visitors described themselves as having no particular religious background or affiliation—similar to the "nones" whose religious identity is not tethered to a particular historic tradition but rests on a more eclectic and flexible set of (sometimes vague) spiritual ideals. These often described being drawn to First Presbyterian by a personal connection or attendance at a music event or special program, and simply deciding to stay.

In many ways, standard social capital explanations for church membership fit the profiles of the majority of prospective members at First Presbyterian. They were thinking about joining because they had married someone who was interested in finding a church, they had a parent or coworker or neighbor who attended, or they had met one of the pastors at a fundraiser or social event in town, liked the pastor and decided to drop in to visit, and then visited again. Yet even among the previously unaffiliated, the jump wasn't a big one—more of a step or a small hop—nothing to push anyone, themselves or their extended family or friends, off balance or trip them up by the move. The services, moreover, were polished, nondemanding, and had the additional benefit of the enjoyable preaching of a husband and wife team.

Lifelong Presbyterians, Fundamentalist Refugees, and Returning Seekers

Two themes dominated the narratives around joining for these prospective new members. First, there were lifelong Presbyterians who had moved to town for work or to be closer to family or to retire; they simply located the Presbyterian churches in the area and went to the one that was closest. As one recent retiree said, "We just moved into town from about half an hour away, and rather than drive back to where we'd been attending, we decided to go here because it was basically the same and was a lot closer. It's a great place to build relationships and spend time with people who share the same faith." Being a lifelong Presbyterian was a central and salient part of the identity of this subset of prospective and current members. "I was born and bred Presbyterian," one older woman said. "I believe what they teach and I can't imagine going anywhere else."

A second theme involved people who were less identified with Presbyterianism per se, but who had come to believe that church membership was important and had been unable to find a congregation that felt satisfactory until they started visiting First Presbyterian. More common among younger and middle-aged adults, these narratives focused on frustration with "Bible thumping" and "fundamentalist" churches, or being put off by pedophilia scandals within the Catholic Church, or their own history of having been loosely affiliated as a child, drifting or walking away, and eventually having some life experience that redirected their attention back toward church membership. One forty-year-old man's story exemplified this narrative theme.

> I grew up going to church with my mother and grandmother. At that point they only had a traditional service and it was pretty bland, pretty boring. I started skipping out during Sunday school, and by the time I was in high school, I just told them I wasn't going anymore. There was football; there was anything other than church. At that point, I started getting into other stuff that wasn't healthy for me. The years went by and by and by. This whole time I considered myself a Christian, even though I was not doing stuff that was very Christian-like. After my divorce I was feeling like I should be connected somewhere. My wife had dabbled in Wicca and I tried to get into that with her, but it didn't make sense. She basically left me and I moved back here to be closer to my family. I tried going to the Unitarian Universalists for awhile, but that wasn't my cup of tea. I even took an online survey to see what would fit with what I believe and it came up Reformed-Presbyterian. So here I am! The second best fit was Baha'i and I was like, uh, No! I joked with my buddies that I was going to stand up in the middle of the service when I first came and say, "I'm not interested in your religion. I'm here to scope out your women!" But in the end, I liked the message and the way it was presented, and the whole deal was very warm. Their pastors are pretty cool and the place is pretty friendly.

Shared Appreciation for Thinking and Common Sense

Within these narratives of connection or reconnection with the Presbyterian Church, prospective members pointed to a range of religious and spiritual goods that attracted them to the church. Many of these goods were gender neutral and appeared in both men's and women's descriptions of what they appreciated about this particular tradition and this particular congregation. For example, both women and men described how much they appreciated the pastors' thoughtful and more intellectual approach to scripture, the common-sense appeal of the sermons, and that the church supported private spirituality without being dogmatic. As one woman in her late fifties said:

> The very first sermon we heard Pastor Patricia preach, she gave us a lot of things to think about which we were not accustomed to. We really like that sort of thing. Both pastors preach sermons where you have something to take home with you and you kind of chew on it all week long. You think about it. And this sounds kind of funny coming from me, I'm fifty-eight years old, but I still find that a challenge.

These sentiments were echoed by men who described themselves as appreciative of the opportunity to "listen to challenging sermons" that have "common-sense appeal." As a married man in his forties described:

> It's very practical, common-sense, get-down-to-basics approach to spirituality. I guess you'd call it middle of the road, not all fire and brimstone type of stuff, but it's a very common-sense approach to developing your spiritual life. Look at what Jesus taught us, and don't get too hung up on stuff that doesn't make sense.

Similarly, both women and men praised the quality of the music program, the combination of both classic church music and more contemporary worship songs, programs for youth, and how they were beginning to feel like they fit in this family of faith.

Gendered Valuations of Inclusion, Energy, and Acceptance

Alongside these shared sentiments, more gendered attitudes and approaches surfaced in talking with women and men who were considering membership at First Presbyterian. When asked what they liked specifically about having a husband-and-wife team as pastors, women were more likely to talk about the leadership appearing to be flexible and open to suggestion. One woman in her fifties summarized these comments, saying, "We were really impressed with the democracy of the church. People have a say in it. And that seems like a great idea. They're pretty open and appreciate differences, and that's nice, too." Another woman in her forties said, "They're open to ideas and suggestions and they're really trying to satisfy the membership by listening to people's suggestions and being malleable."

Men within this group of prospective joiners didn't talk about democratic leadership styles as much as the upbeat balance and energy the pastors brought to their ministry, and the congregation as a whole being open and accepting. As a forty-three-year-old father of two said, "I like the way the message is presented. It's very upbeat. Richard presents things in a fresh, modern way, and Patricia is so full of energy. I wish I could have some of that!" Or, as another man in his late forties, put it,

> I like the energy. They really try to appeal to different types of people. For example, there's very much of a praise type of celebration, lots of music that appeals to youth. Then there's also the traditional as well. So, they're able to walk that line. A lot of churches that you go to, they're one or the other. They're either all praise and it's kind of upbeat new hymns that nobody's ever heard of before or they're the other way and it's all the traditional stuff and nobody ever ventures into the new stuff. And they walk that fence really well here. So I enjoy that part of it.

Again, while both women and men described the congregation as an accepting family, women went on to talk about "feeling really welcomed" and how "you come and are accepted and leave your baggage at the door, it's like family. You're accepted for who you are and trying to become better with God" and how "it gives you a feeling of warmth and welcome and being part of something." Warmth, welcome, and acceptance figured over and over again in women's descriptions of why they were interested in connecting with First Presbyterian. Younger and middle-aged women also mentioned how significant it felt to be part of a community where there were connections across generations. As one twenty-seven-year-old, newly married woman explained:

> We just walked in and loved it. When you come in, you are greeted by so many people, and it's so welcoming. That is really important; we love that about it. It's a place to build relationships. I really like that there are old people. It's really kind of neat to have relationships

with people that have been believers for a long time and have experience. And they are really open with sharing. It's a nice way to have a family, so much wisdom.

Other women echoed these sentiments, saying how impressed they were with how interconnected the congregation was, how the size meant you didn't feel lost and people welcomed you and knew your name.

The men who were visiting First Presbyterian also appreciated the warmth and acceptance they felt while visiting. Yet men were more likely to go on to specify how that was an aspect of their feeling that the congregation was a place where they were loved and could connect in meaningful ways to other people.

In the end it's all about love, it's all about acceptance, it's all about allowing yourself to experience the joy of opening up to other human beings and stopping this, "I'm better than you." That's what draws me. That's what dictates our choice of churches—the emphasis on love more than judgment, and the acceptance that we are all sinners, and we are always going to be sinners, and always trying together to do better.

Both women and men also talked about how they appreciated the church's commitment to social justice and their involvement with a local food bank and Habitat for Humanity. For women, these ministries resonated as examples of how the congregation fostered a personal ethos of giving back to the community. Men, in speaking about the same ministries, described the characteristics of the church's organization that allowed it to leverage change in the community, emphasizing the importance of structure and resources as means of affecting change.

Remedying and Reversing Gender Experience

It might be possible to interpret some of these gender differences as supporting the notion that women are more intrinsically spiritually minded than men—that men appear to focus on the external experience and intellectual appeal, while women focus more on internal values and relational connections. Yet these were not the only ways in which men described the appeal of this mainline congregation. In addition to structure, programs, and personnel, men spoke of the meaningfulness of being connected within a place where they felt safe from the stresses of a harsh world.

> I think the church is a haven, a safe haven, an island of accept-ance and tranquility where things outside might be in turmoil or dangerous and stressful and you come inside and there are people to accept you and you've got a place that's a sanctu-ary.... I think that attendance is important because it forces you to be disciplined. You can say, "Well, I can be spiritual, I can rest on the Sabbath, and I can think about God," but I think that Sunday worship really brings a sense of community and allows you to focus on God and get in touch a little bit better than if you're just on your own.

Men also described the congregation as providing support for developing their own spiritual growth and, most significantly, as providing a venue within which they could yield themselves to some greater good.

> It helps people realize that there is something bigger than them-selves, and in so doing, you kind of surrender your ego and things like that. Things that trap you down in life, and kind of dull your relationships with other people. Gives you a reason for living and a reason for helping people.

At the same time, men also talked about how they found the congregation was helping them develop their own sense of personal spirituality, and provided a venue for them to learn to forgive and embrace responsibility and personal discipline.

> It teaches you how to be a better person and how to be like Christ, which would be a good person. It teaches people to forgive, teaches people that with freedom comes responsibility, [and] you can't just do whatever feels good. There are guidelines for a better living; if you follow the guidelines, you're going to be better off. You're not going to be screwing around and cheating on your wife; in some ways it's a support group for people to stay on a moral track. I think for people to not define morality in some ways is pretty cowardly.

Connecting with this congregation helped men cultivate deeper relationships and their own personal moral commitments. Both relationships and moral commitments require community and personal discipline, and First Presbyterian appealed because it offered the direction, support, and flexibility for men to explore and experience these dimensions of their identity.

Lastly, in terms of gender differences in the experience of moving toward membership, women, but not men, talked about how valuable it was to have a place where they could be quiet for a little while without distraction. Time to think, time to zone out, time to pray was a significant experience for women. Simply having an hour to sit quietly and clear one's mind from the chatter of daily life was a significant good that women found within the sanctuary of First Presbyterian Church. As one mother of two preteens explained:

> I think the biggest thing for me with the role of the church is that it is a relief to have my children go to Sunday school and know that they're getting instruction because that gives me a total channeled time to be with God and to listen and get messages, think and pray, and do all those things. And I think church does that, especially for busy mothers. I think it just gives them that chance to be with God that you can't experience on your own . . . even, I wish you could do it on your own, but it happens more through your church, going to a service for me, at least for me. It re-energizes me and I look forward to that time.

Overall then, when we consider the gendered narratives of women and men exploring membership at First Presbyterian, we find women reflecting on experiences that stand as alternatives or remedies to the ways in which their lives remain limited by working as at-home mothers and everyday subordination (still) in society. The opportunity for quiet contemplation, the encouragement that comes from seeing women in central positions of leadership, and being part of a democratically structured organization resonated with women more than they did for men. Men considered the good they experienced within this congregation as the antithesis of their gender privilege. First Presbyterian felt like a place where they could yield themselves, be supported in developing a spiritual sensibility, and feel safe from the competitiveness that characterizes their everyday world.

Beginning to Belong at Valley Baptist Church

As at First Presbyterian Church, a subset of prospective members at Valley Baptist Church had long-term affiliations with the denomination. About half had grown up in Baptist churches—some at Valley Baptist itself. A few had been lifetime members. Most of these committed Baptists were returning to church after some detour or break in attendance during adolescence or young adulthood. A little over a third of those we interviewed were currently or had been affiliated with other Christian denominations (mostly mainline and Roman Catholic), and were drawn to Valley Baptist because of the teaching, people, and programs. The remainder had little or no background in religion. Some had set foot in a church for the first time just a few weeks ago and had decided they were interested in learning more. This latter group, along with long-term and recent joiners, fit the profiles of those Pastor Mark said the congregation was seeking to attract: "unchurched" members of the community; families struggling with limited employment, substance abuse, and broken relationships; and "mature believers" committed to an evangelical message of salvation and personal transformation who were interested in reaching others.

(Re) Committed Baptists and Brand-New Believers

The primary story among visitors who were long-term, committed Baptists was that they moved into town, looked up Baptist churches in the yellow pages or online, and started visiting what was nearby. The process described by one middle-aged man at a quarterly Saturday Seminar was typical of this group.

> My family's Baptist from way back. So when we moved here, we looked around and found Valley Baptist. I can't remember exactly . . . it wasn't any person, we just, you know, looked in the yellow pages or something, to see what was in the area. Not to "bad mouth" any of the other places we visited, but when we came here, wow! We loved the music and the preaching—Pastor Mark really brings the Word alive. So we kind of feel like this is where the Lord is leading us to get involved to grow our family.

Other people with long histories of affiliation with Baptist churches first became connected to Valley Baptist through personal ties in the community. They were invited by friends to youth group, attended through high school, and then stopped going for several years while in college. Some drifted away during those years—feeling more connected to university parachurch ministries instead of a local congregation. Others were immersed in studies or moved through a period of late-adolescent angst in which they questioned their faith and the relevance of institutionalized religious involvement. Then someone invited them to attend a service, they liked it, and ended up reconnecting again as independent young adults. As one young man in his twenties explained:

> I started going here when I was in middle school with some friends who were in the youth group. I wasn't really connected in high school as much ... my mom's agnostic and kind of pushed me about why I was going and so I kind of dropped out. When I was in college, I wasn't going to church much. Then a friend of mine got saved, and I started going to their college group. He said it was pretty cool and asked me to come. So I thought, "Hey, I'll try it again" as a way to support him. But I liked it—it was pretty fun, so I kept going. I invited my girlfriend and she started coming too. Now we're talking about getting married and think this is where we want to do that and belong.

Most of the visitors who had a history of Baptist affiliation described some period of disaffiliation when they were not connected, and making their way back toward membership from some not-so-distant personal, emotional, or habitual space. If these interruptions could be considered detours, they were not distant or lengthy. People talked about growing up going to a Baptist church with their parents or grandparents; becoming disaffected or drifting away; and experiencing some life transition or relationship that ended up drawing them back toward membership.

Other personal histories involved movement from a more substantial personal or emotional distance. These individuals were in the middle of significant life changes that included a turning or returning to faith at Valley Baptist. One woman in her early forties described a life crisis that reconnected her to a faith commitment she made twenty years earlier.

> I got saved at a Baptist church, but didn't really attend that much. I just said the prayer, but still used to party a lot. I did a lot of drugs

and ended up living in a black hole. Nobody knew where I was, and life just got really scary. I remember praying, "Dear Lord, help me get out of this place, get me out of the hole." Three days later I got a letter from my sister. She had found me. It had three lines in it: "I love you, I miss you, please call me." So I did, and she said, "You let us know, and we'll be there in two days with a U-Haul to bring you home." I waited two months, but then called her, and they came. Once I got moved in, I told my sister I wanted to go to church. They gave me the name of the place they went to, but I couldn't find it. I got really frustrated driving around, so I just prayed, "Lord, direct me to the church you want me to go to" and looked in the yellow pages and found Valley Baptist right there on the page, and said, "Okay, that's where I'm going to go." And that's where I've been ever since. What a change.

Other narratives of distance and return revolved around personal struggles with family, questioning the faith, challenges from agnostic faculty at a university, or getting into a group of friends who were hostile to religion. One twenty-eight-year-old woman's experience typified a narrative that is increasingly common—growing up among the "nones" in terms of religious affiliation.

I always felt like there was some kind of spirit, like there was something more out there, but my parents didn't believe in God at all. You know, we're your typical middle-class suburban family. We don't need God. When I got into college, I hung out with a crowd that was really sort of anti-God; I spent some time just really making fun of Christians, calling them all sorts of things that I won't say on the record. Once I graduated, I figured out that I was making fun of them because I was envious they had this great community and this shared belief. And then when I started working, there were two people at work who were Christians—they didn't go to church a lot but they knew God—and they sort of started me thinking about this big hole in my life that I had just sort of pushed aside and forgotten about. I ignored it though for another couple of years until my dad started going to church with my aunt. I was like, "You got to be kidding me. What'd my aunt do, drug him?" It was just really surprising. And I just sort of watched his process and this real change in his life. And then my *mom* started going to church, too, and they started getting along better. They were just nicer to me, too. And we started having conversations about it, and what Christianity meant, and finally I got up the courage to go to church by myself.

Another man in his fifties talked about becoming alienated from religion while he was in Vietnam, spending years doing drugs, and finally being invited by a new friend to visit Valley Baptist.

I believed in God, but that was about it. I got to Vietnam and started smoking pot over there. When I got back to the States, I started using drugs pretty heavily. I also drank a lot. I was working on the railroad and, really, what else is there to do? I met my wife the year after Vietnam, I think. I was married for like nineteen years and she finally divorced me. I was using a lot at that point. After I hooked up with my second wife, we were running crazy. Our daughter was taken away from us when she was born cause my wife had meth in her system. She went to prison, and I was living alone and was able to get custody. We eventually split. I was out [of the military] for twenty-seven years and high on dope for twenty-three of them. I do believe that God's been watching over me, and I don't know why or what ... [at one point] I shot myself in the chest, not trying to kill myself, but just not knowing what I was doing. It wasn't until I met Emily and she started talking about Pastor Mark and his ministry that I started visiting. I really liked what Mark had to say and it was so easy to understand. I'd been going to AA for awhile, but hadn't been to church until now ... my church was talking to God on my own. One-on-one. But after I met Emily, she got me going and I really enjoyed going to classes and met some people I really connected with. You can just sense it when you walk into the church—they're happy people there worshiping the Lord; they aren't just religious and hypocritical or judgmental.

For visitors who were not lifelong Baptists, some sort of personal invitation or connection was the mechanism through which they first visited the church. Prospective new members who grew up in Baptist households but hardly attended, and people who were transitioning from other Christian denominations or none at all, didn't turn to the yellow pages—they were invited.

Evangelicals Switching to Find a Better Fit

Finding a Better Theological Fit

On occasion, we also heard accounts of religious transition in which a sense of "fit" centered on a conviction that some truth had been missing or muted in the tradition or congregation where they had been attending. As one mother of three explained:

> We were trying to find a place that had really good teaching that was Bible-based. A friend told us they'd heard something good about Valley Baptist. Initially we thought it would be a waste of time to go to a Baptist Church because it would be too conservative—cause we're theologically conservative and socially liberal, and there are hardly any churches that are like that. But something our friend said gave us the idea that maybe it wasn't all that bad—that there were good things happening there—so we went and visited a couple of times. We thought the teaching was very clear and intelligent and true to the Bible as we understand it, and that was probably the most attractive thing. And then the worship, too—that certainly didn't take away from it.

For politically liberal evangelicals such as this, finding a Baptist congregation where they were not in the minority was a challenge. We found fewer politically liberal evangelicals at the mainline congregation (where their politics would nicely fit) and more at the conservative Protestant congregation (where their politics did not). For them, theological perspective trumped political similarity. Although politically liberal evangelicals are a minority within both evangelicalism and within this conservative Baptist congregation, we did find a subset of prospective and newer members who were attracted to the new outreach programs that emphasized social as well as spiritual content and support.

Finding a More Positive Program

These outreach-focused evangelicals, along with "unchurched" people in the neighborhood, were the target population of the church's new leadership team. A full third of those joining, however, were less specific about being attracted to doing community outreach and spoke more about how much they appreciated a good message, an uplifting music program, and a broad array of groups and activities in which they could, but were not pressured to, become involved. The latter figured particularly in the narratives of some of the women we interviewed who had previously been members of other Baptist or mainline churches.

> We'd been members of a Methodist church for nearly a decade, and there started to be some things happening there that we were unhappy about. They had lost their youth pastor and we had young kids, so that's when we started driving half an hour to a different Methodist church. But the commute was not satisfactory and little things they did were different. So about a year ago we decided to look around at other churches closer to home. We spent six, maybe nine, months going here and there different Sundays. Then some friends who went here said, "Hey, you should check it out." So we finally did, and liked it a lot. We were looking for something closer to home and knew some people at the Baptist church, but that's not why we went there. We had heard good things about the church, and that's how we started— through the grapevine.

Over and over again we heard stories of people searching for a program, a community, or a style of worship or music that felt like a good fit. As with the woman quoted earlier, they often made first connections through social networks but were more likely to stay because of the style or types of programs. Staying also related to feeling comfortable with the level of expectations they felt leadership had for participation or service. One family whose college-age son recently died no longer felt comfortable in their current congregation. In their grief, they began to look elsewhere, where they could have a new start in a contemporary and welcoming, low-demand congregation. They found it at Valley Baptist.

> After my son died, we didn't feel comfortable at the church where we were—people were all very nice. But, you know, they never called my husband to see how he was. They'd check in with me, but not him, so when we were grieving, and we still are, my husband says, "Well, look in the paper and see where else we can go." I grew up Mormon and left that and didn't want to go back, and the Catholics to me have always been too formal. I'd been to different churches growing up with friends and stuff—the Presbyterian and Methodist and I didn't care for 'em (chuckles); their services were just too

ceremonial, too formal. We tried another Baptist church and then an Assembly of God. But that was a little far out for me, ya know, when they ask people to go forward for healing or prayer in a crisis or whatever. You go up and tell them your problems and they pray for you. So we tried another Baptist church several times and were thinking about joining. But they called us and said, "Well, you've been here several times, so we want to make you a member now." And they told my husband "and we'll get you involved in things and see where your gifts are and everything else" and that was an instant turn off to him, ya know? Really, our whole life and belief system was totally destroyed after our son's death. And we have to rebuild ... so it was way too much for us. In the end, we ended up trying Valley Baptist because they were the only place we could find that was having a Christmas Eve service. We really liked it and have been visiting for a while. But you know even last week they had a sermon about "in God we trust" and all through that sermon I kept thinking "but do I trust?" I prayed for God to keep him safe where he was in college, and two weeks later he was dead. We've just felt so shattered, not just lost. I know I had more support at our old church than my husband because I'd been more involved than he was. In the end he felt like he wasn't getting anything. Part of that, too, was being with people who had children our son's age. We felt almost like we had a plague or something because people didn't know how to deal with our loss. We just didn't feel like we fit anymore. So we started looking. We knew we wanted a more contemporary-type service, something that wasn't routine but had some variety. That was the Christmas we finally put up a tree again since our son's death. I was having a hard time holding it together, and finally I said, "I've got to go, I've just got to go to a service tonight," and my husband said, "Okay, we're going!" and it [the service at Valley Baptist] was beautiful—the candlelight, the pastor's way of present-ing the story in such simple terms. It hit a chord. So we basically started going there and just recently told them we want to join.

Woven into this couple's story of grief and loss are comments that reflect the importance of relationships and preferences for a particular style of service and expected level of involvement. While this woman laughingly described herself as feeling like Goldilocks in pursuit of a congregation that felt "just right," her comments also touched on a deep sense of desire for community beyond the level of convenient association, and on profound enduring questions around what it means to have faith.

The Religiously Disaffected Giving the Institution One Last Try

Several of those moving toward affiliation with Valley Baptist were making the move from a more enduring sense of disaffection. One woman who had been reared Roman Catholic introduced herself at a Saturday Seminar by joking that she was joining Valley Baptist because she didn't want to have any more kids—then talked in private about being traumatized as a young adult when it was discovered that her parish priest had been having an affair with the mother of a friend. She was first introduced to Valley Baptist by the preschool program.

> I was originally interested in the daycare. I was raised up Catholic, and it was really strict. I didn't want anything to do with church for a while because the priest had an affair with a woman in the parish. But when my kids got older, they started asking me, "Mom, why don't you go to church?" And I kept saying, "I'm not ready. That's good for you guys, but it's not good for me right now. I'm not ready." They wore me down, and I started going more with my husband to the Episcopal church and, once again, the pastor had an affair with a woman at the church. The whole place blew up. But the kids were still going to school here, and I wanted them to learn about God, so we tried a bunch of other places and I didn't like any of them. I didn't really like the people and the music was really old and there was nothing for kids. No kids, no youth groups, nothing. I needed something for my kids to do because I didn't want them to be bored and hate it. So we decided to come here and just fell in love with it. The kids all had their friends from school here, and I liked Mark. I just like everything. I really feel very welcome all the time.

In this woman's narrative, children were instrumental in pushing her back toward regular participation. Her own conviction that learning about God was good, and their enthusiasm for their mother joining them, were significant in moving past a negative experience to begin considering a congregation in which she felt more welcome and at home.

Shared Appreciation for Preaching and Programs

To say that people who are deeply committed to Baptist identity join Baptist churches, or that people who feel dissatisfied with their lives or their religious affiliation begin to look elsewhere, does not explain why they are considering joining this *particular* Baptist congregation. To address that question, we need to turn to narratives of joining and explore in more detail the specific facets of experience and congregational life that women and men say matter most.

As at the First Presbyterian Church, a number of themes ran across interviews for both women and men considering affiliation at Valley Baptist Church. There was unanimity about how friendly the congrega-tion was and how the preaching was upbeat, practical, and engaging. As one woman put it, "I love to sing. I can't carry a tune worth anything, but I love being able to sing along and tap my toes. To be honest, the music is so good; I love the upbeat modern music that I really didn't feel like I needed to try anywhere else. It just felt like the right place to be from the beginning." Another man said, "The songs are simpler and more direct than I'd seen before. I really appreciated that directness and the way we sung to God, not just about God. I was also taken by the pastor's sermon." In addition to the music, the preaching was also a significant factor in both women's and men's valuing their experience at Valley Baptist. One middle-aged woman captured this sentiment saying, "Number one, I'd say the biggest draw is the pastor, because of his messages, I feel they are very timely, very personalized for everyone. And I just really enjoy it. And I like their music too. . . . . Sunday is really a time to refresh and re-energize my faith." One younger woman summarized these ideals:

> The actual sort of teachings are really positive for me and they always hit home, they're always applicable to something going on in my life. It helps me to recharge my batteries every week, remem-ber the reasons I go, the reasons I believe, gives me lessons I can work on which is important because sometimes I don't know what I'm doing. It doesn't feel like some lofty sort of thing going on that I can't be a part of.

For men as well, the engaging and practical focus of the sermons was a significant draw.

> There is a component of the message on Sunday that relates directly to the Word. To me, what he's getting at is how to interpret very

carefully how the words can help us lead our lives in such a way that we keep growing toward Christ, and that's really successful for me and important to me, that they have that ability to reach out in a personal way during the message and to help people along.

Expanded and Unexpected Gender Experience

Although both women and men talked about appreciating the practical and energizing sermons, patterns of gender difference appeared in other areas that were attractive to them at Valley Baptist. Not all of these were in the direction we expected. For example, while women did talk about how they felt supported by new friends, women were also more likely than men to talk about the importance of doctrine and of attending a church where preaching was "biblically based." As one woman who had grown up in a more mainline denomination put it:

> There are a lot of churches that have become very liberal, and I would intentionally not go there. I went to an Easter service once and they didn't even talk about God or Jesus; it was more on social issues. At Easter! I want more of a Bible-based message. I don't really care if they talk about current events. But I think that God's word is important, and if they want to weave it in to a social issue, that's fine, but to not reference the Bible doesn't work for me.

Men, on the other hand, were less likely to emphasize the importance of an evangelical approach to interpreting the Bible or Baptist theological distinctives, and they focused more on feeling a sense of love and acceptance that they hadn't experienced elsewhere. As one man described:

> There's something about Pastor Mark. He's such a loving person— to everybody. It's awesome. Everybody is welcome there, and it doesn't matter what path, where you're coming from, you're all welcome. Now, I don't think all Baptist churches would behave that way. I just know they aren't. But they have a different outlook on who is welcome here. I could go in there in my bathrobe probably, and they might look at me pretty strange, but as long as I'm not naked and a disturbance, I'm there to worship the Lord. And you just see they give their love out so easy.

A number of men talked about feeling welcome and accepted, and went on to describe how much it meant to them to be in a congregation where other men modeled a level of personal transformation they found compelling.

> I went to another church, but it was just too theatrical for me—not that there's anything wrong with praising the Lord, but too much whoop and holler! I just didn't connect with those people. Then when I heard Mark, and the feelings I get ... I can feel the Holy Spirit when he speaks. And then I see some of the other men, I can just see the love they have for the Lord in their eyes. I thought, "Man, I want that." And I hope that's the way I present myself, that they can see that in me, that the Lord has done something in me.

Another man in his forties went on to articulate this theme of personal transformation:

> The reason I started coming is that I can't stand the message at the church where I am now. I want to really dig into the issues of how do we deal with our faith, not just as a Sunday morning thing, but how that works into the rest of the week and how faith can be growing and guiding us in ways that we aren't in control of, that are past conscious decisions, things that go right into our heart and start changing our thinking and our behavior by influencing us inside, much like reading the Word, you don't know what's going to happen to you after you take it in. I think after all my other experiences with faith that this is where I am going and I'm trying to move. Trying to take it out of the straightjacket and put it into action more in a person-to-person way. These are sometimes hard things to formulate in speech. I'm saying, "Lord take me, change me, make me into the person that you would will me to be, that I can be." It's not about realizing myself. It's about realizing Christ. The more I do that, the less I'm stuck on being focused on myself.

These themes of personal transformation, love, intuition, and acceptance appeared again and again in men's descriptions about what they found valuable about being at Valley Baptist.

A few were quite specific about the joy they experienced in "yielding themselves to Christ" in a new and deeper way. One man in his early thirties had become disaffected from the church in high school, and was openly hostile by the time he was in college. Then, as part of a class project, he found himself interviewing self-identified evangelicals, some of whom attended Valley Baptist.

> To my surprise, I discovered that evangelicals were not as simplistic, unidimensional, or unthoughtful as I originally thought. I was taken by their critique of an academic "religious studies" approach to reading scripture. They made the case that the story itself is authoritative—that it's about real events and has an internal consistency, theme, direction, and coherence that I hadn't really thought about before. Plus, they demonstrated a kind of compassion and humility toward others that I really admired and wished I saw more of in myself. A couple of them invited me to church, and I went, really, just to see them. But I was blown away. It felt like being brought to the edge of a cliff. I had this experience of God being real ... right there! And I realized that instead of surrendering to God through the Bible's words, I had been keeping God at arm's length. I didn't surrender or open myself to God, but made a project of deciding what was and wasn't true in the Bible. I had a real conviction in my gut that this was true as well as a fire in my gut that it is God I'm after and not an idea about God; not to follow my ego but to follow God as known in Christ. So I started going, and by the fourth or fifth Sunday, I felt something I'd never experienced before—a feeling of being "at home."

Although not every visitor's sense of the immediate presence of God was as dramatic as this man's, we did find a consistent theme in the interviews with people considering Valley Baptist—that they considered themselves on a journey through which they expected to be changed. For some, that journey involved a relatively short distance in terms of worldview or personal religious practices. And, to be sure, there was a subset of joiners for whom transferring membership to Valley Baptist was simpler than opening a new bank account in a new town. Yet for others, particularly among the men we interviewed, there was a sense of moving from one life location to another in a congregation in which they felt both accepted and challenged to become better men.

Beginning to Belong at St. Andrews

Only a handful of the newer and prospective members at St. Andrews had grown up in Orthodox families and attended churches in Greek, Russian, Antiochian, or other Orthodox jurisdictions. As with the life-long Presbyterians and committed Baptists in our other two congregations, most long-term Orthodox members at St. Andrews had moved into the area, looked online for Orthodox churches, called to speak with the priest about service times, and started attending. Two prospective members were joining because they were marrying someone who was Orthodox and a member of the parish. As one member said, "When you're Orthodox, you sort of go to the church that's in the area that you want to live."

Most individuals just starting to visit or working their way through the church's catechumen program were from non-Orthodox backgrounds. About a fifth were Roman Catholic or Episcopalian and said they were considering the move because of some frustration with either the bureaucracy of their current church or concerns about its increasing theological or cultural liberalism. For these visitors, the sense of personal struggle or distance traveled was not particularly great. The majority of those visiting St. Andrews—nearly two-thirds—were from Protestant backgrounds and were visiting as part of a long process of questioning, reading, and struggle. A third, smaller subset of visitors identified with Eastern religions, Neo-Paganism, or the growing percentage of Pacific Northwest "nones." This group, about 13 percent of our sample, also related extensive narratives of consideration, experimentation, and struggle in their personal histories prior to arriving at St. Andrews.

Making Connections

Visitors from non-Orthodox backgrounds described random meetings on airplanes or attending a spiritual retreat or a cultural festival as what predicated their interest in Orthodoxy and initial involvement at St. Andrews. More than one person was introduced to Orthodoxy via a fieldwork assignment for a comparative religion course. Several first considered the church because a parent or friend had joined, while others picked up a free brochure on a book table or heard a speaker and had their interest piqued.

Switching to Alternative Smells and Bells

Among those coming from Roman Catholic or Episcopalian backgrounds, women and men most frequently talked about their sense of relief at locating an alternative, but similarly liturgical, church that offered stability of traditional doctrine and practice. The experience of one older woman was typical of this group:

> I grew up Roman Catholic, in Catholic schools from kindergarten through college. In the 1970s we were part of the Catholic fringe, very much into the church fathers and mysticism. But it felt unsatisfying; I was offended by the rules and regulations of the Catholic Church, and had questions about so many things. And then things changed with Vatican II so that the things they used to say were so important—you'd go to hell if you did or didn't do such and such—were no longer important. So when we moved here, I started looking for a church, and one day we drove by St. Andrews and my husband suggested we go. I told him, "No, they're Greek and don't let other people in." But he said that wasn't true and we should try it. So we did, and immediately I thought, "I'm home; this is where God wants us." I had a long conversation with Father Michael, asking about divorce, indulgences, the pope, children who die who aren't Christians, all of it. And all the things that had bothered me about the Catholic Church were resolved. I do believe that man is corrupt, not the Catholic Church. But there seems to be more freedom of individual conscience here. I'm a gut person and, my gosh, my gut feels good when I'm here.

For people from other liturgical traditions, the distance between their religious history and their experience at St. Andrews was relatively small. Once basic questions about differences in doctrine or practice had been answered, the transition to becoming a catechumen seemed relatively straightforward.

Hijacked Evangelicals

Those who started from a place of "rabid evangelicalism," as one woman described it, had more expansive narratives of struggle, study, deliberation, and relational work getting to a place where they could consider joining a cohort of catechumens at St Andrews. More than any other group,

formerly evangelical women and men entered the process of joining
through reading, studying, and engaging with already Orthodox others.
One woman who had not quite settled on the question of joining described
changes she had seen in friends, challenges she was encountering to some
of her personal biases, and the need she felt to reevaluate an array of long-
standing beliefs.

> I've been wrestling with becoming Orthodox for about six years.
> When I was in college, one of my friends did a research project
> on the Orthodox Church. She dragged another friend with her and
> they just kind of never came back (laughs). I went on occasion and
> it was confusing, but there was something to it. I saw a light in
> her eyes, like she'd come alive. But I wasn't willing to deal with
> it; I just pushed it into the background. I'd try to talk myself into
> believing that Orthodoxy and Protestantism are really the same.
> But I also started reading. One book was about women who had
> been received into the church, and they were like normal people,
> not "head coverings, skirts and showers once a month," something
> like that (laughs). I started coming to St. Andrews about three years
> ago. I'd visit and then leave, and read some more and then push it
> aside. It has raised questions for me about what do we believe and
> why, and why are other denominations different, and how can they
> really all be true at the same time if they are different? So in the
> midst of that, and reading the Orthodox books friends gave me . . .
> I don't know. I'd love to be Orthodox, but I'm not sure I'm willing to
> go against my family. Still, I don't think I'll ever be quite as content
> in the Protestant Church as I was before.

This woman's experience was typical of a number of prospective members
who were not actively looking for a new church but described themselves
as being "hijacked" by some encounter with Orthodox theology, persons, or worship. Another young woman, a recent graduate from a well-
known evangelical college, described a series of small events that radically
changed her perspective on her religious identity.

> I grew up in a conservative reformed evangelical household—you
> know, the kind where they believe Catholics aren't Christians. When
> I was in high school, I saw a phrase in a music book—"we praise

thee, we bless thee, we glorify thee"—that stuck with me. I didn't know anything about Orthodoxy, or that those lines were part of the prayers before communion. If I thought about Orthodoxy at all, I thought it was a dying old community of Russian babushkas. I hated the idea of icons. But one day during my freshmen year at Wheaton, I picked up a free magazine that had an article on how icons preserve the theology of the incarnation—and it floored me. Not only did it logically make sense, but something shifted in me from thinking icons are probably idolatrous to thinking maybe there's something good there. A little while later I got a CD of vespers music from the library that was so beautiful I started crying, and I was like "What the heck is this? If Orthodox churches are like this, I better check it out!"

Another man described himself as content, even happy, in the evangelical church he and his family were attending until he had an encounter that shook his perceptions of his own faith.

About eight years ago, my parents started attending St. Andrews. I talked with them a little, but we were really content at the evangelical church we were attending and weren't interested in switching. Then one summer I was working for a family friend who had become Orthodox and ended up working side by side with a monk. Yeah, an Orthodox monk! I'd never met anyone like that. He was so quiet! I couldn't believe he'd just donate his time like that, but he was obeying his abbot, who told him to help these people because they couldn't afford to pay someone. I didn't know how to talk to him. I mean, what do you say to a monk? "Hey, how's it going? See the Bull's game last night?" I came home from that job and told my wife, "We've got to look at Orthodoxy more seriously." We weren't going through any big life changes. It was just weird, like when you're walking and trip over the sidewalk because it's uneven—just a surprise. I felt like my eyes were opened to what my faith was based on, and it seemed pretty thin. It feels like I've been waiting for this moment. My dad said the same thing happened to him, too. So we started attending St. Andrews with them but are also still attending our home church. We're trying to decide where we belong.

Surprised Pilgrims and Seekers

Some of those who were visiting St. Andrews talked about being "knocked off balance" and drawn toward Orthodoxy by a variety of significant and specific experiences. One such spiritual seeker described a sequence of crises in which he struggled to find enlightenment through drugs, shamanism, and "self-styled spirituality."

> Drugs weren't really doing it for me, so I started thinking I needed to add some self-styled spirituality—basically to substantiate the need to change my consciousness with mind-altering substances. Shamanism appealed, and I toyed with Wicca for awhile and started getting into this Dream Spell Calendar based on the ancient Mayan calendar. Eventually I met some Hare Krishna's. They were more serious about their faith than any Christian I knew and had a pan-religious relativistic attitude that was acceptable to me, so I started hanging out with them. I lived with them for about a year and a half, getting up at 4:30, taking my cold shower, chanting services a couple of times a day, and distributing books. I was a decent devotee, just not that studious. I'd really thought I'd found the truth, but eventually I started wondering why they called Jesus a prophet and not an incarnation of God. And I started feeling they lacked compassion—that people get what they deserve and to alleviate their suffering would be to perpetuate the inevitable. Then one day I found a New Testament and read about Jesus healing a leper and had this interior perception of compassion and the light of mercy. I thought, "No, no, no! Don't think about that. Jesus: He's not God," and I tried to think about Krishna, but I was really shaken.

He went on to describe being on a road trip to distribute books and meeting a Roman Catholic man who was walking along praying with rosary beads. "I said, 'Hey, we pray with beads too,' thinking I'm going to humor him and then tell him about Krishna." But as they talked, he began to feel a shift in his thinking.

> I started thinking maybe Jesus *is* God ... and I felt the mercy of God in Christ and I thought, "Oh my goodness, there's really something to this!" I was convinced Jesus was asking me to leave Hari Krishna. So I decided to go to church with this guy, and felt very strongly that if I didn't leave them right then I wouldn't

because it felt so hard. So after the service ended, I met up with the other devotees at the van we were using and told them, "I think Jesus is asking me to follow him," and wow … there was a pretty big uproar about that. "You're going to leave pious religious truth for this idiot you met two hours ago?" And they kept arguing with me until finally I realized it was useless and just grabbed my sleeping bag out of the van and left.

He then called his parents, who invited him to come home, and started attending Rite of Christian Initiation of Adults (RCIA) classes at their local Roman Catholic church. Soon, however, he began feeling at odds with some of the requirements and "things that seemed harsh." So when his father told him about a friend who was investigating Orthodoxy at St. Andrews, he got Father Michael's phone number and called their home.

I had a long talk with the priest's wife, and in the end she just said, "Come and see!" So I did. I immediately felt a sense of reverence way beyond what I had felt before, as though I were standing on holy ground. I was sold from day one and started reading more about the Orthodox perspective on ecclesiastical history. The more I read, the more it made sense to me. My parents were like, "Don't jump into this all at once!" They thought maybe I'd become Orthodox in three weeks or something. I attended and read for about ten months before deciding this is where I want to be. It made intellectual sense in addition to feeling these people are standing at the feet of God. I'll be baptized and chrismated at Nativity, about a year after I started attending.

In some ways, this young man's journey epitomizes the spiritual seeking Roof (1993, 2001) describes as the hallmark of the baby boom generation. A child of baby boomer parents, this man was particularly intense in his search for a place that seemed both resonate with compassion and clear in its positions on doctrinal truth.

Other seekers at St. Andrews were themselves baby boomers who related similarly expansive narratives of spiritual searching before arriving at St. Andrews. One woman in her sixties summarized her experience:

I was pretty involved in the whole counterculture, hippie thing in college, like a lot of other people, and was part of a Hindu commune practicing made-for-America Hinduism for fourteen years. I lived in a tipi out in the woods for awhile. Then one day got a ride from a man who invited me to church. They seemed so alive compared to the people I'd been with. So I started going to church, and two months later went up the aisle during the altar call and asked Jesus into my life. That church had a lot of people who had come out of the counterculture movement and who lived communally, and one of the women came every Friday for four months to study the Bible with me in the coal bin where I was living. Nobody told me how I was supposed to change, but I changed pretty radically.

She then went on to describe moving to the Pacific Northwest, where she joined a Four Square church. After several years, however, she found herself struggling with the church's minimalist approach to the sacraments. Then one day she heard a speaker on the radio talking about Orthodoxy. Something in those comments captured her imagination.

I don't remember now what they said, but I was intrigued! What *is* this? Then two days later my daughter called and said she and her husband were looking for an Orthodox church to go to. And I was like, "What?!" and started asking all sorts of questions. I wanted to know everything. She gave me some books to read, and eventually I started driving an hour to the only Orthodox church I knew of. That was about six months ago. Once I decided I was pretty sure of the direction I wanted to go, the priest invited me to become a catechumen and told me I should start coming to St. Andrews because it was closer and I could be more involved. So I did. I also talked with the pastor and church council at my Four Square church to tell them that I was leaving. They took it really well and even "prayed me out" of the church to send me on my way. It was almost too easy and made me think maybe I hadn't really been that connected. Anyway, I've been meeting now with Father Michael and will be received into the church at Nativity. My sponsor is another ex-hippie, so they know just where I'm coming from.

Whether coming to St. Andrews from another liturgical tradition, being thrown off balance from fully engaged evangelicalism, or navigating experiences in a diverse set of religious traditions, this subgroup of visitors ended up at St. Andrews somewhat by surprise. They encountered a person or an experience that turned them in a new direction, after which they moved either quickly or with some struggle toward being received into St. Andrews Orthodox Church.

Turning East

Over time, visitors to St. Andrews began to be more explicit about feeling that evangelicalism was not enough—that it was too thin, emotive, and ungrounded to bring about either the personal or cultural change it intended. Women, in particular, talked about their growing interest in church history and their concerns about how to evangelize a post-Christian culture. One baby boomer articulated these themes:

> I'd been thinking for a couple of years now about how our culture looks more and more like the cultures of ancient Greece and Rome, where Christianity was first introduced. It seems to me that if early believers figured out how to grow the church inside a pagan global superpower with its hedonism and inequality, why does the church today keep acting as though it has to start from scratch in figuring out how to address these things? Then one day I was talking with my husband about all that and he mentioned a book about a bunch of former Campus Crusade leaders who started to correspond with each other about the basics of Christianity. They started reading church history and eventually came to the conclusion that they should be Orthodox. That just blew me away: this bunch of dyed-in-the-wool Bible-quoting evangelical pastors and their congregations joining the Orthodox church! What was so compelling to them? So I got their book and also started reading church history myself—Eusebius, and Timothy Ware's *The Orthodox Church*, and something by Alexander Schmemann, and other things. And I kept having these "Oh crap" moments where something I always believed turned out to be consistent with Orthodoxy, or some Orthodox twist on a doctrine would make more sense than what I believed. In the end, I felt like God was playing chess with me, and I was losing a bad defensive game. Clink, clink, clink, the doors kept closing on my arguments, and in the end I was just boxed in. Either quit the whole Christian project or join "The Church." Crazy. I still think, "Are you kidding me?"

Others talked about their frustration with the lack of substance in the worship music, the concentrated influence of individual pastors, and the fragmentation of Protestantism across cultures and denominations. One young woman in her mid-twenties summarized a number of these concerns:

> I was frustrated by the sense I had from many leaders that if you don't know Greek or Hebrew you better not read the church fathers and mothers because you'll not be able to understand them. But that means Protestantism isn't translatable cross-culturally to a world where people can't read and that seemed off to me since it meant Protestantism can't really be as universal as the church should be. Plus Protestant services don't necessarily reflect the beliefs of the congregation as much as they do the perspectives of the worship leader or pastor or other leaders. So I started reading, and after a couple of months I realized I wasn't really a Protestant anymore. Other things also started to crystallize around things I wished were more part of my Christian experience—more of a sense of sacraments and ritual filled with meaning, and the sense of being connected with other Christians across culture and time though the liturgy. Also, the idea that the church is an actual full Christian body. Overall, I guess a sense of history, a continuity of faith and practice in the physical worship of the church. I'm not sure how to explain that. There's a bit of Docetism to my experience of Protestantism, which seems to guard against the physical. And some of that's good, I mean you don't want to be distracted from God by God's creation, but at the same time I kept feeling like there's something we're missing if we're just intellectualizing the faith.

Bringing the Body Back In

Concerns about the lack of appreciation for the physical or sense of sacredness within Protestantism also appeared as a significant theme in our conversations with visitors at St. Andrews. Over and over again we heard women and men describe how much they valued being able to bring their whole selves to the table, saying "My whole person gets to play, not just my mind or heart." One middle-aged man described how he and his wife had been visiting both mainline and evangelical churches, but they had been dissatisfied with both, saying, "We didn't like how the evangelicals were so exclusive, like when the one pastor talked about people who weren't part of that church going to hell. And we didn't like how the mainline church was an hour of announcements and everything else and five minutes of worship." He then described their first visit to St. Andrews:

> We had heard about the Orthodox church and tried going to the place closest to us, but the time was wrong. So we drove home, looked in the newspaper, and saw St. Andrews and went there! What we saw was worship from the time you stepped into the door until the service was over. And it was worship with all the senses— eyes, smell, ears, everything. We haven't been there long enough to invite any friends, but when we do I'll tell them, "It'll wow you!" Smelling the incense and the icons and music and singing and chanting and floors covered with oriental carpets and icons all over. It's an experience!

Appreciating Mystery and Paradox

A second theme emphasized by both women and men was that their experiences at St. Andrews was helping to resolve troubling tangles and gaps in their current beliefs or the beliefs of the traditions in which they had been reared. Making room for mystery, paradox, and beauty was a significant part of this shift. One young woman summarized these ideas:

> There seemed like there were a lot of false dichotomies in Christianity. There's the physical or the spiritual, or we have complete free will and God is very distant, or otherwise we have no choices, both of which seemed very problematic. Also problematic or missing was a sense of wonder. Something that's infused with a sense of authority. Also, an orientation towards beauty. Obviously some of this I could have just gotten by changing Protestant churches maybe. But I wasn't sure if what I was looking for existed except for probably in heaven. But it felt like it existed and like I was moving towards the Eastern Church. So, those are some of the questions that brought me to St. Andrews.

Others talked more specifically about how they were drawn to St. Andrews because the sacraments were envisioned as both mysteries and means of grace. As one catechumen said:

> I don't know where I turned a corner and became somebody who believe[s] that it was truly the body and blood of Christ, whatever that meant. I mean transubstantiation, trans-whatever-ation, because I know there's all kinds of different terms. It doesn't matter in Orthodoxy; it's both. It's both the bread and the wine and the Body and Blood of Christ, all at the same time, which is totally emblematic of Orthodoxy where normal, everyday things become sacred in a mystical, mysterious way. I love that. There's also humility, this paradox where you have a church claiming to be *the* historic Church where the fullness of truth lies. Other churches, other religions even have elements of truth, but the Church claims to be the place where the fullness of truth is. Another paradox is that here's this incredibly seemingly structured liturgical system with all these certain ways of doing things, especially in the worship ... that's also completely un-legalistic. For instance, fasting, you know Wednesdays, Fridays, and all these long fasts and shorter fasts and fasts before Feasts. There's the ideal fasting "rule," but you do the best you can do and you always try to do better. I don't know how these two go together, but they do. Or finding women in a hierarchical, patriarchal church who are amazingly accomplished and their spirituality is immensely valued. They are honored in the church. And the whole Mary thing. I started seeing Mary as more than I'd ever seen her as a Protestant where she's just trotted out at Christmas as the young maiden in the manger scene. But she's actually central to our salvation because she provided a body for God. And if there's no body that dies and is resurrected because it is *God* incarnate, well ... there's no hope of resurrection for the rest of us. It's also a patriarchal church. So if you're a feminist and you don't look too deeply into things, you think patriarchy and hierarchy immediately spells disaster. But the fathers *and mothers* of the church are both enormously important for spiritual direction.

One young father in his mid-thirties also commented on dogma, doctrine, and mystery:

> One of the things I like is that there's some stuff the church says it has always believed, then a lot of other stuff we're not sure about or can't fully explain. Even with the sacraments: they don't try and explain them in a really rigorous way. They admit they are mysteries, and that's what they call them. I really appreciate that over the scholastic way. I just think it meets the world in a better place because it says both what it knows and what it doesn't— that we can't really know a lot of this stuff. And I appreciate that humility.

As we listened to people unpack their experiences at St. Andrews, we were surprised at the frequency and depth to which narratives focused on doctrines and approaches to doctrine as significant in their consideration of whether or not to become members. We also were surprised at both the diversity and direction of gender differences that appeared in these accounts.

Bringing Other Facets of the Gendered Self to Play

Given that Orthodoxy is the most explicitly patriarchal of these three traditions, we fully expected to find substantial differences between what women and men said they liked about the church. We were ready to hear men say they appreciated being part of a congregation that valued a male priesthood, or women opining on the involvement of children and support for traditional roles. That is not what we heard. Instead, we found a diverse range of perspectives among both women and men, as well as some of the same themes countering cultural expectations of femininity and masculinity as we heard at the Baptist and Presbyterian congregations.

Women Engaging the Spiritual Disciplines

Women were more likely than men to talk about being interested in Orthodoxy at St. Andrews because it offered "tools for change." Describing the prayer book given to her by her sponsor prior to her joining the church, one woman said:

My godmother gave me a prayer book, which I just love. I can't
come up with the discipline on my own. I've never known how to
pray and still don't feel like I do; but I feel like I have a chance
now because I have a rule of prayer. The prayers are so beautiful,
so right on, and so old. To know that thousands of Christians have
prayed this before me, that I'm part of the historic Holy Catholic
and Apostolic Church is truly amazing to me.

Other women emphasized the salience of spiritual disciplines for spiritual formation. For example, one graduate of another regional evangelical
college, who was generally skeptical about the value of the institutional
church, found herself surprised at St. Andrews by the notion that spiritual
disciplines could actually be transformative.

I heard some guy speak at a conference about Orthodox "spiritual
formation" and it really blew me away. I've always been pretty suspect of the institutional church—you know, like a house church
with "real" relationships is so much better than sitting like lumps
in a pew listening to some guy preach. Worse, getting dressed up to
sit like a lump in a pew listening to some guy preach. Even worse
to listen to some guy preach in a ritualistic routine service. But after
hearing this guy talk about the history of spiritual disciplines within
the Orthodox church and how they offer the opportunity to actually
be changed to be more like Christ, I started to realize I'd never taken
the institution of the church seriously as something formative . . .
and that maybe I needed to rethink that perspective.

Other women described their own surprise at valuing formal confession
and delight at being linked with a spiritual godmother who sponsored them
in the process of joining. Others went on about how they were learning
that formal prayers could shape personal prayer, and how fasting during
prescribed days and seasons was helping them become, as one woman said,
"more consistent in my faith and closer to the Lord."

One of the things that has been a draw for me is the fact that it
seems to encourage your walk with the Lord, that it's designed to
help you grow spiritually. The idea of confession and some form of
accountability seems good. Whereas in a typical church, I come on
Sunday, and sit for an hour and a half and then I go home. I know

the Lord works individually in a person—if you read and spend time in prayer, He does speak and convict us—but it seems as though there isn't an accountability. Lots of churches are trying with small groups, but it doesn't really happen.

Women Working Through Doctrine

Women were also much more likely than men to talk about their immersion in reading church history and theology. "There are things that really appeal to me—the history of the church, the stability of the worship, the substance—particularly when I compare it to the evangelical church in America and how thin and distracted it is," one graduate student in her late twenties said. "It wears me out having to figure out what to read or what to preach on or what to sing," said another, "so coming to worship at St. Andrews is a relief in a way, but also really challenging since there's so much that's just a little bit different, sometimes a lot different, than what I've believed before or how I've tried to live out my faith before. Certainly a lot more than twenty minutes of Bible reading sitting under a tree—you know, Jesus and me."

Another woman who had also immersed herself in reading church history before starting to visit at St. Andrews said:

> The connection to history has been amazing to me. For example, the woman at the well: she had a whole life outside of the lines in the New Testament. Those lines weren't her whole story. And the church says she has a name—Photini. It makes sense when you think about it. If those people's lives were transformed by the Lord, they were surely changed and there was more to them than gets recorded. Maybe it's just my experience, but it seems like in Protestantism the message is you know who Jesus is and you know who the apostles are, but once you turn the last page in the Bible, that's it! The church stops and then doesn't start again until Martin Luther. There is this huge gap. I have never had a church history class, but I've looked since at the synoptic roots of church history, and it has left me with a lot of questions.

The number of times we heard women talk about the importance of working through history and doctrine and the challenge of spiritual disciplines was something of a surprise. Although men sometimes mentioned one or two favorite authors or books that had been helpful in orienting them to Orthodoxy when they first started coming to St. Andrews, the women read a *lot*, and often read for many months both before and after starting to visit St. Andrews. Among those who went on to become catechumens, there was even more reading—sometimes a book or portions of a book a week while attending inquirers' meetings with Fr. Michael.

Risking Potential Relational Loss

Women were also more likely than men to express concern that joining St. Andrews presented a risk for straining relationships with family or friends. Several reported having hard conversations with parents, pastors, or siblings about their interest and involvement in the church. Two were worried about others perceiving them as "leaving their husband behind" and were counseled by Father Michael to "take it slow" so that their partners could have time to do some reading and thinking of their own. In addition, while some women described themselves as "blown away" or "smitten" the first time they visited St. Andrews, more often women described feeling put off and confused even while feeling compelled to keep reading, visiting, and struggling with the idea of being received into the church. One young woman from a Roman Catholic background captured this sentiment:

> My first time visiting I was mostly thinking about my feet hurting and when was this service ever going to get over, and what was the priest doing popping in and out of the altar like a cuckoo clock. I was feeling pretty defensive. But I promised myself that I would try and seek the truth and be honest and I would try to seek the will of God, wherever that be. And I began to pray, "God, I don't want to become Orthodox, but if that's your will, ok." I have to be open to whatever God has, and I promised myself that I would try. There wasn't really any super decisive moment. It was a long process.

Strengthening Men's Networks and Connections

Although a few men shared similarly long stories of study and struggle, most of the men we interviewed seemed less troubled by the transition to Orthodoxy at St. Andrews. A substantial subset was considering membership in part because they knew someone there, or they had a wife or parent who had become interested or already joined. Men also seemed more likely to discuss how much they appreciated being part of something less individualistic and more connected. One man in his forties captured this perspective:

> I've spent most of my adult life in the Protestant churches, and I'm getting a little weary of the individualism and the "let's make it up on Sundays" sort of approach—the very thin view of history and the "worship" of the Bible, as though there was the New Testament church with the New Testament, and after that you skip to Martin Luther. The centrality of the sermon is a problem—you're at the mercy of the speaker. If they're a dolt, you're wasting your time.

In addition to appreciating a tradition that was less individualistic, men were more likely than women to argue that other traditions placed too much emphasis on "personal spirituality." As one man in his late twenties said, "Protestant churches don't seem to have a very intense sense of community. They tend to be very focused on individuals' private beliefs. They'll have a disagreement within the church, so they start another church across town. So you know there is no acknowledgment of the authority of a broader community outside of that particular congregation or group of individuals."

Men's Care for Children

Men also, to our surprise, talked more than women about how much they appreciated the involvement of children in worship services, and how the presence of children added to their sense that becoming part of St. Andrews was "like joining a big, messy, extended family."

> I really like that our children are right there with us throughout the whole service. They don't go off to a different place and learn different things; they learn right along with us. We love that everyone's kids are in the service. My daughter's friend walked up today and slipped her hand into mine as I was standing there. And I looked down to see a beaming little smile. It was great! We're like family.

Another older man agreed with this sentiment:

> Children are always there. And the young people participate by reading Psalms and prayers at the end of the service or serving as altar servers or singing in the choir. The little ones can lie on the floor if they get tired, or move around. No one worries about that. A child

will come up to you in the middle of the service and put their arms around you, or you can put a hand on their shoulder. It's just very loving as far as children are concerned.

Having opportunity to interact in worship services allowed men to become "uncles" or "older brothers" to the congregation's many children.

Becoming Like a Little Child

In contrast to their experiences in other congregations where children may be sent off to Sunday School before the sermon, or may not be present at all, having children present with all their distraction and moods and modest ability to attend seemed to help men do the same: to connect, to attend, and to learn little by little the rhythms and routines of worship at St. Andrews.

> I don't feel like I'm out there on my own anymore; that I don't have to have all my own understanding, that there's something out there that I can rely on better than myself. I like that there is a real sense of community. After liturgy we sit and have lunch, and I've made some good friends there—they seem pretty upfront about who they are—everybody knows everybody is a sinner. Everybody knows that life isn't always easy, so that's been wonderfully comforting as well. I feel more relaxed, less tense. I don't feel like I have to put a face on in front of anybody, like I can be more honest about my struggles.

Other men echoed similar sentiments, emphasizing "the absolute warmth and caring of the people," how they felt "at home" when they walked into the church, and how they felt like "you're not in this alone, you continue to work to get better in the company of other people who also fall short."

Conclusion: Gender and Joining

Although these data do not explain the greater proportion of women in the pews, they allow us to explore the religious sensibilities and preferences of women and men who are considering membership in these congregations. First Presbyterian and Valley Baptist offer more gender-specific programs than St. Andrews, and it is at Valley Baptist that we found the most gender difference in what prospective members say they appreciate about these congregations. Women and men from evangelical backgrounds bring with them to Valley Baptist the same range of complementarian and egalitarian gender ideals that are hallmarks of evangelical identity.[1] So while church programs and rhetoric celebrate motherhood and men's spiritual leadership, the things prospective members say they actually value about the Valley Baptist are much broader. Women at Valley Baptist emphasized valuing the church's evangelical theology and "Bible-centered preaching" more than men. Women at St. Andrews and First Presbyterian also placed more emphasis on theology and doctrine as attracting them to the congregation than did men. In contrast, men in all three congregations described how much they valued the opportunity to connect to other men, identify and deepen their moral values, and feel accepted. At First Presbyterian men talked about feeling safe and described the church as a haven; at Valley Baptist and at St. Andrews they talked about their appreciation for children's programs and engaging with children in services. Men also talked about the opportunity to give themselves to others and yield themselves to God. Overall, then, what men thinking about joining these congregations say they are looking for is more than thoughtful preaching or a "good worship experience"—it is a place, space, and community in which they might engage dimensions of their personhood that extend beyond the narrow cultural scripts of individual accomplishment, status, and power.

The differences we find in what women and men value across congregations go beyond, even invert, normative ideas around masculinity and femininity. If women are more religious than men, that religiosity does not appear to be particularly well linked (in these congregations at least) to interest in networking, resources, or safety. Nor does what men value neatly map on to ideas about masculinity tending toward rationality, individualism, or leadership, or even religious experience. The degree to which these are shaped or reshaped by involvement is something we turn to next.

5

Growing

NOT EVERYONE WHO visits a church joins; and not everyone who joins seeks additional growth or involvement. We begin this chapter by assessing the factors that people consider important in helping them connect more deeply into the life of a congregation. We focus specifically on the notion of spiritual growth and explore the ideas, programs, and practices that new members say help deepen their faith and religious practice.

Conceptualizing Spiritual Growth

Students of physical and psychological development have created elaborate explanations for the specific stages, tasks, changes, and ends of physical, cognitive, and emotional growth. Sociologists have applied a similar perspective to individuals' religious life—describing increasing knowledge and connection to one's religious tradition as "spiritual growth" or "spiritual capital."[1] Deepening one's understanding of a tradition's texts, rituals, expectations, idioms, and even jokes, as well as collecting meaningful experiences within a congregation, are all elements of "mastery" and "attachment" dimensions of spiritual capital.[2] Changes in personal behavior and religious participation (becoming more involved in programs or organizational leadership) or shifting relationships with family and friends are also identified as intrinsic and extrinsic elements of spiritual growth.[3] These are related, of course, as changes in what people think and believe shape how they invest their time; and how people invest their time reshapes what they believe and think.[4] Specific programs of spiritual mentoring[5] and ongoing efforts to encourage the integration of faith and practice help religious institutions cultivate a shared vision of spiritual growth within congregations.[6] In this chapter, we focus on spiritual growth as reflected in growing knowledge and salience of religious experience.[7] In Chapter 6, we turn to the implications of growth for involvement in service within and outside of these congregations, including ideas about how faith intersects with broader social and political ideals.

Learning a New Vocabulary

Becoming part of a congregation involves learning a new vocabulary—both some specifics related to a particular tradition, as well a local congregational "dialect" around matters of faith. People who are new to a tradition or its local expression need time and practice to gain some facility in the language of faith. We found it was relatively easy for clergy, long-time members, and congregational leaders to talk about the what, the how, and the goals of spiritual growth. But early conversations with very new visitors were a different story. People who had just started attending, especially those from different or no previous religious backgrounds, often struggled to respond to some of our questions about the meaning and means of spiritual growth. With these observations in mind, we returned to each congregation to talk with small groups of regular attenders and members at each site. Adding conversations within these focus groups allowed us to observe a little of the process through which ideas about the how and why of spiritual growth are encouraged, developed, and conceptualized.

What, then, are the vocabularies of spiritual growth within these congregations? Are there core ideas, values, or beliefs that clergy and other leaders encourage new members to adopt or embrace? What, if any, are the activities, practices, or rituals members and attenders are encouraged to participate in as a means to help them spiritually grow? And what are the contours of that notion of spiritual growth itself among long term, newer and prospective members?

First Presbyterian Church: Valuing Learning, Personal Process, and Connection

Clergy Ideals: Growing in Knowledge and Shared Experience
Clergy at First Presbyterian envision the church as a place where people can deepen their understanding of their faith and become engaged within the community by helping others. These themes appear again and again in printed sermons, bulletins, and newsletters around Christian living,

stewardship, and service. From Pastor Patricia's perspective, spiritual growth and service are inseparable elements of congregational life.

> What's the purpose of the church? One, the church is a place where we grow our faith. Whether that be in our head, through classes, or through worship with the heart, music. It's also supposed to be a place where we work on representing Christ's concern for the world in an outward way. So, that would be caring for the poor and the weak and the hungry and whatever. They have to go together though; they can't really be separate, because if you're growing in your faith, you want to be about what Christ called you to do, and if you're being about what Christ is calling you to do, and feel that your unique gifts as an individual are being used with the church, then your faith is growing.

These two ideals were embodied in the congregation's current new member seminars that encouraged prospective members to identify their spiritual gifts and "plug in" to areas of service. Patricia was largely responsible for organizing and leading these seminars, so her work and her vision for the church as a place of worship and service were closely connected.

When we talked with Pastor Richard, his vision for the church also reflected his main areas of leadership—Sunday morning worship that emphasized time for clarifying beliefs about God, an opportunity to feel connected to God through the music, and a time to rest and recharge through the rhythm of keeping a Sabbath day—or at least a Sabbath morning. As Pastor Richard described:

> What's really important is the church as community. We have a cafeteria approach to religion in the United States. You know, "I'll take this idea over here from something on TV, I heard this idea at church, and the Bahia', they have some good things going on, I'll take that, and I got this from my psychologist." It's not very systematic, and sometimes ends up being kind of a goofy mix of things. I think that a community identity can help us sort through some of that. The real blessing of the church today is we live in such a fragmented society. You need a place to go where your time is not up for sale, where you are in community and people can deepen their knowledge of God through worship. Especially through music—that's an incredibly

important outlet for people to feel connected to God. Sort of get the heart and mind component of Presbyterian worship—that gives a rhythm to the week and a chance for people to recharge by stopping work and having a day of rest and reconnection. I think most people who feel like their life is frantically crazy and out of control, when they get into a Sabbath rhythm, they realize that's part of life that they really need, and that's good for them. And marking their weeks with time on Sundays when they come to church has a positive impact on the structure of their family and personal life. A lot of people get the sense of really being recharged through worship. It's the eye in the midst of the storm for a lot of people.

Although Pastor Richard did not talk as much about service or involvement in church ministries, both he and Pastor Patricia emphasized themes that have long been part of Presbyterian subculture. The church is a community in which people can engage heart and mind, thinking and belonging, rest and reconnection. The number of services, the configuration of the sanctuary, its programs, and its styles of music may change, but the overall purpose of the church is to help people to grow in understanding their faith, shared experience, and responsible, compassionate use of gifts and resources. To grow spiritually is to grow in these things.

First Presbyterian Church Members: Growth as Individual Journey

When we talked with members at First Presbyterian, they were somewhat less clear about these ideals. In our focus group discussions of the topic, participants made the case that each spiritual tradition has its own ideas about spiritual growth, and so it would be presumptuous to try and define either the process or its goals. Over and over we heard comments such as "It means many different things to many different people." Women, in particular, seemed to resist the notion that growing in their faith could be defined any more specifically than "a process" or "a journey" or "development over one's lifetime." When pressed to define growth more specifically, women said things such as "You're going to hear a different definition from every single person you talk to." Men were also careful not to sound evaluative in describing their understanding of what it meant to be a Christian and to grow in one's faith and connection to the church. Both women and men went out of their way to preface their comments with disclaimers such as "I don't want to offend, but ..." or " I don't know about other people, but for me," rather than appear critical of a specific ideal. There was very little effort to speak to another person's comment—either to agree or disagree, expand or refine, as though doing so would imply there was a right answer to the question. One focus group member summarized these comments, saying, "I'm not sure what the phrase really means. But, whatever it means, it is not something that is finite where you get there. Everything you do is continuing." Other than the idea of respect for a variety of personal journeys, the discussion was pointedly vague.

A second theme in focus group discussions was that spiritual growth involved clarifying one's life purpose. Perhaps because the church had organized several study groups that had read Rick Warren's (2002) *The Purpose Driven Life*, we regularly heard spiritual growth described as an intentional plan or purposeful journey. You must have a purpose. Otherwise, as one man said, "You shut your doors and go on vacation." Living intentionally, thoughtfully, or purposefully was described as a way to cultivate a more complete worldview and become a more well-rounded person. As one woman put it, "For me, the purpose of spiritual growth is to grow in a feeling of wholeness. Completeness. That your mind and your emotions are joined. For inner security and outer action. You keep working on it." As with other members of this mainline group, her ideas around spiritual growth were that it is largely a generalized effort to live life in reference to some greater good—a moral orientation that underlies a sense of security, intentionality, and coherence in life. Being willing to keep "working on it" provides a context for understanding life's struggles and difficulties, a roadmap for moral behavior in relationships, and a sense that the process is the point.

Consistent with the ethos of respect for individual perspectives and experience, members of this discussion group engaged in very little actual discussion. Instead, they offered individual perspectives in turn. The following extended segment illustrates this pattern of talking in parallel with, rather than between, participants.

R1: [reiterating her point made earlier] Spiritual growth is a growing feeling of wholeness, where you connect mind and emotion with reality.

R2: A journey that is really not a guided tour ... we have to take it on our own. The way you interact with people on a day-by-day basis, the way you look at solving problems on a day-by-day basis, I think that might be a part of it—developing a better way to relate and to move through things.

R4: A deeper everyday deeper connection with God; just trying to think of Him daily.

R6: Like setting goals—I heard years ago you shouldn't set goals. You should set directions, because once you get a goal, you're there and you stop. I think it is the same kind of constant layer on layer of development.

R4: Knowing you are not alone, knowing that whatever obstacles that you always have someone with you. That he is a presence in your life as long as you acknowledge him.

R3: It isn't a solo journey. It is a united journey for everybody.

R4: Not just about your relationship with God, but in terms of bettering relationships with those you come in contact with all the time.

R5: At work, I deal with a lot of people who get hurt or are feeling bad, and of course it's not okay in company policy to talk about it, but after they leave I keep it in my mind that I need to pray for that person. I think it has a lot to do with how you allocate your time and your focus. When you are praying, you are asking for a bigger picture than you have, and when you study the Bible, you are looking for a bigger picture, or whether you are reading a devotional thing, or whether you just sit under a tree and admire and just drink up the greatness that *is*. So you don't forget the bigger picture of life.

R6: If you get to the point where everything you do is, God is in what you do . . . it just becomes part of your whole life and actions. Like when you talk to somebody or do something that you are actually God's messenger on Earth.

R3: [laughing] If you get there, let me know!

R1: Letting God work through you to become a better person, but you can't do it on your own.

And in response to a question on what helps a person to spiritually grow:

R1: One of the main things on a spiritual journey is that we have to have constant prayer because we are not doing it on our own.

R2: Small-group Bible study.

R3: Small groups just form . . . because it can be difficult in today's society . . . you can't just walk up to someone and start talking to them about Christianity. Because some people are very uncomfortable with that and so, you know that bonding relationship if I needed to go to them they would help me and we would say prayers together and we can connect that way.

R1: It just seems like prayer and going to church and the small groups and all those things are *things* that you do, but I think spirituality is a thought process. It is internal; it needs to be reflected in your relationship with other people, but it's a thought process.

R2: A lot of churches are more emotional. I like that this place is more intellectual. That's more my personality.

R3: It all comes down to what you are more comfortable with. We're more comfortable with the more sedate things.

R4: It's just like, people learn differently. Visual, auditory, it's kind of the same thing.

R5: It's a process not a destination, any specific goal. I guess your goal is to continue the process!

In terms of the more specific goals and means of spiritual growth, our focus group participants again seemed to take care to frame their comments as "not the only way" a person could grow, or that "personal freedom in spiritual practices" is important. Thinking positive thoughts, being mindful of the needs of others, being attentive to how God might be present or visible in ordinary things—each of these was reflected in the discussion of how people can grow. The group was also in agreement that small groups were helpful, and that Bible reading would be a good idea, but as we talked further, they admitted that none of them regularly read the Bible other than what they hear being read during services on Sunday mornings, and none were regular participants in small groups. There was also general agreement that prayer was also important—not in any routinized way but in the form of "praying throughout the day" or "offering up a little prayer" when encountering a difficult situation. Yet when the discussion shifted to the relevance of church attendance, the level of conversation increased and a number of speakers began to comment on how church attendance was important because it created a space for them to think about important moral issues and talk about these with other adults.

One of the benefits of including focus group conversations in the research is that they provided the opportunity to observe our subsets of regular attenders thinking out loud in a small group. We anticipated focus groups engaging in some—albeit polite—debate, hearing individual perspectives echo themes that appeared in bulletins or sermons, or observing the participants work together to build a group consensus on a few select topics. Maybe even pull out a white board and run the discussion as a meeting. What we did not expect is that focus groups at First Presbyterian would effectively work as personal interviews in parallel. Yet, whereas little consensus emerged on what spiritual growth might look like or how it related to being part of a local church, what we did observe was consistency in affirming the importance of respecting individual perspectives, appreciation for the idea of growth as an ongoing process, and deference rather than definitiveness as the hallmark of the local congregational culture.

Individual and Gendered Notions of Spiritual Journeys

When we posed the same set of questions to individual women and men at various stages of the membership process at First Presbyterian, most also described spiritual growth as a personal process and talked about the importance of respecting diverse perspectives. One man in his late thirties simply said:

> My faith is my own business. The church is nice for the fellowship, for support, to share your beliefs and your views and to talk with fellow believers. You're only there for an hour, an hour and a half, though. As far as it helping my spirituality, my religion, you have to walk it throughout the week. Or else you're a hypocrite and a lot of people go to church and aren't really spiritual.

Similarly, a woman in her mid-seventies explained:

> My Christianity means to be more tolerant to people who are different from me. And to be more forgiving and so forth. To be a better neighbor. I'm not so sure Christians are any different from anyone else. But if I go someplace and see somebody who has a need, then I will try to address that need in one way or another. But sometimes I think we do too much pushing our values on other people, not meeting them where they are. And that's what I suppose I've learned in the church.

In addition to reiterating themes of individualism, tolerance, and civic engagement as hallmarks of spiritual growth, visitors and newer members were more likely than those in the focus group to go on to be specific about the meaning of spiritual growth, how one goes about growing, and the ways in which they felt they had been growing since becoming involved with the church. Both women and men talked about the purpose of the church as "spreading the good news" and doing good. One older woman summarized this perspective, drawing on a quotation from the Old Testament book of Micah.

> What's the purpose of the church? To glorify God, that's what the catechism says [she laughs]. And, well . . . what does it say in Micah? "What does God require of you? But to love justice, and mercy, and to walk humbly with your God." So for me, that's the mission of the church. Now that involves mission projects. That involves working with the youth group. That involves cleaning the church if you have to.

Similarly, a middle-aged man who had just started visiting said:

> I think the church gives you the opportunity to come together. You still have differences, but to come together in a community where you can demonstrate your faith. Also, there's power in numbers, and you can do things in a church community that you might not be able to do on your own. So there's an opportunity to have an effect on the community and to do good works . . . and then there's the education piece and modeling so that the kids can see, "do this." It's a good place to be and there's things to learn.

Overall, men were more likely than women to talk about the organizational utility of being part of an institution one purpose of which is to do good in the community. But women also described being drawn to First Presbyterian because of its reputation for service—whether the food pantry, Habitat for Humanity, preschool, or providing facilities for AA meetings. They talked about appreciating these things even if, as one woman said, "I'm not one to go out and build houses in Haiti, but that doesn't mean I'm not concerned about the poor."

In the personal interviews, women were more likely than men to talk about the importance of Bible reading, and the ways in which Sunday worship provided a quiet context for personal reflection. Several had been part of small-group Bible studies, but in most cases they were short-lived, topical groups. Some of the older women were or had been involved in Women's Circle meetings for many years, as had their mothers before them. Fewer talked about trying to participate in the newer programs for working mothers or at-home mothers with small children. Given that the perception that women are more religious than men is based, in part, on higher rates of attending services, we were particularly interested to hear women describe Sunday morning worship as an important spiritual discipline, yet in the next breath go on to include a caveat: if you didn't go, you could still be spiritual by being mindful of God, whatever you were doing. One woman in her mid-forties captured this sentiment:

> I think regular church attendance is really important. I was raised that way. I think it gives you discipline. Adults benefit from routine the same way that kids do. Still, there have been times in our lives when we have not made spiritual connection with a church and it's ok.... The Sabbath means that you recognize God and that you are being spiritual that day, so I don't have a problem with people who choose to do other things than go to church, but for myself, I really feel like it serves a purpose for me.

Other women were more explicit about the relative significance of Sunday worship as a means of spiritual growth.

> How important is going Sunday morning? It probably depends on the person. I don't know, for some people it's something that they feel they would really need to go a lot. By the same token, I think that you can believe in God and worship God without attending church as well. I think it depends on the person. We go as much as we can when we're home, but we don't change our plans around making sure we go to church on Sunday.

While some of what we heard from women and men in personal interviews at First Presbyterian could be interpreted as support for standard narrow gender stereotypes—of women's caregiving and men's pragmatic instrumentality—more often than not, people considering membership described their experiences at First Presbyterian in non-gender-stereotypical ways. The same man, for example, who was explicit about the size of the congregation making it possible to leverage resources for doing good also talked about the congregation as a place to grow through being part of a community.

I think that attendance is important as a discipline. You can say, "I can be spiritual, I can rest on the Sabbath and I can think about God," but I think it really brings a community sense and allows you to focus on God and get in touch a little bit better than if you're just on your own. It strengthens and renews your faith. Sometimes you have that consistency, sometimes you don't. If you're not attending on a regular basis, you don't think about your faith on a lot of days. Being part of the community really helps.

Other men talked about how becoming involved with the church gave them the opportunity to seek spiritual advice, to have a spiritual mentor with whom to talk, to not miss out on opportunities to be more effective in serving others, and to grow. Finally, for some men, small groups were particularly important sources of spiritual growth and fellowship. As one young man in his late twenties explained:

You don't get a whole lot out of church on Sunday mornings because it typically tends to be one person talking and everybody else listening. You can get things from that but I think that when ministry happens it happens in a setting where people can express what is going on in their lives, share, and get feedback from one another. I think that those are definitely things that can be way more helpful when it comes to spiritual growth.

Or as a man in his early thirties put it, enjoying nature with your family can be just as spiritually rewarding.

I think it's all personal choice. If someone doesn't go to church, it doesn't mean they are going to hell. Part of me, I don't know, I just don't believe in that. I don't look down on someone or judge them or anything like that because it's all personal choice. It's all in what you believe. Church is important to spiritual life, but we often have other things going on. We're really big campers, so in the summer I think we'd be lucky if we went twice a month. Going out and camping and being a part of nature is its own kind of worship, I think.

Although there was somewhat more consensus among focus group participants that Sunday morning worship was an important means of spiritual growth (not surprising given the group itself was selected from regular attenders), neither focus group participants nor conversations with individual visitors and regular attenders suggested that reading Christian literature was a significant source of spiritual growth. A handful of members mentioned Rick Warren's *The Purpose Driven Life*, several of the older members had read works by Marcus Borg or Dietrich Bonhoeffer, and a few middle-aged members mentioned reading Kathleen Norris, Thomas Moore, or Phillip Yancey.

Overall, then, the themes we heard most consistently across clergy, focus groups of current members, and individual interviews with visitors and new members at this mainline congregation involved metaphors of spiritual growth as a personal journey and individual process. Beyond these core ideals, we found women and men expressing different ideas about spiritual growth in non-gender-stereotypical ways. Men emphasized the importance of community and connection—even if that did not involve regular attendance on Sunday morning. Although they were somewhat more likely than women to consider the instrumental benefits of being part of an organization that could leverage greater resources for doing good, men also described how valuable it was to have a spiritual mentor, be part of a small group, and be encouraged to think about and apply their faith through the discipline of Sunday worship. Women, on the other hand, focused more on their individual experience in worship, of praying for others, and personal Bible reading. In most areas, the women and men at First Presbyterian were largely in agreement: spiritual growth is not a one-size-fits-all proposition, but a deep and personal process they are challenged to integrate into their everyday lives.

Valley Baptist Church: Biblical, Individual, and Experiential

Clergy Ideals: Changing Lives Through Practical Preaching and Small Groups

From our observations of the local culture, teachings, and literature distributed by Valley Baptist, we would expect to find members and regular attenders describing the concept of spiritual growth as focusing on personal transformation through a relationship with Jesus Christ, becoming a better person through participation in a church community, and the centrality of evangelism to Christian life. Although the pastor and staff occasionally used the language of spiritual journey, they framed that journey as one from which the traveler emerges as a different person, rather than growing in appreciation for the changing landscape experienced along the way. Nearly all conversations on the topic with church leaders included some discussion of how the church's core mission was to "see lives transformed by people coming to faith." Transformation is not the same as growth—it is growing into someone different. All the steps may be modest, but the goal is substantive and lifelong. Toward that end, Pastor Mark described specific means of growth—prayer, small-group Bible study, and Sunday worship—as all serving the larger good of personal transformation.

> We don't have a lot of rules, but the things you need to do to grow in Christ are in the Bible—make sure you're talking to God often, pray; stay close to God's people, definitely in church, or wherever else you go for that matter, too; and when God impresses something on your heart, gives you something to do, do it. There's a lot of other stuff; there are youth groups and women's Bible studies and men's accountability groups, or this softball team that they can plug into. Education classes, Sunday school; sure those are available, but clearly on a different level. Our goal is to see people transformed—to be able to go down the line and absolutely every person could say, "I am a different person today than I was three years ago, because God has changed this area of my life." New believers that's easy to spot, because they say I have put faith in Christ and he's brought conviction of sin to certain areas and I see a new-found peace. But we all need conviction of sin and greater faith in Christ. God has a next step for everyone. For that reason, we don't stress initial decisions as much as some say our tradition would, in terms of did you cross the line, did you put faith in Christ? That shift to seeing spiritual life as a journey totally changes things. Every person in their spiritual life has one next step God is asking them to take right now. And so everybody's on an equal level. For some people that may be to put their trust in Jesus Christ. For others, it may be to deal with bitterness and unforgiveness in their heart. But everyone has a next step to take. Maybe some seventy-five-year-old woman who's been in our church for fifty years, but she stays because God's really convicted her and she's praying in a new sort of way. That's a life being transformed. It may be someone who by all outward standards is an upstanding Christian sort

of person, but is looking at their marriage in a new way and there's new relational dynamics happening there. Or maybe someone who suddenly has a new heart for strangers and aliens, for people of other ethnicities. Or people having a soft heart, being less divisive in terms of the body of Christ and suddenly having a bigger heart for God's kingdom. Whatever it is, it's lives that are truly being transformed into the image of Christ.

The emphases on small groups, Bible reading, and Sunday worship celebrations are infused in the church's Saturday Seminar orientations, sermons, bulletins, and outreach materials. Each of these is intended to support the broader goals of the leadership: to see lives transformed.

Valley Baptist Church Members: Being Saved and Applying the Bible
Compared with new members at First Presbyterian, we heard much less ambivalence on the topic of spiritual growth at Valley Baptist in our focus group discussions. Not surprisingly, members at this conservative Protestant church were particularly clear about how a person begins to grow—by putting their trust in the "person and saving work of Jesus Christ" and making a public confession of faith. Without this saving experience, the idea of spiritual growth doesn't even make sense. From there, applying a common-sense interpretation of the Bible to everyday life is at the center. One older man in a focus group discussion summarized this perspective:

> I base my beliefs on what the Bible teaches. And if it's not in the Bible, then I am not interested in it. And the Bible says there is one mediator between God and man and that is Jesus Christ, and if we aren't willing to accept that, then we can't even meaningfully talk about spiritual growth because to me it has nothing to do with sincerity; it has to do with believing what the Bible says about Jesus.

As he spoke, others around the table nodded in agreement, and several spoke up to reiterate the point that effort or intent alone is not sufficient for growth, but that faith in Jesus, not "works," is essential.

Individual and Gendered Notions of Personal Transformation
The centrality of "putting your faith in Christ" and applying the Bible to your life ran through the personal interviews with women and men at

Valley Baptist as well. Understanding the Bible was particularly impor-
tant in women's descriptions of their experience and ideas around growth.
As one woman in her fifties who had recently attended an introductory
Saturday Seminar put it:

> One thing we really like about Valley Baptist is they really try to
> teach the Bible, to help you grow through Bible teaching. They don't
> have a lot of what I call "canned" Sunday school classes where you
> read from a book or some packaged curriculum; they teach the
> Bible. The point is to help you become a believer in God and help
> you grow, and the only way to have that is through faith and belief
> in Jesus Christ.

Both women and men described the goal of growth as becoming "more like
Jesus" and "growing in their relationship with God." That included some
of the same personal characteristics emphasized at First Presbyterian—
most notably compassion and caring for others. It also included notions of
thinking differently and making different life choices. As one new member in her mid-thirties described:

> I think each person, once they become a Christian, should be dif-
> ferent from the person that they would be if they hadn't become a
> Christian, right? So, God only knows how far each person has come
> in following Christ. It depends on where you started, so it is some-
> what artificial to compare Christians and non-Christians. I think
> you really need to compare pre-Christian and post-Christian. As a
> Christian, I should be hearing from God and following him ... and
> that would mean different life choices depending on what I hear.
> I should have more patience, more compassion, you know, be chal-
> lenged in reading the Bible and listening to the teaching at church
> to think differently, to become more Christ-like, less self-centered,
> more open to God and Him using me. You know? You take some-
> one like me, who looked pretty good on the outside whether I was a
> Christian or not. Only God knows how a person needs to change to
> be more like Christ.

"Becoming more like Jesus" and "personal transformation" are pretty lofty
goals. They are very personal and somewhat difficult to define, as another
young woman noted:

Becoming like Jesus is the common, number-one answer that is repeated over and over. But like, what is that? That is what we have to figure out on our own . . . and that is where we have to be reading the Bible and the book learning comes in, and the life experiences. The experience of growth is different for each person, but I think everyone is looking at the same goal.

Women in the focus group discussions and personal interviews were explicit about the need to grow in understanding of their faith and "recharge" their faith through worshiping with others.

I think it's pretty important to sort of get that recharge every week. It helps me to remember all the reasons that I go, the reasons that I believe. It helps strengthen my faith, and it gives me lessons that I can work on, which is extremely important because sometimes I don't know what I'm doing. I mean you talk about living the life of God, but I don't know what that is. So part of the way I learn what that is by going to church. I'm sort of slowly figuring it out. I mean, I could just sit down and read the Bible, but I don't think that I'm going to just understand everything that's in there. Attending service and listening to the teaching helps to explain things to me that I would miss on my own.

Especially for women who came to Valley Baptist with little or no prior experience with Christianity, Sunday worship is an important opportunity for them to literally "learn the story."

Noting that "you can't do it on your own, you need to surround yourself with others that strengthen you," women talked about growing through the experience of worshiping "with people like you," in a "safe place" that "feels good" and "gives you opportunity to learn how to have a better life." Relationships were part of this, but women focused more on the good of worshiping with a group more than specific relationships through which "God works out all the rough edges that are on people and changes us."

Men were even more specific in describing relationships in which they cared for others and the experience of worship as a context for spiritual growth. In fact, in the personal interviews men talked more about relationships than they did about the need for Bible study or prayer as the means through which they saw themselves "becoming closer to the

Lord." The church is "the house you come to worship in and care about each other and worship the Lord," one new member said. "I know I'm not where I'm supposed to be yet, but I try every day to get a little closer to the Lord. That's what it's all about." Another, a retiree who had just started visiting, emphasized the idea of relationship with Christ in the context of relationships with other believers as the defining aspect of his faith.

> I don't have a strong desire to be anything but a Christian. I'm not looking to be self-realized; I'm not focusing on "enlightenment." That is not my deal. My deal is to be a Christian. Going with Jesus' love wherever that goes. I don't want anything getting in the way of that. Being part of the church is important to grow your faith, to have the input of brothers and sisters in Christ in your life. Some people can do it on their own maybe. But I think it is helpful to share, to have a full experience, you need to go to church. It makes you grow faster because it helps you keep Christ at the center of your thoughts . . . to be connected with the body and the people that are there, to feel that connection.

One professional man in his early forties summarized this perspective:

> I see the church as a place where people come together to strengthen each other, encourage each other, challenge each other . . . to be God's people, God's hands and feet in the community, reaching out to others. It is a unique place for people to just be together and be enriched. And a safe place for people to go and to be encouraged. It is really about God. It's really about your relationship with God, spiritual food. You know, having that openness . . . it's there for the community, to serve people. But it's primarily about people's relationship with Christ.

Although we may have heard slightly more emotive language from younger men in the congregation than we did from older men, these themes of connection, relationships, and feelings experienced in worship were consistent across age, family, and employment status. This is not to say that these conservative Baptist men thought Bible reading or questions of doctrine were unimportant. We would expect them to affirm the centrality of the Bible as a means of spiritual growth and guidance; and they did.

Still, we noted that men in the personal interviews put less emphasis and spent less time talking about the authority of the Bible than they did in the focus group discussions—as though the focus group provided a venue for a more formal presentation of Baptist ideals. Compared to women, men in both the group discussion and the personal interviews spent more time and went into more detail about the salience of relationships, personal connections, and experiences to their sense of spiritual growth.

One of the main settings for those relationships was the church's many small-group fellowships. Nearly two hundred people participate in these small, home Bible studies (more than half of those who regularly attend). Men talked about these groups as fostering greater accountability to God through greater accountability to each other, as well as an opportunity to "give themselves" to others. One young man summarized this perspective:

> Some people just go on Sunday mornings. I think it's pretty vital to be there regularly for the teaching aspect and keeping Christ at the center of your thoughts, but it's also to be connected with the Body—to feel that connection. We're here to strengthen and encourage each other, to challenge each other. I think involvement in small groups is the next level. That's where God is challenging me, to give back and not just receive—to be involved and be able to give myself. Two years ago I don't think that was the case. I was there mostly to receive; now I want to give back.

Along with connecting to others through small groups, women and men at Valley Baptist talked about prayer as a means of spiritual growth. Using slightly different language than the Presbyterians, they described prayer as helping them to "see God working in ordinary things" or "rejoice in everything," and "thanking God for helping me find something that I'd lost." Each of these little things, they said, could be understood within a larger narrative of Christian faith and life. As one woman explained:

> It is taking the experiences that naturally happen to us in this life and saying, "What does this teach me, what am I trying to learn through this?" I don't think that things happen just randomly, I think they happen for a reason whether it's a little thing or a big thing, and so I try not to read into stuff but you know when something big happens I think, well what does this teach me, how can I use this? That is the "how" of spiritual growth for myself.

Even when suffering through a period of depression or significant fam-ily problems, people at Valley Baptist emphasized that gratitude prompts them to grow personally and spiritually. Particularly among those who had little previous experience in a church, starting to "pray a lot more" was one of the biggest changes they saw in their lives since starting to attend the church. One newer member in her late twenties came to Valley Baptist with an understanding that prayer was being like a little child kneeling beside the bed saying, "Now I lay me down to sleep . . ." or a family saying a formal prayer before Thanksgiving dinner. Her time at Valley Baptist opened up that notion to the idea that prayer was (also) a frequent and more ordinary thing, like a conversation with someone.

> One of the biggest changes is that I pray more. I didn't really know how to pray. The whole idea that it's okay to be in a constant dia-logue with God, talking all the time, that prayer doesn't have to be super formal, on your knees, head bowed, kind of thing. There are certain things you should do during prayer, but whether or not you do that is up to you. I also started reading these books, *The Bible for Dummies* pretty much [she laughs]. But it's really interesting for me to get kind of the short version of the different books in the Bible since a lot of it is new. So reading those and just learning how to pray.

Prayer, Bible study, small-group fellowships, and the experience of wor-ship Sunday mornings were what the pastor and elders envisioned the church being about. For the most part, there was a fair amount of coher-ence between those ideals and the emphases of newer and existing mem-bers in this Baptist congregation as well.

St. Andrews: Salvation, Struggle, and Spiritual Routines

Clergy Ideals: Becoming Like God (Theosis) Through Liturgy, Prayer, and Sacrament

In Orthodoxy, Father Michael says, the goal of spiritual growth is nothing short of "*theosis*"—a theological term for becoming united to God through the process of salvation. That means weeding out "the passions" of self-centeredness and learning to enact loving compassion through the disci-plines of prayer (with the church and alone), fasting, regular confession, participation in the Eucharist, and giving. Communicating those ideals to a congregation, most of whom have recently transitioned to Orthodoxy from other religious backgrounds, can be a challenge, as Father Michael described:

A Christian has been given that most intimate of knowledge and communion with God. We would say it is unique. Not that people in other religions aren't trying to seek the truth and God. But you know, for the Christian who believes that God is a personal God, who loved us so much he was willing to die for us and experience everything for us, that kind of understanding of God is going to hopefully produce a different kind of life. Human beings are very similar; we share the same nature, we struggle with the same things, but the way we live our life is not the same. Hopefully being a Christian means living one's life in a way that communicates God's love in a unique way. That's how Christ says that they will know us, right? The love of God and love of neighbor, those are tied together. So what does it mean to love God with all your mind, heart, soul, and body? For those that are able to truly achieve that with God's help and to be people of prayer, to be praying continuously, because Paul says pray continuously . . . well, there are some people that are able to do that and they literally shine. You know when you're in the presence of a Godly person; I mean a true holy man or woman. You can just see it. They don't even have to say anything. You just feel the presence of Christ coming through them. And, you know, certainly there are those who are able to move mountains and perform miracles through their prayers. But that's not that common, but that's what we're all called to. We're all called to be that light, to become like God.

Growing toward that ideal involves participating as much as possible in the life, liturgy, and routines established by the traditions of the church. Worshiping together, he says, is one of the most obvious places to begin:

When you're starting out, attendance at liturgy is very, very important. Even in the lives of the truly holy men and women in the Church, it's only after being immersed in the worship and services and life of the local church community that you might get to the point where you can somehow be removed from the physical Church worshiping together in the liturgy. But those people are very few. They've developed such a close and intimate and strong relationship with God that even if they're physically separated, they're still very much united spiritually. But, for most of us, almost all of us, being involved as much as possible whenever the church is meeting together to pray is important. Christians are not supposed to be just Sunday devotees, right? It's a daily walk with Christ and so how do we do that? You immerse yourself as much as you can in the life of the parish, it's absolutely important for one's spiritual maturing and for each other to help carry each other's burdens. I would think a truly dedicated and committed Christian Orthodox person would be attending not only the Sunday services, but any other weekly services that may be happening and would be participating in whatever other activities are going on at the church: educational, support parties, charitable ministry, whatever it is. But it's when the Church comes together as a Church, that the sacraments, the mysteries are possible, not anywhere else. So, you can do these other things, you can read on your own, you listen to speakers and read other books and instructional materials to increase your learning and your knowledge of the faith. You can do charitable work anywhere. It doesn't have to be in the congregation. You can take in and give support to other people as necessary wherever you are. But the worship of the liturgy and sacraments is what's indispensable.

St. Andrews Members: Explaining Salvation as an Ongoing Process

Given the centralized, liturgical, and creedal nature of Orthodoxy and given the relatively long and doctrine-focused nature of the catechumen process, we would expect to find members and regular attenders at St. Andrews to be able to articulate a clear and coherent narrative around the process, means, and ends of spiritual growth. Indeed, compared to the other two congregations, the Orthodox discussion group collaboratively tried to explain church teaching and tradition—so that the group as a whole constructed a fairly cohesive narrative around the concept of spiritual growth. At the heart of this discussion was the concept of *theosis*. Whereas people at Valley Baptist described salvation as a decision to accept Jesus Christ as savior based on his death on the cross as "payment for our sin," the members of St. Andrews made the case that it was impossible to assume anyone's salvation was a "done deal." To be sure, spiritual growth begins with an initial faith commitment, they argued, but conversion was not synonymous with salvation. One member summarized this portion of the discussion:

> Salvation is the process of being saved, not "I'm saved" now. That assumes you could know. It's more like this: Christ has come along with his lifeboat and saved us . . . we get in, but in the lifeboat on the journey back to shore we can mutiny, we can jump ship, take over as though we are the captain, things like that. So salvation is a process of getting back to home.

Beginning with similar vocabulary as those at First Presbyterian Church around spiritual growth as a process, people in the St. Andrews focus group went on to specify the purpose of that process as reuniting with God and becoming the whole, healthy "rational sheep" that God originally intended. As one woman explained, "The goal is union with God. Loving God and loving people. And it is being able to be what God designed us to be in communion with him and in communion with other people. It's union with God for me." To which another man added, "In Orthodoxy, the idea is returning to what God created me to be. That is salvation. I was made in the image of God, and coming back to Godlikeness is the process of salvation." The journey is one in which a person takes small, daily steps of repentance "from trying to take the finite things you think will fulfill, and finding the infinite that really does fulfill."

While members of First Presbyterian described spiritual growth as a journey that is sometimes a struggle, men and women at St. Andrews described the journey itself as struggle through which growth takes place. As one woman remarked, "It's become clear to me that salvation is in the struggle; it's not in the overcoming of the struggle, because Christ is the one that overcomes that struggle in us. We do the work, make the effort, but Christ makes it complete. It is the process for us that's important." The context for this struggle is the community, where common practices and core beliefs cultivate a sense of solidarity in that process. As one woman said, "Everyone has the desire of fulfilling this thing where we are all going for the same goal."

Gender Parallels in the Use of Spiritual Tools

Participants in both the St. Andrews discussion group and the personal interviews talked about the same spiritual practices Father Michael described as core disciplines for spiritual growth. These spiritual rules or tools reshape routines every day—and because there are so many things to *do* and services to attend, opportunities for spiritual growth are never hard to come by. As with training for an athletic event, women and men described committing themselves to a daily spiritual routine in order to cultivate spiritual growth. The sense was that if a person keeps "acting like a Christian," soon those actions will sink in and become a part of who you are. As one man who had recently joined explained:

> I try to imitate people that I admire and respect. And the person I admire and respect the most is the person of Jesus Christ. To imitate him means to follow and imitate, act like, do things ... love, act like love, do loving things and love might occur. Fake it 'til you make it, as they say in AA. Orthodoxy gives you a chance to act like a Christian. Here are all the wonderful techniques they give you. Just do it. God will take care of the rest.

Another, a young woman from an evangelical background who had just started attending, said:

> By its nature it requires a lot of you, if you are going to actually actively choose to participate. It requires more of me, more of my participation throughout the day. Orthodoxy is structured so that you are praying throughout the morning and the evening. Fasting is something that comes and goes in the week and seasons. In contrast, before starting to come here, I was in a really great evangelical church where I might choose to go to a Bible study, but there is nothing that really required of me other than I come on Sunday. I guess "required" isn't the right word, more like what is assumed or understood it's going to take for me to really grow in my relationship with Jesus. At St. Andrews the assumption is that it isn't enough to come on Sunday and do your thing and go to Bible study, if you want to really be rooted in Jesus, and to really be able to quote-unquote "fight the spiritual warfare" around us, the assumption is that you just need all of this—you would need to be praying and you would need to be fasting in order to really truly be able to grow.

Both women and men described the usefulness of having a structured set of things to do to help them stay connected. As one woman in her late twenties said, "I need this; I can't come up with the discipline. I've never known how to pray, and I still don't feel like I do, but here at least I feel like I have a chance because I have a prayer rule and know that thousands of Christians have prayed this before me."

The basic outline of these spiritual disciplines is framed by the institutionalized traditions and cycle of services and readings provided by the Church: whether attending services, weekly meals after church, the Eucharist, icons, incense, a calendar of fasting days and daily scripture readings, confession, and daily prayer routines. Overall, this is a very low "free rider"[8] congregation—where most parishioners and frequent visitors see as good those little sacrifices involved in exercising the spiritual disciplines offered by the church. Together, they say, these offer a well-considered path that a person interested in spiritual growth would be wise to follow. As one woman explained:

> Take the Church calendar. In the morning I can look and see what the scripture verses are for today and who the saints are or who the martyrs are we are celebrating; and I can see if it's a fast day. The calendar is shorthand instructions on how to be a Christian. Read the instructions, and that's how I am to be a Christian today. So today I eat this and today I do this and then I learn to cross myself and learn to pray before meals, and I learn to pray in the morning, and in the evening I light a candle, and before long you've got this whole sort of rhythm of Christianity. And to me that is just hugely beneficial because without that I just go on into my own natural rhythm and my own natural rhythm is basically hedonism.

Although not everyone described hedonism as the alternative to following these spiritual disciplines, there was general consensus that what you feel like doing, or think up to do on your own, or consider a good idea might not actually be so.

Individual and Gendered Perspectives on Corporate Practice

In the personal interviews, both women and men at St. Andrews talked about how attending worship services helped them stay focused and provided a sense of being "in this together." They talked about not feeling alone and appreciating being in community. They also described a "weirdness" in which they felt both a sense of accountability (to a community; the priest; a godparent or sponsor), as well as a sense of personal freedom around individual practice. Individuals can, and do, they said, read what they wish, fast or not fast, go to confession or not. One newer member mused at length about this balance of community and relationships of accountability:

> I've been thinking about how Orthodoxy is just weird in its ability to do two things at the same time—holding the sense that the community or "body" of Christ is the Church and that's what is central, not the individual. But then that you are a unique person and individual. It is weird to me that Orthodoxy focuses on the relationship between priest and the believer. It sometimes seems as though Orthodoxy is both more personal and less personal than Protestant groups I've been a part of in the past. There's less input from a whole crew into your spiritual life. But there's pretty specific and authoritative input from your priest, as well as potentially the priest's wife, or your sponsor. At some level it has started to shift my experience to being one where my Christianity (what I'm doing, feeling, or not) is not anybody else's business. That feels more individualistic than close Protestant small groups, say, where multiple people are encouraged to be involved in keeping others "accountable." But at the same time there's more accountability because you have confession and a greater sense of being part of a body that is being saved. You're accountable to a spiritual father or mother. So the individual is not off the hook, but in the end maybe the struggles are just a little less public? I'm not sure I'm getting this straight, or really have a clear idea of how it works because I'm so new. But that's some of what I've been thinking.

Another recently retired man who had attended a Bible college in his twenties went on to be more specific about the experiential dimensions of his faith:

> Well, where I am now, I would say that being in the Church is everything. It's not something "pious." It's not something that's intellectual. The Greek have a word for it, they call it the *nous*—the eye of the soul. It means, at the core of our knowing, at the core of our soul, our mind is to be in subjection to our *nous* rather than

our *nous* to our mind or intellect. There are intellectual dimensions to faith, but you know and experience God in the *nous*, not your intellect. Being at liturgy is part of that, because it's something you experience, you know by experience. The Orthodox faith is one to be experienced and not a set of intellectual propositions to be grasped.

Two places where we heard slightly different nuances in women's and men's narratives around spiritual growth were that men seemed to talk slightly more often about the good they saw in confession and went into more detail about their appreciation for a more corporate notion of salvation.

> The church is a family, where you live out your faith and come to experience salvation, which is a family thing and not an individual thing, cause we're all in this together. At one time, I would have thought of salvation as very individual, as just between me and God. I almost see salvation as bigger than the Church; it's the whole of humanity [that] is trying to find God, whether they know it or not.

To be sure, women also talked about the good of being in a community when it came to mutual support during seasons of fasting, particularly Lent, and a communal sense of Orthodox Christians around the world praying similar prayers. Yet other than these two slight differences in emphasis, the women and men at St. Andrews were remarkably similar in their descriptions of the means and ends of spiritual growth. One woman who had been attending an inquirer's class summarized this perspective:

> Being part of the Church is the means by which we become more like Christ. We participate in the life of the Church and in doing all this "stuff" we are conformed into his likeness. At the same time, the Church is the end itself. It is the Church for which Christ died. It is the Church, the whole Church, that the Holy Spirit preserves and empowers and transforms and keeps throughout time. If you want to talk about the "perseverance of the saints," it is the Church that we're talking about. You don't make it on your own, you are saved with these other people. The Church is called the Ark. Get in it! So yeah, participating in the ongoing services and life of the Church is a pretty big deal.

Conclusion: Growth as Learning and Experiencing Congregational Culture and Theological Tradition

Narratives of spiritual growth at these three congregations are consistent with theories of spiritual capital and research on spiritual formation that emphasize the centrality of gaining proficiency in the narrative and language of a particular religious tradition. Congregational culture provides a context for these processes—processes through which religious traditions offer a diversity of models and means for growing in experience and belief.

The degree to which spiritual growth is understood as a journey, or a journey toward a specific end, varies across tradition. Within the mainline Presbyterian Church, understanding growth as a personal journey and open-ended process echoed teaching within the congregation on tolerance and respect for diverse perspectives. Members were reluctant to specify either the means or ends of spiritual growth, but rather emphasized how spiritual growth is a personal matter that involves an increasing ability to recognize transcendence in ordinary things and growth in personal integrity and compassion. At Valley Baptist, concepts of spiritual growth reflected core teachings about the need for new birth and integration into small "family" fellowship groups. Immersion in the church's worship celebrations, Bible reading, and small group ministries each contributed to a sense of identity as being part of a robust and distinctive religious subculture. At St. Andrews, the importance of practicing spiritual disciplines was articulated and reinforced through sermons, bulletins, the church calendar, prayer books, new member catechumen classes, and informal conversations. Both the means and ends of spiritual growth were clear: to become like God through gradually being weaned of self-indulgence and expanding one's ability to love and care for others.

Somewhat surprisingly, we found smaller gender differences in ideas about spiritual growth within the congregations whose teachings were more specific about the means, ends, and meaning of growth. At First Presbyterian, where definitions of growth were most individualized, women emphasized Bible reading, quiet reflection, and appreciation for Sunday morning worship services, and men were more likely to emphasize organizational resources and personal mentoring as means of growing their faith. At Valley Baptist, women and men were in agreement that growth centered on being born again and continuing to change to become more like Jesus. At the same time, women were more likely to talk about the importance of understanding the Bible and the good of worshiping with others, whereas men talked about the importance of being in safe, open, and caring relationships more than they talked about Bible study or prayer as the vehicles through which they experienced growth. At St. Andrews we found both the most specifically defined teachings on the means and ends of growth as well as the most consensus among women and men on those things. Where newly Orthodox women and men differed is that women were more likely to emphasize congregational support for practices such as fasting or prayer; and men were more likely to talk about the salience of confession in their experiences of growth. Working to grasp the concept of *theosis*, embracing paradox, struggling together and individually to pick up the tools of prayer, fasting, and generosity appeared in the narratives of both women and men.

Finally, the degree to which the bodies of believers are engaged in the process of spiritual growth also differs across these churches. Although it is important not to overgeneralize either to these congregations or the traditions in which they are located, it does appear that a different degree of embodiment is encountered in each. At First Presbyterian, growth comes through quieting both body and mind—by creating a rest and openness apart from the demands of everyday life within which the mind can re-engage with the beauty of music, a depth and richness of color, and a reasonably outlined faith. Eating and drinking are small but symbolically rich. At Valley Baptist, bodies are more active, not only listening, singing, and thinking, but standing, clapping, embracing, and occasionally getting very wet. Bodies are encouraged to be more active and emotive as reflective of the faith itself—positive, upbeat, and engaged. At St. Andrews, additional senses are called into play along with the mind and the heart. Bodies at St. Andrews stand, bow, kneel, sit, eat, drink, smell, and hear—often multiple choruses or dialogues at once. Overall, then, spiritual growth involves both increasing understanding of the language and story of one's faith and increasing facility in the practices in which believers engage. Our observations and conversations within these congregations point to the additional salience of the body and embodied practice in ordinary, lived and corporate expressions of faith.

6

Giving

CHURCHES ARE A place where people grow. They are also places where people give. In this chapter, we take up this second dimension of congregational culture and assess the ways in which joining shapes men's and women's involvement across congregations. We begin again with outlining what clergy would like to see happening within their congregations and move then to explore gendered narratives of involvement, volunteering, and ideas about the articulation of faith to politics and social change.

First Presbyterian Church: Philanthropy and Civic Engagement

First Presbyterian Church has a strong culture of philanthropy and civic engagement. With the average age of parishioners in the mid-fifties, financial giving has been consistent and adequate to cover salaries and maintenance of an historic building. Yet the aging of the congregation has begun to generate some concern about how well the church will be able to manage expenses in the not-so-distant future. Bequests are welcome, but short term; and increasing empty space between parishioners seated in the pews highlights the need to address membership attrition for the sake of the community as well as the budget.

Changing Demographics and (Re)creating Ways to Be Involved

One effort to increase membership and create opportunities for giving was initiated after a subset of the church's leadership attended a seminar on church growth. An early Sunday morning service was added in the hope of transitioning to being more of a "seeker-friendly" church—complete with Power Point sermon outlines and contemporary praise music. The membership never really settled on the changes, however, so after several years of churning on the question, Who are we and what do we offer?, the church conducted its own survey to see what members liked and didn't like about the new model. Opinions were mixed and with attendance stagnating, the pastors decided to revamp again. They created vision teams, dropped back to one service, and focused the new-member process on cultivating a sense of connection to the congregation by becoming involved in its ministries and service programs.

One element of this emphasis on connecting through service was a revitalization of the office of "deacon" (an elected and ordained position within the Presbyterian Church that focuses on service and caregiving ministries) which had existed at First Presbyterian without much focus for several years. They began a parish nurse program and created a volunteer position to coordinate visiting and transportation for parishioners with limited mobility. They also developed, or began to more actively promote, a host of other ministries and activities, including the annual financial pledge drive; a men's breakfast group; hosting "coffee hour" after Sunday services; sports teams; groups to help brainstorm new educational programs; food pantry volunteers; sewing for missions; and "church mouse" cleanup teams. They promoted and celebrated Habitat volunteers; youth and adult choirs and special music; facilities clean-up crews; retreat planning; a group tasked with researching a remodel of the sanctuary and preserving the historic building; and hired a youth pastor in an effort to attract families with children. As Pastor Richard explained:

> Service can be within the church itself—serving as leader for youth or adult music, drama study programs, or helping with the financial and physical stewardship of the building, or working with Habitat for Humanity. All of those are essential to keeping us up and functioning in this place, as well as sharing the good news. We're trying to focus people on finding their purpose through becoming involved in ministry as soon as they join. For some of the older people, that's a challenge since they come more from social habit—a kind of 1950s model. Sometimes I think we focus too much on change, but we're trying to find out who we are as a congregation, and that's in flux.

Children's ministries were also revitalized, as the church expanded youth programs and increased the visibility of youth in Sunday worship. They incorporated older children into special music programs and began to regularly invite younger children to come to the front of the church, sit on the steps to the altar, and listen to a short, simpler version of the topic of that Sunday's sermon. The pastors encouraged the congregation to use these opportunities observing children to "consider who you were as a child," to remind members that "Jesus welcomes us as he did the little children," and to "have faith like a child and enter in." Children dramatize, sing, and speak about faith in a way that adults in the congregation say point to the mystery, openness, and joy associated with faith. Their presence encourages older members, in particular, to envision a future for the church and affirms its history and place in the community.

Valuing Opportunities and Reasonable Involvement

In our personal interviews, women and men both talked about appreciating the idea of being part of a congregation with a revitalized youth program, as well as one involved in the local food bank, Habitat for Humanity, and occasional service missions. One woman, a nurse in her mid-forties who had recently joined, summarized the comments we heard over and over again from newer members:

> I think that they have a really good missions program, both in this community and then outside the community. They've done really well with Habitat for Humanity; I think they've built three houses now. Let's see . . . and they've built a church in Haiti, the youth program has done trips to Mexico. They help the local food pantry and do a really good job at helping within the community. When they don't always have money for other things, they still continue to be able to do missions and that's tremendous.

Both newer and longer term members were appreciative of the kinds of service the church provided. Yet, despite the growing number of service opportunities and the strong ethos of the congregation around giving, we found very few members actually involved as volunteers. One part-time staff member who had recently been hired to help coordinate volunteers talked about the challenges she faced helping the church "move from a model of we provide these programs and services for you" to one in which members were encouraged to be more actively involved.

> Now that they've hired a youth pastor, I think the biggest change for me is I will not be recruiting volunteers for working with youth. But I'll still be recruiting for other things. For the size of the congregation I think we have a lot of staff people, and because of that I think that we have a habit and a tendency to heavily rely on staff. There is a potential for me to empower a lot of people to do ministry in the church, but that doesn't seem to be our tradition. We are in a habit of "we do it"—as in the staff does it—so that volunteers aren't really that essential. But we're in the middle of a huge transition, and we are really being intentional about enlightening people about their ministry and their call and giving them the permission to then do it. It is going to be a real challenge. But that is the exciting part. It is very challenging, but it is really fun because I believe that the heart of the Christian relationship is the love of God and the love of one another, so there you go. Find out what you love to do and you've got all three!

Older Members: Trimming but Still Involved

To be sure, older members at First Presbyterian often described long histories of volunteering—providing meals on wheels, hosting coffee, giving regularly to the budget, participating in mission projects, wrapping bandages, and sewing. Many of these activities were fairly gendered when they were younger. None of the older men, for example, reminisced about their work with the sewing circle, or older women their weekends with friends doing church maintenance or building homes with Habitat for Humanity crews. But both women and men described being active teaching Sunday School, collecting food for the local food pantry, and serving on committees. They described their work as "wonderful" and "good fellowship and way to get acquainted," as well as "a way to get to be more a part of the church." "I like giving our resources—the idea that we give back. That's very important," one woman in her late fifties said, "Philanthropy is a Presbyterian philosophy, it's the Presbyterian way!"

At the same time, older members also talked about trimming their volunteer efforts or refocusing them on activities that were social as well as philanthropic. "I think probably at this point in life I would be better off dealing with older people than with little kids," said one retired woman in her mid-sixties. Her husband, interviewed later that day, said similarly, "I'm more interested in support for retired folks now more than youth. I've been helping a little with this Wednesday morning breakfast program to encourage the men of the church to get together. There's a bit of study; it's primarily fellowship and support. I guess if we had a couples club, we'd be big pushers of that, but that's about it right now." Older members occasionally spoke about beginning to feel "pushed" or having their "arm twisted" as interest in recruiting volunteers increased and their own energy levels dropped. This was all the more apparent as the church shifted to a new-member process that emphasized strengthening congregational commitments through increasing members' involvement beyond Sunday morning services.

Younger and Newer Members: Selective, Gendered, and Time Poor
Enthusiasm for volunteering was even more muted among younger, newer members, particularly women. For some, fitting church volunteer work into overbooked calendars of school activities, lessons, family trips, household maintenance, and full- or part-time employment seemed impossible. More than one woman laughed out loud when we asked about volunteering and then went on to explain:

> Volunteering? Well, we don't really have time to do that, but if we did we would. It's a great idea! Right now we're happy if we can make it to church on Sunday. We really try because we'd like our kids to go to their afternoon programs. But my husband and I both work and the youth groups start at four forty-five. My daughter's involved in swimming and other things we've tried to participate in, have been during swimming lessons, so those have been a "no-go," too.

Although not all mothers with school-age children laughed at the thought of adding more to their already busy lives, the idea that volunteering was a good idea in principle, but not a current practice, was a common theme among new and prospective members.

A second theme among newer members at First Presbyterian was that some felt they were not yet connected enough to the congregation to volunteer. Connection came first, then service. A few talked about having been involved elsewhere before starting to attend the church, and making a conscious decision to wait until they had formally joined before starting to volunteer. Others described resisting invitations to participate more widely while they weighed options and considered schedules. One woman whose family was in the process of joining described not wanting to volunteer until they were confident they would be more than sporadic attenders.

> We've been really holding off on doing more until we make a spiritual commitment to the church. That sounds contrary to what I just said about volunteering being important, but . . . well, we're big on acting as a family, and a commitment to the church is a commitment that we're going to make as a family. The kids have been really involved in kids' programs and Sunday school and choirs and all that. And both my husband and I have been in choir in churches we belonged to in the past . . . but I'm struggling with whether or not I can make it an extra time a week to join the choir. The pastors keep inviting us to do things, but we're taking one event or one activity at a time. I think eventually we'll get our niche and get to the place where our talents are. We just want to settle in first.

Men were less likely to describe volunteering at church as a challenge or as conflicting with other work and family caregiving responsibilities. They were, in fact, quite likely to talk about embracing opportunities to serve as part of their involvement with First Presbyterian. They described helping out with youth programs, teaching Sunday School, helping with small-group studies, and donating professional services. One younger man who had just recently joined said:

> You know, Christians should walk the talk. They should be caring and loving individuals who are unafraid to talk about God to people who are willing to listen. I think that they should volunteer for activities that benefit people; they should not erect monuments to themselves or claim credit for whatever it is that they do, but simply do it because they're Christian. On the flip side, many great acts of philanthropy are done by Christians, but you don't ever hear about them.

For these men in their thirties and forties, involvement as a church member appears as another facet of the institutional and personal commitments that are markers of adult masculinity.[1]

Reasonable Faith and Civic Engagement

Overall, members at First Presbyterian were clear that faith informs civic engagement, particularly at the local level. Volunteering at community organizations—whether the Rotary Club, Habitat for Humanity, or the local hospital—was an expression of this ethos. Even among those who were not themselves active volunteers, the *idea* of volunteering and the value attached to it was an important part of their identity as church members. "It's very important," one older woman said. "It makes you feel good to do good." Others described it as follows:

> The purpose of the church is to love and support the congregation; that's number one. Number two, I think, is the mission in the community, whether it's the shelter or food pantry, or Habitat for Humanity. There's less interest in international missions, we've had a couple of teams doing Habitat type stuff, but that's harder to get people to commit to things that involve a lot of travel.

Sentiment was fairly consistent across older and younger women and men in that the church does best when it focuses on local issues and stays out of national politics. One woman in her forties summarized this sentiment:

> I don't like when the church takes a political agenda. When any church takes up a political agenda, really. I think people, as individuals, can take up political agendas because of their faith, but I disagree with the organized church taking a political agenda. People can be an influence on the local level. They can be an influence on the national level when they vote. They can be the yeast in a group that they are in, but they don't have to make a big noise . . . they can just be a gentle soul.

"Not being pushy" but "being tolerant" of other political perspectives was something we heard over and over again from both women and men. Women were especially adamant that the Presbyterian Church as a whole, and individuals within it, avoid engaging in what they considered misguided tactics of the "Christian Right." As one older woman explained, faith and civic responsibility are, and should remain, separate spheres.

I don't think Christians should involve themselves in trying and make society more "Christian" per se. I think they should be involved in society for humanity's sake. I couldn't disagree more with the Christian Right. They are so wrong about the policies they push around nation building. That's not even our charge—we have a Constitution that the government is supposed to abide by, and as Christians we have the Bible and that's what we live by also. So we serve both—we can be good citizens and try to do good in our community because of our faith. But that doesn't mean imposing your views on others.

Most newer members were similarly put off by what they considered the "intolerance" and "pushiness" of conservative Protestant political groups, and they made the case that many of the issues those groups opposed were personal not political, and generally best left to personal conscience, not the voting booth or picket line.

Valley Baptist Church: Building Community Inside and Out

Pastor Mark and the elders at Valley Baptist Church are also interested in getting people involved in the church and its ministries. The congregation has a long history of youth and family programs, as well as outreach in the community. Although some of those programs had faded prior to Pastor Mark's arrival, the collective memory of the church as a cornerstone in the community is still very strong. In addition to its slate of Bible study groups and holiday celebrations, the congregation now offers an ESL program, addiction recovery group, and prison and homeless ministries. Even with all of these new programs, Pastor Mark argues that their first priority is not to get people to start volunteering or give money, but to connect to and support each other.

I'll say over and over again: we want people here, number-one reason, because they believe that this is an environment and a community where God can work in their life to bring about transformation. That's why I want people here. Not because they found a place to serve, not because they found a place to learn, not because they found people they like, but because they believe this is an

environment and a community where God can work in their life
to bring about transformation. Again, I would tell someone, if you
could only do two things, come to Sunday worship celebration and
get involved in a community group. But remember, what happens
on Sunday mornings is not body life. There's some really good stuff
that goes on there, but when the New Testament talks about all the
dynamics of the church about teaching one another, serving one
another, and the healing and forgiveness that happens, and the
prayer and expression of gifts, generally speaking that does not happen on Sunday mornings with hundreds or thousands of people.
That's a good thing and very important, but what we want is people
to really be connected to Christian community.

Although Valley Baptist faces some of the same challenges with a graying congregation and aging building as First Presbyterian, its success in
adding young families has improved the health of its budget, at least for
the short term. A core group of families and retired individuals provide
a baseline of support, while the leadership works out how to best teach
the concept of regular giving to a younger generation unaccustomed to
the idea. "We don't expect visitors to put anything in the donation plate,"
Pastor Mark explained, "that's the last thing we want them to think we're
about. We try to be creative in helping people give."

The church has had two fundraising drives for major building repairs,
and after a sermon on the parable of the "good steward" one year, gave
each family an envelope with twenty dollars cash and told them to make it
grow so they could give. Several weeks later the church held a celebration
service in which people shared the ways they had turned their seed money
into something more and thanked God for the good of additional funds to
run the church's ministries. Eventually, the congregation stopped passing
a collection plate altogether and put a box for giving at the back of the sanctuary, so that the physical process of collecting money was as decentered
as its discussion.

Running on a Core Group of Volunteers

In our personal interviews, members and visitors alike spoke enthusi-
astically about the church's teaching and ministries. They talked about
the revitalized children and youth programs, of the special services and
outreach to the community, the prison ministry, the Christian School,

and how the church was "reaching out to people in need." Half were at least occasional participants in midweek community Bible studies. Yet few were actually involved as regular volunteers. Fifty people might show up for a fall clean-up party or to decorate the gymnasium or sanctuary in preparation for a Christmas or Easter program. But other than large events, the day-to-day teaching and caring ministries, outreach, and upkeep of the church are managed by a relatively small number of people. If First Presbyterian has a history of relying on staff to run programs, Valley Baptist relies on a core group of very involved volunteers.

Gendered Domains of Service

Because volunteers are relatively few, we want to be careful not to over-generalize gender differences in involvement. Leaders talk about welcoming men and women into all sorts of service, and there are no formal rules proscribing women's leadership in positions other than pastor or elder. Nevertheless, the culture of the congregation is highly gendered. All of the church's programs are ultimately the responsibility of the pastor and elders (all of whom are men). Women serve as support staff, lead the children's and women's ministries, and plan and participate in women's retreats. In 2005, the church hired a woman to be principal of its Christian school. During the time of our research, all but one of the church's adult Sunday School classes were taught by men (and in that class, one of the elders sat in as a way to avoid offending the sensibilities of more conservative members who might think a woman teaching inappropriate). Overall, Valley Baptist runs more gender-specific programs than either of our other two congregations, highly sentimentalizes Mother's Day, has special "moms' mornings," and until very recently referred to women and women's ministries as "ladies" and "lady's ministries." In many ways, the congregation's programs echo and reinforce the patterns of separate leisure sociologists have observed in working-class families for much of the twentieth century.

Women are visible greeting people as they enter Valley Baptist Sunday morning, are up front giving a welcome, doing announcements, and helping to lead worship music. When we talked with newer members about their involvement, we found women mentioned being involved in a wider range of ministries than men, and more frequently mentioned volunteering with children, youth, and hospitality ministries. They described volunteering as a way to "put your faith into practice" and "feel good about being with others who share the same beliefs" and as a natural extension of their other paid and unpaid caregiving. As one newer member said:

> I think that if you want to become a disciple of Christ and follow Christ and do his work, then that's going to involve a commitment to the body and to other people. How that might get worked out for each person is going to be different. Apart from Sundays, I go to a small group once a week. And about a month ago we took on the children's ministry. Before that, we were trying to figure out what we should do to do more, and the children's ministry seemed a good fit because I work with people all week, so doing that here makes a lot of sense. Plus, we have two kids, so we thought, "Let's work with the kids!"

Men, on the other hand, were more likely to talk about helping with the high school group, setting up multimedia, or volunteering for work parties.

At the same time, both women and men serve as Sunday morning "greeters," volunteer to serve during fellowship time after church, prepare food for picnics and special events, and help organize outreach programs such as "Christmas Compassion," where members distribute cookies, baskets of food, and blankets to people in the neighborhood. The gifts are an expression of practical kindness as well as a way to remind people that the church is there to offer welcome, support, and resources for change. One newer member described her involvement in these programs as growing out of a strong sense of reciprocity, saying,

> I've always found people to help and lend a helping hand, so I got involved in Christmas Compassion. In the summer, we walk around downtown and give people cans of cold soda; at Christmas we take baskets to people in the neighborhood. There were people who helped me, and you just want to do the same thing for other people.

This same woman also helped in the nursery, served as a greeter Sunday mornings, and volunteered at the local food bank. Most of her efforts, however, were devoted to one of the smaller, yet more intense, ministries Valley Baptist ran visiting people in prison and supporting families struggling with poverty and substance abuse.

I've been helping one of the elders who runs the prison ministry. He really has his hands full; there are so many people who need help. Like Amy. She has a couple of kids, and I just happened to go by her place the day she was getting arrested. She was high, and she kicked her baby across the room. So they arrested her and took the kids. She's clean now. She's actually getting out of prison soon and just needs a little help to kind of keep her on track. Or my friend Amber—we met when working at the grocery store. We weren't making much money and were going to get an apartment together, but she was still partying and I'd just walked away from that life, so I couldn't do it. I lost track of her for a while, then got reconnected when we were handing out baskets at Christmastime. She had breast cancer and pretty soon was on hospice. I was with her when she died. That was pretty intense. I met her mom through that ordeal and helped her get on her feet because she was home-less and didn't have a job. The church also helps connect people to the food pantry and other resources in town like the one that pro-vides temporary free housing. You have to be in the right spot, too, to help, and the person has to be ready to receive it. So it's been a learning experience. It's hard to know where people are at, and it's true, some people are just using the system. But Pastor Mark says if we're not being taken advantage of once in a while we aren't being generous enough, so we just go along and help people as the Lord gives opportunity. That's what the outreach is for.

As in other research on American evangelicals,[2] we found the church's ministries focused on personal relationships and support for individu-als and families in need. Although they also supported international and evangelistic missions, most of Valley Baptist's ministries were local. As one man who had recently joined explained:

One of the things that made me want to dig deeper and become a member here is that this place is all about reaching out to people, encouraging people to attend, helping the community, especially people in need. They have a lot of outreach ministries for people who really need things financially. I guess I don't see the church as being involved in politics. I know some people are, but the church as a whole? No. It's about peace and joy in the Lord, and reaching out to people in need.

Or as another new member, an engaged woman in her twenties said, "Christians should lead by example. If we want to change society, we need to be changed ourselves. We need to love people, and then we'll see more people experiencing that change."

Personal Faith and Personal Politics

Whereas the majority of the members at Valley Baptist are fairly conservative, the pastors and staff describe the church as not committed to any one political perspective. Nevertheless, the congregation celebrates right-to-life Sunday, and it supports a group for gay men seeking to live in celibacy and men struggling with pornography and sexual addiction. Yet in our personal interviews, only one person brought up the topic of abortion and gay rights as things Christians should try to change. She framed her argument in personal terms:

> If someone asks me, I'll tell them I'm not a personal believer in abortion. From my perspective, the woman has already made a choice by choosing to have sex. It's not right. It makes me so angry. (Pauses) I'm not trying to be radical here. I'm not going to burn down a clinic or anything 'cause that's not right either! But I'm not going to vote for someone who supports abortion. I don't know how I feel about the case of rape or incest, but it shouldn't be a form of birth control. I also think Christians should be more vocal about homosexuality. I had a coworker who died of HIV and I really liked him personally. But it is really hard to separate being loving and supportive from their lifestyle. Plus the cost of everything, I don't want to have insurance go up or be denied for some child because we're spending money on drugs for people doing stuff they shouldn't be doing. Plus the Bible seems pretty clear that it's wrong.

Appealing to the Bible, yet framed also as personal perspective, this woman voiced opinions we suspect others in the congregation were reticent to share lest they play into stereotypes about the reactionary "Religious Right." As one woman explained:

> I think we have to be very careful in the political arena because Christianity is diverse, but the ones we see in politics are the extreme, right-wing, almost scary to me, sort of groups. They would

have us get rid of all sorts of people and that's very frightening to me. I think that we should have an influence and it should be political, but you have to be very careful in your portrayal of Christianity and what that means. Right now we have such a bad reputation. You say the word "Baptist" and people are like, "Oooh, I'm staying away from you, because scary fire and brimstone stuff." So I think most importantly we need to have an influence on a personal level. That's where individuals can have the greatest impact, by talking to their families, talking to their neighbors and their coworkers about what Christianity really is.

Overall, discussions about broader social and political activism in this congregation mirror the contours of American evangelical politics in general—with the majority leaning to the right on matters of abortion and gay rights, while a persistent (and perhaps growing) minority are politically progressive and describe themselves as primarily concerned with social justice. One young woman summarized this range of perspectives and articulated a more liberal evangelical viewpoint:

I think it's hard to say there should be a specific "Christian-like" agenda, because God is beyond politics. And people at the church are all over the map. You know, there are people who are very strongly antiabortion and, I don't know, maybe home school so they can teach their kids creationism and all that. And then there are people who are really on the left end of things. Like me! (She laughs.) What Christians should be doing is communicating the message of God's love to other people. That a relationship with God is possible, you can have a relationship with God and forgiveness of your sin. That's the center. Christians should be providing housing for those that don't have it, providing food, providing child care, you know, all of those things to show people God's love. That would be what I would want.

None of the men in our personal interviews talked about the need to oppose either abortion or gay rights. Most did not talk about politics at all, and the few who did were more progressive than we anticipated—describing being "bugged by the church's division of roles for men and women," and believing as one man said, that Christians should not get sidetracked by the issue of abortion.

Christians should speak from our sense of moral certainty about justice, not get sidetracked by single issues such as abortion. That's not the cornerstone of Christianity. When taken to extreme, it is an issue of hate and no longer about justice. It is a distraction away from more important justice issues such as wage justice or the environment and what we call the developing world and what's happening to those people, and are we doing the just thing by helping.

Overall, then, members of this theologically conservative congregation were generally, but not uniformly, conservative in their perspectives on issues of gay rights and abortion. Yet rather than finding faith motivating believers to political action, faith is primarily personal—shaping voting, perhaps, and the impulse to give to those in need, but mostly focused on helping people encounter the love of God and begin a relationship with Jesus Christ.

St. Andrews: Mercy and Service

The two areas that have posed the most challenge for leadership at St. Andrews have been meeting expenses and helping new members acclimate to Orthodox practice. More globally, as part of a national and international network of churches, St. Andrews struggles to build its identity as an Orthodox church in America—one that remains faithful to historic practice and celebrates its Eastern and Mediterranean roots, but is distinctly American in its organization, volunteer structure, and gestalt. The parish also struggled financially. Early on, they could only support Father Michael on a part-time basis. Eventually he went to full-time, but the church regularly ran a deficit month to month, eating into funds they had hoped to use to build a new building. The issue was not having quite enough members. As at our other two churches, a small number of families were donating the majority of the funds the church needed to cover costs, and although the membership was growing, most members had modest incomes and were modest givers. Toward the end of our research, the adult membership had finally grown to the point where giving covered costs and monthly budget reports were no longer running in the red. Since then, the membership and their giving have continued to grow. The church holds an annual stewardship campaign around Christmas and an annual meeting in February, at which time it votes on the budget and any significant program or ministry changes. Most recently that involved the decision to use funds from a substantial estate gift to pay off the mortgage and move forward on the purchase of property on which to build permanent church facilities. The church also encourages additional financial giving during major feasts of the year, and those funds pass through to various local and international charities.

The Limits and Challenges of Patriarchy

St. Andrews offers members numerous opportunities to serve in the parish and the wider community. Because the church as a whole is organized as a patriarchy, serving in positions that potentially lead to ordination as a priest (e.g., altar server, subdeacon, and deacon) has historically been reserved for men. In all other areas of parish life, women and men are active and visible. Men and women both serve as readers, choir members, and chanters; both hold office on the parish council and other special committees, lead the church's building/vision committee, manage Sunday School programs for youth, and help support college outreach. Women and men are also both representatives of the church at a local child abuse prevention center founded by the parish, and both help organize food drives and gift collection around the holidays, as well as collections of school supplies in late summer to support low-income families. Men are also as visible as women in managing children during services and in the kitchen doing cleanup after weekly postliturgy potlucks. We asked whether that might be an idiosyncratic characteristic of this particular parish, but Father Michael's wife, Katherine, said it was not. In fact, she was surprised that *we* were surprised to find men in the kitchen. "To me, as someone who grew up Orthodox, it's not surprising at all. That's how we were raised, with the men in the kitchen cooking as well as the women, and with the men engaged with the children, as much as the women."

(Un) Gendered Service in a Patriarchal Church

When we asked newer members at St. Andrews how they were involved in the church's programs and ministries, nearly everyone talked first about increasing participation in the church's *services*. When we specified that we were also interested in how members were involved in the practical life of the church and the broader community, nearly everyone then went on to talk about some level of involvement in the church's annual ethnic food festival. Most of the early phases of planning and preparation are run by a small group of men and women who cook for months ahead of time, together and alone, organize the rental of equipment, strategize the flow of hundreds of guests through food lines, hire a band, and lay out the arrangement of tables and displays. On some days, there are more men than women in the church kitchen preparing food. As the festival approaches, the team grows and more men and women join in, ordering additional food and beverages, spending hours doing setup, grilling hundreds of pounds of meat, and spending hours clearing tables and keeping up with dishwashing during the course of the festival itself.

Other areas of service are too idiosyncratic to generalize, given the size of the congregation. One woman leads a burial ministry; one man drives the church bus; one woman runs the church bookstore; one woman coordinates teams of volunteers to clean up after Sunday potlucks (with a rotating schedule of families being responsible each week), while one man typically stays behind to finish sweeping the floors; and two families regularly donate excess farm produce for parishioners to share. In the end, the overall life of the church and the ways in which women and men participate and serve are remarkably ungendered. They are fairly unspecified by age, as well, as children of all ages stand with their parents during services as they are able and play at their feet when they are not. Children who are interested in music mingle with adults in the choir, standing or sitting on a set of tall stools so they can see the music. Older children occasionally read psalms at the end of Vespers or prayers at the beginning of Matins, and a whole cadre of adolescents stays overnight on Good Friday, sleeping on the floor of the church's hall and taking turns reading through the Psalms and the Book of Acts in the sanctuary beside a table decorated as the tomb of Christ.

Celebrating, Accepting, and Struggling with Patriarchy

To be sure, the all-male priesthood came up in numerous conversations, and on occasion members described men's and women's responsibilities using language similar to what we heard among some very conservative evangelicals. One young mother who had recently transitioned from a conservative evangelical congregation reflected on the male priesthood as one of the things she liked most about the church.

Yeah, I love the all-male priesthood. You know, Orthodoxy is the first place that I've ever found with strong men who were there because they wanted to be there. I just feel like our culture has so blurred the idea of men and women. I just find it completely refreshing, beautiful, and comforting that men's authority is just not a question. I mean of course people question it, and there are the discussions that happen, but the male priesthood it is clearly the tradition that has been given us. And it is not to slight women. When I'm told I can't be a priest, I don't take it personally. Submission is not a male-female issue. Everyone is in submission in the Orthodox Church, even the Patriarchs. The head of the Church is Jesus, so it is a Christian issue—being submitted to Christ. We all get to work that out in different ways. But I definitely feel like it's a wonderful thing to have a husband who desires to lead his family and to raise sons who will grow to want to be men, and daughters who would like to be women. We can celebrate our differences and that's a beautiful thing.

Few women were quite so specific in their ideas about the importance of celebrating and maintaining gender difference. More often, women described being neutral or reluctantly accepting of the restriction of the priesthood to men, and they were uniformly careful to make the case that the Church values both men's and women's ministry and participation. At the same time, over half of the women with whom we talked experienced some struggle around gender, especially women coming to St. Andrews from churches in which there were no gender-prescriptive paths to service. One graduate student described the course of her own struggle in detail:

Well, men are priests, and up the hierarchy from that as Bishops, Archbishops, Metropolitans, Patriarchs. But women do just about everything else. There's a debate I guess about the role of women as deacons; it's acknowledged that there were women deacons in the early church, but that practice fell out of favor in mostly patriarchal societies. So in principle women could be deacons now, and I guess are so in some churches, but the principle of moving slowly to change cultures and individual churches, where culturally that would be seen as inappropriate, is . . . well, they seem happy to leave it alone or at least move slowly. At St. Andrews, I see women and children reading, chanting, singing, moving around the sanctuary to turn on the lights, move the gospel stand, check and refill candles. When I see guys doing things like cooking and cleaning up and women doing things like leading worship by reading, the whole rigid "only men are priests" thing seems less important somehow. Plus Father Michael seems so clearly to me to be doing a "service" when he's doing the priest thing. Evangelicals talk about men as servant leaders, but I see Father Michael actually doing it—they call it serving at the altar. All the movement, all the words, all the prayers, all for our sake. Lifting all of us, drawing us all in to worship, looks more like serving than leading or directing. Certainly he's not exercising authority over the congregation as a male at that point. His maleness doesn't seem that important. Plus there is a lot of slipperiness and "gender bending" that I see at St. Andrews; such as when Father Michael comes out to join the congregation bowing before the cross. Leading the congregation in being humble rather than simply standing up front and telling us how to think about the Bible. All those things help me not get too bent out of shape, or feel like I'm being put in a box or slotted into positions where authority is reserved for men simply because they are men. That's certainly not the case here.

Some men also struggled with being part of a patriarchal church, as one retired man who had recently joined said:

This has probably been an issue for me my whole life. I am a man who loves rodeos and I like to crochet, so I don't see things as gender specific. I used to have a real question with why women couldn't be priests in the Orthodox Church. And I now understand a little bit more. It isn't because they're female; it's because of the iconic theology of Orthodoxy. The priest is an icon of Jesus, so you need an icon that's a man because Jesus was a man. If the incarnation doesn't matter, then the physicalness of Jesus as a real man doesn't matter. But that's not what Orthodoxy says. The historical Jesus—the God-man with a real man's body—matters. So the priest must be a man to rightly be an icon, an image, of the God-man Jesus. That's the only place I hear Orthodoxy say something gender specific. I don't see a specific gender thing other than that. Overall, I think gender in America is pretty messed up. Evangelicalism has a long way to go because they have Dobson and that element, preaching that men are from Mars and all that. It's persuaded itself that men and women are totally different—that men should be tough and always the leaders, and women should be at home with the kids. It's pretty messed up.

We were not surprised to find that the idea of being part of a patriarchal church was problematic for some members. What we did find surprising is that some younger women described their experience in this patriarchal institution as helping them work through the misogyny they experienced elsewhere. One woman who had recently joined said:

> I actually didn't like the idea of being a girl most of my life. It didn't seem fair that the guys got to do cool things and the girls didn't. But more than that, it seemed like there wasn't respect in the Western world for what it is to be female. I knew that had to exist some- where. And I've actually learned to be okay with being female and maybe even appreciate it through Orthodoxy. Part of that is recog- nizing the part of Mary that is really cool. If she hadn't said okay to being Jesus' mom, there would be no incarnation and no salvation. She is God's partner in our salvation. Without her cooperation, we are not saved. When Jesus dies, He takes a body through death—the body Mary gave Him—and when Jesus rises from the dead, it is the body Mary gave Him that raises and makes our resurrection possi- ble. So priests might be men because they are an icon of Christ, but a guy can't be mom, like Mary, who gave Jesus that body. So God made us different, but God made both sexes good. It wasn't until I became Orthodox that I finally felt like I was in a community of people who really believed that.

In the end, questions of whether or not women might serve as deacons or altar servers or priests moved to the background for most members as they worked to understand and practice and serve within the church. As one former Baptist explained:

> On the surface it would appear that the Church's ideas about men and women conflict with what I believe. But the ways I see peo- ple interacting around gender seems to mesh more than I would expect—much more than the Baptist church I was going to. On the

surface, St. Andrews appears really traditional with the male priest
and all, but after being there for a while it seems different—oppo-
site the Baptist church where they present themselves as really open
to everyone, then you hit a wall and you realize they have all sorts
of rules about what women can and can't do. So I'm getting to a
place where something about tradition humbles me. Who am I to
come up against two thousand years of how this is how the Church
works—we're not talking about a Church that is five years old here.
It at least slows me down, and I have to realize that there are a lot of
people who have thought through this, so it is okay for me to give it
a little bit of space. The other thing is that the Church really highly
honors Mary and you hear about women all the time in the services,
so it isn't like they don't honor or respect them. So it does make me
kind of go, okay, I need to have some humility in how I approach
this. I think I need to actually sit back and watch a little bit and consider what's going on there.

Individual and Institutional Perspectives on Faith and Social Change

Finally, we asked newer members at St. Andrews about their perspectives
on how their faith relates to politics and interest in shaping America. We
anticipated the congregation to be fairly conservative, and to some extent
found that true in the aggregate. However, taken individually, we found
perspectives ranged across the political spectrum. One subset of members
who had come to St Andrews from conservative evangelical backgrounds
described the articulation of faith to politics in language similar to that
of the more conservative members of Valley Baptist. They talked about
being "concerned about the direction our country is headed in," worried
about "secularism in the public schools," were opposed to health care
reform, gun control, abortion and gay marriage, and were highly skeptical about climate change and science in general. Others who had grown
up in Orthodox churches expressed similar opposition to abortion, gay
marriage, and "big government" but did not carry the same skepticism
about climate change or the reliability of scientific research. Another subset of newer members located themselves at the other end of the political spectrum and talked about their concern with policing and racism,
thought health care reform had not gone far enough, were not opposed

to gay partner rights (although most expressed concern that legalization of same-sex partnerships be understood as distinct from the sacrament of marriage in the Church), and did not want to make abortion illegal. One new member who had grown up in a mainline Protestant congregation and transitioned to St. Andrews from an evangelical emerging church summarized his observations of the congregation:

> I've never been in a church where people had such varied perspectives. There are everything from fundamentalist conservatives to really hippy dippy liberals. I think it is pretty safe to say the church has Socialists and avid Democrats as well as staunch Republicans. What seems more important is that there doesn't seem to be a political directive from the pulpit. There's one message about loving your neighbor and caring for all, and you have to work out where you take that as an individual voter. That seems different to me— I've been in liberal churches and conservative churches where both feel like you're being told what's right. Here we prayed for Bush and now we pray for Obama ... and some people have to work hard to do that either way.

Overall, St. Andrews could be characterized as generally conservative but also eclectic in the range of political perspectives held by its members. It mirrors the mix of political perspectives that are espoused by the national church jurisdictions that also cut across standard US political classifications of liberal and conservative. Most Orthodox jurisdictions (Greek, Antiochian, Serbian, Albanian, etc.) are officially prolife and are opposed to euthanasia, but also opposed to capital punishment. They are skeptical of what they consider the uncritical positions of the United States toward Israel (Palestinian Christians are mostly Orthodox), believe that the "New Israel" is the Church and not the modern State of Israel, and are cautious about efforts to overthrow autocratic leaders in Iraq and Syria because those governments provided a semblance of protection to religious minorities.

Gender, Mercy, and Serving the Poor

Given the cross-cutting political perspectives of Orthodox jurisdictions in the United States, it is not that surprising that we found a range of perspectives on the articulation of faith to politics at St. Andrews. What we did not find were significant gender differences in where those political sentiments lay. Both women and men talked about the need to work for social justice as an expression of mercy. One woman who worked as a teacher in a low-income school district highlighted this theme:

> It's easy in our country to be apathetic towards our community and what's happening in it, to be critical of or ignore the underprivileged. It's very easy to be judgmental and not merciful. I think God has extended so much mercy to us that we should stand out as people who desire justice and desire to be merciful to others. Someone who is connected with God should be going in that direction at least. Sadly, some Christians stand out in terms of judgement and hypocrisy. And that's not what I want. You want Christians to be the people that are merciful and that are really interested in seeing justice.

Other women talked about how Christians should "first pray and then help the poor and needy," "be merciful," and "provide a safety net for children who have nowhere to go." Men also talked about mercy as a vehicle for social change, how Christians should "be like Mother Theresa, love the poorest and most needy," and "make a difference not by power or force but by being willing to change myself first, to have compassion and be brought to tears by the meanness of the world." In most cases, helping individuals and helping groups that then help individuals were the main outlets for doing good. People collected supplies for school children, donated to special collections for missionary families, and attended fundraising luncheons for the child abuse prevention center.

A few members considered individual needs within the context of broader systems of social injustice. One young woman spoke about "the need to look at systems and try and change them, while recognizing that those systems are all in a fallen world and without God's help change isn't going to happen," or as another man said, "The Church needs to be a different kind of community in a pluralistic society." Still, for the most part, the connection of faith to social change focused on the local—working within the community to do good to individuals and families in need.

Conclusion

As women and men became integrated into these diverse congregations, we found unexpected gender differences in avenues of participation, giving, and service. Moving toward membership, joining and growing appear to create space in which women and men express values and experience community in ways that often challenge, even reverse, cultural stereotypes around femininity and masculinity. When it comes to giving—whether money, volunteer time, or connecting faith to broader social and political concerns—we find the gender experience within congregations not only to be different, but different in unexpected ways.

We found the greatest gender differences in ministry and service within our conservative Protestant congregation, Valley Baptist. There, a small subset of women and men were involved in ministries to people in prison or struggling with substance abuse, or they served as part of the "welcome committee" that greeted people as they entered the church each Sunday morning. Other avenues of service were much more gender specific, with pastor, elder, and most other formal leadership roles reserved for men. Women's volunteering focused on ministries specifically for women, supporting staff and programs for children. We were surprised to find nearly as many gender-segregated avenues of participation at First Presbyterian. Although both women and men talked about having opportunity to read scripture during Sunday services and serving as greeters and hosts during Sunday coffee hour, they also described participating in a wide range of gender-specific activities, whether men's breakfasts or women's circle, men's and women's retreats, or men's maintenance work parties or women's leading various children's programs.

In terms of broad areas of service, the least gendered congregation was the one specifically described as a Patriarchy in its clerical organization. To be fair, St. Andrews is a smaller congregation and so some of the "everyone is involved in helping everywhere" may be as much a function of the number of hands available as it is a congregational culture that makes most, but not all, service gender inclusive. Women may not serve as priest or deacon (as they may not serve as head pastor or elder at Valley Baptist), but they are as likely to participate in weekday and feast day services; serve as chanters, singers, and readers; and participate in maintenance and Sunday potluck dishwashing as are men. The limitations on ordained positions within the Church are a struggle for many transitioning into Orthodoxy from other, less restrictive traditions. Yet even among these former evangelicals, Methodists, Presbyterians, and Pagans, there is a recognition that while there is no perfect institution, there is room within this one to grow, give, and change.

7

Changing

PEOPLE CHANGE. THEY change when they become members of voluntary organizations. Simply passing through time and place, they change. Participating in a local congregation is no different. Some congregations, such as Valley Baptist Church, are explicit in celebrating their identity as centers of personal change. In less evangelical congregations, the idea of personal journey captures a more understated notion of change. There is no judgement regarding what a person is changing from or changing to, other than it be toward something kind and good. People change, and congregations provide a venue within which they may do so, somewhat more intentionally than might otherwise be the case.

In this chapter, we explore the concept of change and how new members understand themselves to be changing as the result of their participation in these three congregations. We focus specifically on personal change, change in relationships with others, and the experience of some members and prospective members who after three years are no longer affiliated. Across all three domains, we explore and assess gender differences in reasons for and experiences of change within this diverse set of congregations.

Reshaping a Sense of Self
First Presbyterian Church: Getting to Church and Growing in Grace

About a third of the newer members at First Presbyterian Church didn't think they had changed much as a result of being part of the congregation. Believing is something they take for granted, and their participation at First Presbyterian is a place to affirm common beliefs and values rather than seek personal transformation. Women in particular said things such as "I don't think my prayer or spiritually have changed much," or "Being part of this church hasn't changed my faith much" and "I was brought up as a Christian, so that hasn't changed at all." A few emphasized how being part of the church encouraged them to "do the best that I can and hopefully someone will be able to see that and I am able to impact them in a positive way" and to "set a good example so maybe others feel this is a good road they should take, too." The more ambivalent men seemed puzzled by the question and then settled on the notion that perhaps they were a little friendlier as a result of being part of the church, were more compassionate, or were better friends.

Other members were much clearer in terms of identifying ways in which they saw themselves changing since being part of the congregation. Women at First Presbyterian talked about being renewed in their faith and appreciating the opportunity to "get outside myself." A few mentioned praying more and the simple fact that they were making an effort to get to church services. The most frequently mentioned area of change by women was the sense that they were becoming more tolerant, less critical, and open to difference. One older member explained her growing patience with politically conservative friends, saying "We have some good friends who are pretty conservative. I listen to them and I don't comment, I don't argue. I might go home and blow my stack, but it's not my place to tell them what to believe. If they can see that we have something that they haven't got, then great. My faith has deepened, and I don't take life quite so seriously." Another, younger, woman who had just recently joined went on about she felt more empathetic and less critical of others.

> You know, just the bit I've attended has made me a little more aware of my immediate surroundings and the way I react to people. I'm not so harsh. I try not to be so harsh and critical anymore. If someone's doing something that I don't like, I always try to think that there probably is a good reason why that person is behaving that way. I try to give them the benefit of the doubt, more often than I did before.

In addition to being more tolerant of the foibles of others, some of the newer members at First Presbyterian described growing appreciation for styles of worship that were different from what they were used to. As one younger woman explained:

> It definitely has changed my idea that worship has to all be done in one way. I think that's important. A lot of people get wrapped up in the way they worship, like that's the only way. I have seen different ideas, like Patricia's version of a more meditative style the way she does her praying. They have services outside; they can really embrace nature and just things I hadn't really thought of that way. They definitely have taught me new ways.

Men at First Presbyterian also talked about change—most in terms of practical involvement. They described becoming more active in the youth and music programs and getting to church services more regularly. Men also talked about how being part of the congregation had helped them become more aware of God during the day, growing in their appreciation for different styles of worship music and being challenged to focus on the grace of God rather than whether what people are doing is right or wrong. One young man who had come to the congregation from a conservative evangelical background summarized these themes:

> I don't know if being here has changed how I think about my faith, but it has changed how I apply it. If I'm having a conversation with someone, it helps me focus on helping them to see how Christianity is beneficial to them rather than explaining things as "this is right or this is wrong." I came from a conservative church, where things were either right or wrong. I think that can be good in some respects, knowing where boundaries are. The emphasis here is the idea to love and to try to understand people before trying to pass judgement, or assuming that because you follow the rules that you're better than someone. Grace and helping people become whole is emphasized. That is something that I really enjoy about the church. There is a feel of really wanting to help people. And I think sometimes in conservative churches where right and wrong are so emphasized, the love factor and grace factor is kinda missed out on and not understood as well. It think there is a place for trying to please God; I also think that understanding that God loves us even though we make mistakes is [an] important factor.

The flip-side of the grace thing is they have a very difficult time really setting any kind of boundaries. The pendulum really swings the other way, maybe in circumstances where they *should* apply some more boundaries or discipline, they tend to err on the side of caution and don't because they're trying to support, say, a person in leadership who maybe shouldn't be there.

A sizable minority of interviewees at First Presbyterian did not seem to think they had changed much as a result of being part of the church. Most, however, did believe they had changed. For some, that change was simply getting to church more often. But values and perspectives also changed, and they changed in ways consistent with the broader congregational culture that values tolerance, diversity, and doing good.

Valley Baptist Church: Supportive Relationships, Economic Stability, and Individual Values

Given how the theme of personal transformation saturates sermons, bulletins, small-group discussion, public testimonies, and special events, we were not surprised to find newer members describing how being part of Valley Baptist Church had changed their lives. Men considered these transformations across a relatively narrow band of experience, behavior, and belief. Some described graphic accounts of their lives using drugs, struggling with unstable relationships and employment, or serving time in prison. These men were clear that people at the church had been instrumental in their being saved and their jobs, families, and relationships becoming more stable and rewarding.

It's not that Christians don't mess up, but I think in general there's less of that here than in the general population. There's help maintaining a moral point of view so families stay together. To stay away from things like promiscuity that are going to drive relationships apart. I am really glad to have felt protected many times by my faith. It helps keep the other stuff away.

For men who struggled with unstable employment or drug abuse, being part of the Valley Baptist congregation provided an informal connection to men who modeled stable family lives and an opportunity to gain some facility in the language of the middle class.

Here it's all about coming to worship the Lord and care about each other. It's not about who you are or how much money you've got. On Easter, I don't know if they were homeless, but a couple of guys came up and talked with me, and I realized that I used to do dope with them. You know, at some churches they'd look down on you, but I don't feel that ever from anybody. I've probably met everybody in the church and I've never felt that at all. Some of the men, one of the elders especially, have really helped me a lot. I know I'm not where I'm supposed to be yet, but I just try every day to get a little closer to the Lord. That's what it's about.

Men also emphasized how they thought they were becoming (or wanted to be) gentler, less self- centered, and more connected to others since being at Valley Baptist. One newer member captured these themes saying, "I think that Christians participate in the world with a gentler spirit. They are kinder and more careful about the way they relate to one another. Not that other belief systems don't produce gentle people, but I think being a Christian helps me with that and I see that in others."

Women at Valley Baptist had more to say and a wider range of areas in which they described themselves as changing. One subset of changes were practical: women described praying more, getting up on Sundays to go to church, reading the Bible for the first time ever or in years, and worrying less about day-to-day concerns. One woman whose husband was in prison described some of these changes:

Getting to church is important because it shows that I have faith in the Lord. It's just me and my kids right now. We're struggling little by little; you know, it's hard for me to keep this house and pay rent but since I've been at church, I just don't even worry about it; it's in His hands and I'll let Him deal with it because otherwise I'm going to stress myself out and let my kids see that I'm stressed. I've always believed in the Lord, so the biggest change for me is maybe just getting up on Sunday morning. I wasn't used to it. But now I get up and I'm happy to be up. I go to church every Sunday and I talk to John, one of the elders, or the pastor. They help me. Last month they helped with rent, so I shouldn't have a problem. My kids' dad is in prison, but now he's a Christian inside there and he talks to John and the pastor sometimes. He'll write and tell me to go to church and to bless my filthy mouth and I'm like ok, I'm calming down, but that's how I was raised, you know, with foul language and I'm so used to it so it slips out when I'm angry. Not as much now, I'm trying to do the best I can. I know I have to do it on my own, and it's really hard sometimes.

Increasing levels of involvement were significant for women who drew on the church for practical support. In the same way that men with marginal employment benefitted from personal networks and an entry into more middle-class modes of work and family, women described benefitting from Valley Baptist's financial resources, access to children's programs, interpersonal communication, and guidance in navigating bureaucracies. The resources of the congregation are a backdrop of support to women struggling to be independent and "do it on their own," providing a vocabulary of "middle-class respectability" and a network within which to practice it.

Along with feeling more independent, women also described a sense of increased agency since becoming affiliated with Valley Baptist. One young woman who had recently joined the church summarized this perspective:

> I feel like I can make a difference and that I can change things in my life. The church has helped me clarify some of those things for myself. I've found this new sense of comfort with myself and what I'm doing. And it's made me more aware of my values and that it's okay to not agree with other people. Not that there aren't grays or that I'm passing judgement on someone, but now, for example, when things happen at work, I'm more able to say, "That's inappropriate, you can't do that, you can't say that to me." So there are things like that. I have more confidence.

Becoming more confident, clearer, and more assertive in articulating their values, even when those ran counter to peers, was one of the areas of personal growth we heard most frequently from women. Confidence in working through value conflicts was also significant, as another new member explained:

> It's taken some shifting, figuring out what my real values are based on what I believe and not based on what the television tells me to believe or my husband or my family. It's almost a relief to clarify where I'm at, and I think Valley Baptist has really helped

me to do that for myself. To figure out "Okay, I used to think this issue was okay, but now I'm looking at it from a different angle and maybe it's not." I've been rethinking a lot of different things. For example, my views on abortion. It's a big issue. I'm trying to figure out how to balance out my feminist side with believing that at conception this is a baby, this is a soul. You just don't have the right to kill it. And sort of trying to balance that with the idea that it is a woman's choice, it's her body. The church doesn't talk about it directly, but some of the things they do talk about have made me start to think about that differently. So, there's a struggle there, that's kind of where I'm at right now. I just think people in general need to be a little more accountable for their actions, but that's easier said than done, and I'm sure that I've taken the easy way out many times.

Overall, while both women and men at Valley Baptist talked about changes in their religious practices and described how church was helping them cultivate more stable work and family lives, women focused more on their growing sense of independence, agency, and self-confidence since becoming part of the congregation.

St. Andrews: The Work of Worship and Refining Faith

When we asked people who had grown up in Orthodox households about how they might see themselves changing since arriving at St. Andrews, some said their faith hadn't changed much because "every Orthodox church is basically the same," but they appreciated "being part of a church where people are pretty open and the church feels like a big family." A few described their faith becoming more personally relevant because, as one man said, "in Orthodoxy there's a lot of going to church, so growing to be an adult and making the faith your own has been important." Or, as another man explained, "I don't know if my faith itself has changed, but our priest is a really good educator, so I feel like I'm learning something new every Sunday." For a few families that had come to St. Andrews from very ethnically based congregations, learning a different style of music, slightly different versions of traditional prayers, or praying for a slightly different slate of hierarchs and saints during liturgy took some getting used to, as one newer member explained:

It is really interesting that most of the parishioners at our church weren't born Orthodox. One man's father was Brethren, so becoming Orthodox was a big change for him. We have people from a lot of different backgrounds. It's just neat to be around people like that. Very well-educated, too. We have people in the church with advanced degrees, so that's interesting. We also have a lot of kids. I've lived in places where the Orthodox church I was going to had very few children. St. Andrews is growing. You might not see that in an Orthodox church in a city where there are a lot of elderly people, or in a mostly immigrant church, you know what I mean? Some of that is just demographics.

Most of those who were new to St. Andrews were also new to Orthodoxy, and the changes they experienced as they were received into the Church felt substantial. As at our other two congregations, both women and men talked about reading the Bible and praying more. They also talked about continuing to study to learn more about Orthodox perspectives on the faith. Neither of these is particularly remarkable, given the lengthy catechumen process and the numerous services and guides for private prayer. What we did find remarkable was the number of areas in which new members said their perspective on the church as an institution had changed as the result of being at St. Andrews. Men talked about a growing appreciation for "worship being a form of work," describing both the physical demands of standing during services, as well as the way in which the physicality of worship reminds them to attend to the ideas behind the motions of the services. One older man who had recently joined captured this sensibility:

There's so much to it because whether you are in the service for a long time or a short time, you are totally involved. What you are doing keeps the question of what it means in the front of your mind. Why are there icons; why is the Eucharist done the way it is; why are there no chairs, just a few pews around the edge for people who need them. You stand for the whole service. If you're old like me, I have to sit down every once and awhile, but during the service, most people don't. All the way things are done make you want to think and learn more.

Women who were newer members also talked about the physicality of the services and a shift to thinking about Sunday worship as a place to "work out their salvation" rather than a vehicle for evangelism or learning about the Bible. As one young woman explained:

> I used to think about church as somewhere you take your friends so they could hear about Jesus. But that's shifted. What I see happening at St. Andrews feels a lot slower, but deeper and more genuine. It may not rack up the numbers, per se, but seems more real to me. It has made me realize that it doesn't require much of me to ask my neighbor to go to a church where I don't really have to talk to them and it's really fun. They are going to enjoy themselves cause the music sounds good and it's fun and different and they might just want to come back on their own, versus my having to actually engage in a relationship and be gracious and actually live it. I feel like it requires a lot more, and I think that is better just cause probably being a Christian shouldn't be very easy. Plus it has made me think about things that I just hadn't even thought about or hadn't been involved in my faith at all. I think it has changed how I live it out by just the mere practice of love and just the way that prayer is structured. Not so much that I once believed this, and now I believe something else, but it has taken what I had and helped it mature and grow to more than it had been before.

The ideas of deepening an existing faith and refining specific beliefs and practices were common themes among women who had transitioned to St. Andrews from strong evangelical Protestant backgrounds. For some, concerns they had had about icons, the Eucharist, or fasting "just faded away" or shifted and were "no longer a question for me anymore, something just clicked into place and finished it." Speaking about her struggle with a number of doctrines, one woman from a Reformed background explained:

> It wasn't hard to wrap my brain around the idea that the Orthodox baptize infants because that's similar to the church I grew up in— the child joins the church on the basis of the parents' faith until they decide to make a commitment of their own. The harder, newer idea was the sacrament of Chrismation, where a child is baptized, then anointed with oil, symbolizing the anointing of the Holy Spirit. In doing those at the same time, the child becomes a Christian and

is empowered to live [and] grow in the Christian life. Anyone can choose to walk away, but the Orthodox bring a child fully into the church from the start. It underscores a deeper sense of we're all in this together. That salvation is in the Church, together, not me and Jesus reading the Bible under a tree—you know, that worship in private or with a small group was just as good, if not better, than whatever happens Sunday morning. But I'm beginning to see Liturgy as something bigger; as a mirror of worship in heaven. Walking into the church, we join the saints and angels and archangels who are constantly worshiping around the throne of God. That image is a lot more potent than the vision of a hip praise band and a good sermon! I don't mean to make fun of those things. I value them a lot, and for most of my life they've been the whole point of Sunday worship. I'm just starting to see Sunday morning as more, and the sacraments as significant for our healing and salvation, not just memorializing or a token, but doing real work on our behalf. A lot of these ideas were really hard for me. What pitched me over the edge in the end was how the theology of the Eastern churches seems to hang together a lot more coherently than the theologies of the Western churches. There is still a lot we can't explain, but not so many contradictions or inconsistencies or weirdness.

Overall, women seemed to read and struggle more than men with doctrine before resolving on the idea that not all doctrine can be finely parsed or defined. Rather than trying to "figure it all out," women spoke of embracing "the paradox of truth claims and humility," or "having high ideals and taking people where they are," of "being and becoming, rather than doing," and "reading the Bible from a totally different, enriched perspective after reading it for years and years."

A second area in which women and men described themselves as changing was their sense of self. Women spoke about feeling more confident and peaceful, saying "For the first time in my life, I've felt little doubt," or "I feel more peaceful and patient." Men emphasized how they thought they were less judgmental, more tender hearted, more relaxed and secure, and not alone. As one man in his early thirties explained:

I think being part of St. Andrews has given me a satisfaction that I don't have to know everything on my own, and that there is something out there that I can probably rely on better than I can rely on myself. I don't feel like I'm out there all alone. The good thing about St. Andrews is that they really do have a sense of community. After liturgy we all sit down and have a lunch, and it is really good to sit down and talk to those folks. I've made some good friends there; they are honest people. Everybody knows everybody is a sinner. Everybody knows that life isn't always easy. So that's felt wonderfully comforting as well.

Reshaping Relationships with Family and Friends
First Presbyterian Church: Church as the New Neighborhood

Many of the same people who thought that being part of First Presbyterian had not changed them much on a personal level also felt church membership had not substantially changed their relationships with family or current friends. Some who had very recently joined said that it was too early to tell. But others who had been members for a year or longer said membership had not appreciably improved or challenged relationships with others. In some cases family lived too far away or religion was not a topic of discussion, and so it didn't seem relevant.

Solidarity and Shared Family Experience

Where becoming a member at First Presbyterian had changed relationships with family, those changes were in what people did together—primarily going to church. A couple of men described going with an elderly mother, or starting to pray with their children before bed, or attending because their wives asked them to. One woman said the only change she saw in her relationship with her husband was that she felt some sympathy for the learning curve he was experiencing as a first-time church-goer.

My husband has not been raised in a church. So he's a little nervous about it, but it's not a bad thing. He's just wondering what's going on. I grew up going to church so it feels natural, but it's really different for him at age thirty-eight all of a sudden attending church. Everything is new. He didn't know what Advent was. He had to ask my son because I wasn't sitting next to him, and they were going on and on about it being Advent and he had no idea what they were talking about. So he's a little nervous. He's not against it. It's just all brand new for him. He comes all the time and he listens and sings along with the hymns. We've attended a small-group session on Wednesday nights once, and he listens but he doesn't ask questions. He has a lot that he wants to know, but he's too nervous about asking. The kids are teenagers, and they come because we go and they have to.

Talking later with her husband about the experience, he explained:

My grandmother was Jehovah's Witness, and I went with her a few times when I was a child but that was it. My wife grew up going to church, so when we got married, she said she'd like to start going again and I said sure. If it means a lot to her, then why not? It's a little uncomfortable. The teachings are hard to follow without having had a whole lot of religious exposure. I don't even know who Mary Magdalen is. But we're making a conscious effort to get there. I think it teaches you how to be a better person and to be like Christ—which would be a good person. It teaches you to forgive and that with freedom comes responsibility. You can't just do whatever feels good; there are guidelines. So it's kind of a support group for people to stay on a moral tack. If everybody could behave in a little bit of a religious fashion, the world would be a much better place—any religion for the most part as long as it's a religion of peace and tolerance that helps you amend your faulty ways.

To the degree that membership at First Presbyterian changes family relationships, it does so primarily through adding an expression of family solidarity and shared experience.

Expanding Networks of Friends

Friendships were different. Across age and gender, we heard women and men at First Presbyterian describe the significance of the congregation in forming friendships and developing networks of support. For them, the church is the new neighborhood in which people expand connections beyond family ties. "We have a lot of good friends there," one older woman explained, "and that makes it easy to talk to someone if you have a problem." "It's the center of our life right now," said another elderly woman.

One older man who lived with his wife in a nearby retirement community listed a couple of neighbors that were friends, and then went on to say, "One of those is a retired minister who goes to the church, and the other two are also members ... well, and I guess there's Mary, but we claim her as a cousin. Really we are certainly better friends with any of the people in the church than we are with anyone in our neighborhood." Women and men with younger and teenage children also described the significance of the congregation in terms of integrating their social lives. As one woman in her late forties explained:

> What's different for us is that we've made some significant friends and that puts a new dynamic into the equation. Our neighbors are okay, I mean they don't seem turned off that we go to First Presbyterian or that we practice going to church. They have their own beliefs and that's not a problem. But overall we feel much more connected to people at the church than to people in the neighborhood.

For men, the function of the congregation as a source of meaningful friendship was particularly important. Men described it as a place where "people just really care about each other and have a family-like atmosphere that you want to continue outside of church." "I think we've gained some significant friends, and we haven't even been there that long," one middle-aged man explained. "Not that we didn't enjoy the people at the church we went to before or don't like our neighbors. But here we've had opportunity to socialize a lot more with people outside of services, so it has integrated our social life. None of our neighbors go to the church." Another man who was also new to the area similarly said:

> Many of my friends go to church there, so it's a real positive thing for me. This can be a pretty cliquey community in that there's so many people who have grown up here, they go to high school, they go away to college, they come back, they have family. And if you are new, it is hard to make friends. I have a lot of friends who go to the church—probably most.

For these men and women, the church now does what neighborhoods used to do: provide a community of connection, support, and shared experience.

For families whose calendars overflow with competing responsibilities from school, work, and other kin, the idea of consolidating friendships "under one roof" is efficient, even though it loosens connections with the people who physically live next door. Yet, there also, women and men at First Presbyterian said that relationships with non-Presbyterian friends were being changed—if not adding friends, at least helping them "understand a little bit where other people are coming from" and "becoming more intentional about showing God's love rather than just talking about it."

Valley Baptist Church: Shifting, Strengthening, and Expanding Relationships

The effects of joining Valley Baptist on relationships with family and friends were more substantial. Although a few newer members said that family and friends simply thought "it was nice that they'd joined a church" and left it at that, the majority described a more thorough reworking of relationships.

Women talked about friends who were surprised to hear they had "become a Christian" and were no longer interested in partying. "I don't really have a lot of new friends yet," one new member said. "I told my friends I wasn't going to party anymore cause I'm a Christian, and they were like 'Oh, wow, okay ... that's good, I guess.' I get a lot of support from the pastor and a couple of the staff, but am still working on making friends." For women whose affiliation countered the beliefs or values of family and friends, joining Valley Baptist was particularly challenging, as another woman explained:

My husband believes that church is a cult, so he's not incredibly supportive—although the longer I go, the more comfortable he's gotten about it, so now he's more okay with me going but he doesn't want me to talk about it. One of his concerns was that the church was going to tell me that I have to leave him since he's not a Christian. So I met with Pastor Mark and he said, "Never, no, you just love him, you love him more and more, you're not leaving him." And that was really assuring for me. I think it was reassuring for my husband, too, for me to tell him the church just doesn't work like that, you have nothing to worry about. As far as my in-laws and things like that, I don't think they even have a clue that I go to church. It's not really something that's comfortable to talk about with them because their views are very similar to my husband's, so I kind of don't really go there with any family. It would be a lot easier if my husband were going.

It was not uncommon for us to hear wives who were attending alone describe their husbands as resentful of their involvement because they were less often at home and were developing an independent set of friends. This willingness to invest themselves in a congregation without their husbands runs counter to the stereotype of evangelical women as subordinating their interests to husbands and children. To be sure, there remains a strong undercurrent of sentimentalized motherhood and personal sacrifice within the women's ministries at the church. Yet among women themselves, membership was experienced more as a source of increased agency and empowerment, particularly when family or friends were opposed or thought it odd.

Most women had husbands or other family who also attended. For them, being part of Valley Baptist seemed to strengthen relationships and a sense of connection. As one young woman explained:

I think we just share a closeness now. Some shared belief, some commonality. I didn't get along with my dad when I was younger, very headstrong, very independent, had my own views, so there was a big division for a while. Since I got into college, graduated, and started working, things have gotten a lot better. But now there's just a softness to our relationship. I don't know if that makes sense, but it wasn't there before. There's kind of a hardness to both my dad and I, and now we've just both sort of softened and we're sort of on to the same path.

Sharing deeply held beliefs is no small thing. For women whose family and friends already identified as Christians, the decision to join Valley Baptist was significant. "Taking the same path," "getting on the same page," and "sharing the Lord" were all dynamics of these changes that had the potential to enrich relationships with family and friends.

Men emphasized a somewhat different set of themes in describing how relationships had changed since joining Valley Baptist. Fathers were emotive and personal, speaking about the importance of their faith and the desire to pass that on to their children. As one father of three explained:

I grew up in the church and had dropped out for a while when I was in college. My dad had died and I was really hurt by that and I didn't know how to deal with that in the faith context and so I didn't. It wasn't until I was about thirty that I started to think about it again. I got married when I was thirty-four, and my wife and I started going to church right away. We thought it was very important for our kids to have access to that community of faith. So to have my kids grow up in a church that is really a Bible church is very important to me.

A few men also talked about losing friends after they "got saved" or friendships that shifted or diminished in importance after switching churches. One young professional captured this transition:

We're not as connected to people from our old church. So, yeah, it's changed some. Some of the old acquaintances have dropped off and we've gained a bunch new. We still have good friends, but the people around the periphery have been swapped I guess. Not the really close friends or family. I guess it is us wanting to be more challenged in our faith. They probably see us as being more religious than they did when we were in the church we used to go to. I think it's more in the front of our minds and some people aren't comfortable with that.

Overall, men who were newer members at Valley Baptist saw themselves as being challenged by other men in the congregation to be better fathers and friends. None of the married men attended alone or had wives who resented or resisted their participation. And while the salience of relationships with people who were not also members might shift, the tenor of those friendships remained positive, even if they got together less often.

Saint Andrews: Challenges and Choices

Women and men who were transferring to St. Andrews from other Orthodox churches said that their participating had not had much effect on relationships with family and friends, other than allowing them to expand and deepen friendships in their new location. The parish was friendlier than some they had attended, and there seemed to be more opportunity for doing things with other families outside of Sunday liturgy or Saturday Vigil. Women and men who were new to Orthodoxy were much more likely to talk about how some friends or family thought their participation was "weird or wrong" because Orthodox doctrine and practice seemed so different from their previous affiliation.

Men Considering Community and Connection

Some of the men who were considering being received into the Orthodox Church at St. Andrews talked about waiting until they were sure about their decision before talking with family or friends. "We want to make sure it's where we want to go before discussing it with them," one older man said. "It's something they don't even know about at this point, not because we're afraid, but because we want to make sure we know what we're doing and know more what we're talking about so we're prepared to explain it to them." Other men also described tensions in their relationships as they were in the process of joining and trying to explain their decision to friends at their current church.

> For a while we attended St. Andrews and also our home church. And one week that church had a missionary from Russia who commented that less than one-half of 1 percent of Russia is Christian. And I thought, what? There's 200–300 million Orthodox Christians in Russia, and many were martyred for their faith under Communism. They don't count? So that perspective that Orthodox aren't "real Christians" was hard. When our friends heard we were attending an Orthodox church, they were like "Don't they make you wear skirts and buns and that sort of thing?" Nobody knows anything about it. We eventually stopped going, not because of the people (we still have family there) but because it is just such a different way of understanding and spirituality. It's not a negative thing, it's not a holier than thou thing, that's just a different level of understanding. You can only understand so much if that is all you're fed.

Over time, friendships for many men shifted, as they did at our other two congregations.

Men's relationships with family were generally less affected, but were still a concern for men whose partners were vehemently opposed. As one middle-aged man described:

My wife associated Orthodoxy with Catholicism and was very adamant against me looking into Orthodoxy. In fact, she told me that it was probably one of the stupidest things I'd ever done in my whole life. So I was a little hesitant to go to services, because I asked my daughter, "What's it like at home here when I go to these services?" and she says, "Mom is stomping around." It did make me hesitant to go to a lot of things because it meant that my daughter was left with a lot of crap. My wife's never gotten used to it.

In some cases, partners don't adjust (the wife of the man just quoted eventually asked for a divorce). In other cases, partners reconcile themselves to being in different places most Sundays, and swap holiday visits to the other person's congregation if they attend elsewhere. Occasionally, we heard men talk about how a partner or prospective partner's opposition caused them to rethink their interest in joining altogether. As one man in his late twenties explained:

This has been a pretty significant challenge for my girlfriend. I'm looking for the truest form of worship and she's looking at it from a different perspective, maybe a more relational perspective. She's a Christian convert from Mormonism and there are things about the structure of the Orthodox Church that seem similar and wrong to her. She's not as hardcore into the truth aspect as I am. So we've had a lot of conflict trying to resolve these things since we're not focused on the same goal.

This particular young man, along with a handful of other men who were attending without the support of their wives, stopped attending because of the strain it was creating in their relationships.

Women Navigating Opposition and Reconciling with Family and Friends

Women who were transitioning to St. Andrews from some other background also described shifting relationships with family and friends. Those who were moving from evangelical or fundamentalist Christian traditions talked at length about the tensions their decision had created. Some were grilled by pastors who argued that their current tradition was "more Biblical" and they could "develop the same habits of spiritual formation on their own." At times these conversations were quite extensive, as clergy, parents, and friends tried to talk women out of making the move. One young woman described this experience:

> I met with my pastor a couple of weeks ago and he asked me to explain why I wanted to be received into the Orthodox Church at St. Andrews. He talked to me for nearly two hours and gave me some books to read. I thought that was it, but then he invited me to dinner and he and his wife grilled me some more. They think it is their fault and are pretty upset. After I told them I had decided to go ahead and join the church, he called me and asked me to come say goodbye. He basically read me the riot act for an hour and a half. He told me it is all empty ritual, and vain, and didn't I know Martin Luther had come to free us from all that? It was pretty rough. My mother was the same way—very opposed. I got her to come visit with me, and she hated it. She grew up Christian Science and said it reminded her of that "all cold and ritualistic." That's hard because she usually has good instincts about things. We had some pretty heated discussions, but eventually when I told them I had decided to join the church, they were a lot calmer and supportive than I imagined they might be, my mother especially. They made it clear they didn't agree, but said they weren't surprised and loved me and wanted me to know that. So that was a relief.

Some women described a "huge eruption" in family relationships and with friends who said "they thought I was joining a cult" or "equated icons with idolatry." Some said it took months and months of regular conversations in order to help family and friends resolve their concerns.

Not all family and friends were so strongly opposed to women's interest in St. Andrews. "We thought the elders would flip out when we told them," one former Baptist said.

> But it turns out, you're not as important as you think! A couple of elders looked pretty uncomfortable when we told them, what can they do? Baptists are all about individual conscience after all, so in the end they asked a few questions and wished us well and that was it! We're pretty sure they think we're heretics, but they can't help it—it is just too big a jump.

Conversations often involved some puzzlement on the part of family and friends who knew little about the Orthodox Church. As one young woman from an evangelical background described:

> One of my best friends continues to make pretty pointed remarks. She loves me and so says she's happy for me if I'm happy. But she has absolutely no interest in it herself and has let me know that she's perfectly satisfied where she is. It's not something I'm shoving in people's face. I'm just, you know, sincerely going this direction and it's interesting to see how people react. A lot of people are just very interested. For the most part, people don't know enough about Orthodoxy to have an opinion. I mean, you can see them going through their mind, searching, Orthodoxy ... Orthodoxy ... ? But there's hardly any data, so they don't know how to react, which is kind of nice. If I said I were going to join the Catholic Church, they'd flip out. But Orthodoxy? It's kind of floating out there vaguely associated with Russia, with Greece, but that's about it. And that's kind of an advantage. Most people don't have much baggage, because they don't have a clue. They kind of say, "I'm happy for you.... I think."

Women who grew up in Orthodox congregations and started attending St. Andrews because it was the closest Orthodox option, experienced none of these challenges. But women coming from other religious backgrounds, particularly those switching from evangelical or Pentecostal congregations, encountered a stiff headwind of puzzlement, questions, opposition, and incredulity. Nearly all of these relational challenges faded over time, but in the process of joining, women felt at risk of radically reshaping relationships because they chose to be received into the church.

Why People Don't Stay

After years of observing services, talking with clergy, and interviewing current, prospective, and newer members, we returned to these congregations to ask the question, "Why is it some people don't join or, once joining, don't stay connected?" Because membership is voluntary, congregations themselves are keenly interested in understanding and assessing what happens when community fails, as much as they are in recruiting, supporting, and retaining members. Churches are not different from other organizations in that regard. In addition, many churches operate on the same underlying assumption that "bigger is better" as do other US institutions. Growing numbers are interpreted as a sign of programmatic success and validation of the group's message and purpose. Member loss may be interpreted as undermining the plausibility of the congregation's teachings on transcendent and deeply personal moral issues, or a failure to meet the aesthetic or programmatic tastes and desires of their members.

Explaining Declining Church Membership in the United States

One of the reasons congregations lose members is related to changing demographics. Unless congregations actively recruit new members and retain the children of current members, membership inevitably shrinks through mortality. Churches may also find themselves shrinking because older members slowly stop attending due to decreasing mobility or the cognitive challenges associated with aging.

Rather than focusing on involuntary congregational attrition, most research has focused on assessing and understanding why people voluntarily choose to leave. People drop out and disaffiliate because they no longer find the faith itself plausible.[1] As sociologist Peter Berger[2] argued in *The Sacred Canopy*, pluralism and empiricism appear to undermine the plausibility of religious belief. Although the United States has not yet experienced the degree of secularization Berger predicted, a growing number of Americans are reporting a loss of faith and a gradual shifting toward a more generalized sense of spirituality removed from historic religious traditions or institutions.[3]

People also leave particular congregations for reasons related to the life course. One spouse may switch affiliation in order to attend the same congregation as his or her partner. After a divorce, one or both parties may drop out or start attending a different congregation where they can have a fresh start. In much the same way that some couples begin to consider religious affiliation after they have children, so too couples may leave behind those affiliations after children are launched and grown. In addition, as the practical needs of family members change, church participation may become less relevant and attendance may decline or cease altogether.[4]

A second set of explanations for why congregations lose members has to do with changes in the salience of religion in US culture. Survey research shows a growing percentage of Americans identify as "none" when asked about their religious identification. Although there is some debate around the degree to which that trend indicates a growth of agnosticism or the loss of connection to specific religious institutions or denominations or both, the observed outcome is lower rates of attendance and less robust identification with the broad metanarrative of Christianity or the articulation of that narrative to the experience of lived religion. From this perspective, changing patterns of attendance are related to changing beliefs, as members move elsewhere or drop out entirely because the story no longer resonates or fits.[5] At a more personal and relational level, a loss of faith is sometimes related to a personal hurt or unresolved harm.[6] Still, in much the same way as high rates of remarriage signify that divorce is primarily about the rejection of a particular partner rather than the institution of marriage itself, so too, personal hurts are often associated with switching congregations rather than abandoning belief altogether.

Congregational Culture, Clergy, and Membership Change

What about our three congregations? In this final section, we explore explanations for leaving and overall membership change. To address these questions we compared congregational membership lists across the intervening years of our fieldwork and talked with a sample of people who were no longer attending based on contact information they had provided. We also talked extensively with clergy in order to assess the shifts in personnel, programs, or physical space they thought might be reshaping the climate and culture of their congregation, and returned in 2016 for a final set of conversations with clergy and staff to see how their congregations had changed in intervening years. Within our small sample of congregations, we find three distinctive patterns of overall congregational change: one of decline, one of relative stability, and one of growth (see Table 7.1).

Table 7.1 Congregational Membership (2002–2016)

	First Presbyterian	Valley Baptist	St. Andrews
No. of members in 2002	420	396	60
No. of members in 2009	378	330	79
No. of members in 2016	248	356	132
Membership change	n (%)	n (%)	n (%)
2002–2009	−42 (−10%)	−66 (−16%)	19 (32%)
2009–2016	−130 (−34%)	26 (8%)	53 (67%)
New members	n (%)	n (%)	n (%)
2002–2009	105 (28%)	141 (42%)	43 (54%)
2009–2016	100 (40%)	220 (61%)	76 (58%)
No longer attending (%)[1]	n (%)	n (%)	n (%)
2002–2009	147 (35%)	207 (52%)	24 (40%)
2009–2016	230 (61%)	194 (58%)	23 (29%)
Retention: n (%)[2]	n (%)	n (%)	n (%)
2002–2009	273 (65%)	189 (48%)	36 (60%)
2009–2016	148 (39%)	136 (41%)	56 (71%)

Notes: Based on reviews of current church directories, 2002–2003, 2007–2009, and 2014–2016.

[1] Percentage of the 2002 congregation no longer attending in 2009; percentage of 2009 congregation no longer attending in 2016.

[2] Percentage of the 2002 congregation still attending in 2009; percentage of the 2009 congregation still attending in 2016.

First Presbyterian Church

In 2009, First Presbyterian was a slightly smaller congregation than it had been in 2002. Membership overall had declined about 10 percent, and the congregation had become somewhat grayer, in line with denominational trends.[7] These seem like modest changes. However, inside the congregation was much different. By 2009, more than a third of the 2002 membership was no longer attending, and over a quarter of the members were new. The congregation had entered a period of changing leadership as well, as Pastors Richard and Priscilla left the church for other positions. The move was unexpected, but the policies of the denomination—to assign a two-year interim pastor—provided enough structure and support for a pastoral search committee to form, survey the congregation, and begin to envision what the church's future might look like. Despite these efforts, and although the rate of adding new members across the years remained steady but slow, overall membership continued to decline. Between 2009 and 2016, total membership had dropped by a third, and only 30 percent of the original 2002 congregation remained—an established civic-minded group intent on maintaining the community they had come to feel was home.

Valley Baptist Church

Although all three congregations lost members because some died or moved away, the substantial proportion of voluntary membership loss at Valley Baptist was related to the departure of the congregation's charismatic pastor. Four years into our fieldwork, Pastor Mark was recruited to lead a much larger church in another state. The congregation was stunned when he announced his departure midsermon one Sunday morning. As he concluded with encouragement that the church is bigger than any one leader, the elders brought an easel with white poster paper to the front of the sanctuary and challenged members to sign in affirmation that their commitment was to the congregation and its ministries and not to a particular preacher. People came forward slowly, and then in greater numbers, until page after page of signatures appeared.

Pastor Mark's departure left a terrific gap at Valley Baptist. In the four years of since his arrival, he had transformed the place into a revitalized center of neighborhood outreach and ministry. The man the congregation hired as his replacement was less innovative and charismatic. Members described him as more typical of a Baptist pastor—conservative, amiable, family oriented, and generally more concerned than Pastor Mark had seemed about changes in US culture and how Christians should be different from "the world" by living out more conservative values around gender, family, or politics. The music program also changed, as the praise band leader followed Pastor Mark to his new congregation (significant promotions for them both). Although the new music director also played guitar and was accompanied by a group of three (usually women) background singers, the dynamics of the music became more muted with fewer people standing or raising their hands to sing, and clapping began to sound more tentative than celebratory. Efforts to incorporate Spanish speakers into the congregation stalled, and worship services seemed to revert to a less innovative, more conservative traditional evangelical style of preaching, music, and outreach. By 2009, the total membership had declined 16 percent—a relatively modest drop since 2002. Yet over half of the members who had been attending in 2002 were no longer there. A core of the 2002 membership remained through the transition, but more than 40 percent of the congregation was new, and the leadership was kept busy forming and reforming home fellowship groups, identifying new leaders, and evaluating the congregation's slate of programs and ministries as the church navigated its new identity.

Three years into the tenure of Pastor Mark's replacement, Valley Baptist was in the process of recruiting again, as the elders reevaluated the effectiveness of their initial choice and began to search for a leader whose vision was more aligned to the outreach-focused ministries begun under Pastor Mark. After a three-month search, they recommended that the congregation hire the principal of the affiliated Christian school—a younger man who served with several others as fill-in preachers when the pastor was away, and had an established history of support within the congregation. Over the next several years, the membership at Valley Baptist stabilized and began again to grow. Between 2009 and 2016, the church added 220 new members. The former principal, now head pastor, attributed some of the influx of new members to changing leadership in other area churches. Five congregations had had clergy retire or move elsewhere, and during those transitions many new families migrated over to Valley Baptist. Yet the church had not simply attracted new members. It had also lost nearly two hundred of those who had been attending in 2009. Overall growth was about 8 percent, but over that seven-year period, four hundred plus people had come and gone from this evangelical congregation. Less than a quarter (22 percent) of the original 2002 congregation was still attending in 2016. Yet, despite the turnover, the leadership remained upbeat and optimistic as it created new fellowship groups and managed programs for youth and a growing singles population in a revitalized and energetic congregation.

St. Andrews

The congregation at St. Andrews also changed over time. Between 2002 and 2009 the congregation grew by about a third, adding forty-three adult new members and losing twenty-four. By 2009, the congregation was just shy of eighty adult members—60 percent of whom had been attending since 2002 (about the same proportion as had attended across those same years at First Presbyterian Church). Choir and youth programs expanded, as did educational opportunities for adults.

In 2016, Father Michael was still serving as priest, and the congregation had added two subdeacons and two deacons to assist with services. Seventy-one percent of the 2009 congregation was still attending, and the overall membership had grown again by two-thirds, to 132 adult members and about 50 children. The church continues its quarterly inquirers' classes to introduce the church to the broader community, has expanded its music and children's programs, and recently added an auxiliary for women and men who wish to be more involved as volunteers. Although not all prospective members joined and not all new members were still attending at the time we finished our research, only twenty-three members (about 29 percent) who had been attending in 2009 were no longer listed as members in 2016. Forty-five percent of the members who had been at the church in 2002 were still attending in 2016—a proportionately larger core than remained at Valley Baptist or First Presbyterian. Whereas St. Andrews remains the smallest of our three churches, it is now a medium-sized congregation[8] that has outgrown its current location, and is beginning the process of building permanent facilities on land it purchased in a residential area on the edge of town.

Personal Explanations or Membership Loss

Just as these congregations experienced different trajectories of membership change, so too, they exhibited distinctive patterns around why those changes were taking place. Findings from our interviews with a subset of former attenders and with clergy, staff, and key informants at each site confirm the findings of previous research—that most membership loss is because people have moved, died, or are no longer physically able to attend. At the same time, we found people also leaving for personal reasons: because programs or pastors change; because of the loss of a significant connecting relationship or personal hurt; and some, because of a change in beliefs. Summary data from interviews with a sample of those no longer attending are presented in Table 7.2.

Table 7.2 **Explanations for No Longer Attending, 2002–2009**
(Number Interviewed and Percent)

	First Presbyterian ($n = 20$)	Valley Baptist ($n = 20$)	St. Andrews ($n = 24$)
Moved/distance	9	7	19
	50%	35%	79%
Died	5	2	1
	26%	10%	4%
Health	1	1	1
	5%	5%	4%
Pastor/program change	2	5	1
	11%	25%	4%
Loss of connecting relationship	0	4	2
		20%	8%
Doctrinal differences	3	1	0
	15%	5%	0%

Notes: Numbers reflect a sample of individuals listed in each church directory in 2002 who were no longer listed in 2009. Information on members who had died was provided by church staff.

First Presbyterian Church: Geography, Demographics, and Doctrine

Nearly half of those in our sample of mainline "leavers" were no longer attending because they had moved out of the area. A quarter of the sample had died, and one person no longer attended because of health reasons. Geographic mobility also resulted in new members as expanding professional jobs and relatively low housing prices brought a steady stream of new families into the area and into the congregation.

When we contacted former members who had left First Presbyterian for other reasons, a subset described themselves as leaving because they felt the church no longer met some personal, aesthetic, or spiritual need. A few described leaving because of doctrinal differences with the pastors and had moved to a different congregation before or during the transition to a new leadership team. In these cases, former members said they felt the church was not traditional enough or not on the right track theologically. They explained how they thought the Presbyterian Church seemed to have as lost its connection to historic Reformation theology and was trying to be "too broad an umbrella" under which diverse, and sometimes incompatible, theological perspectives were equally valued and welcomed. These individuals had switched membership and started to attend an evangelical congregation, become Roman Catholic or Orthodox, or moved to another Presbyterian/Reformed church in the area.

The loss of the organist also had a significant impact on some members. Organ music had been a fixture in the congregation for many years, and the director had maintained a high standard of choral music and regular productions of classical ensembles or piano pieces. Even among members who were still attending at the end of our study, the loss of this classic "high-culture" element as a regular feature of worship services felt like diminution of tasteful, traditional, Presbyterian worship. Finally, for those who had come to the congregation from conservative Protestant or Roman Catholic backgrounds, the loss of having a woman in the preaching rotation seemed to diminish the depth of worship experience, and so eventually left the church as it transitioned to a new male head pastor.

Valley Baptist Church: Geography and Relational and Leadership Loss

We heard some of the same explanations for people leaving in our conversations with former members at Valley Baptist. Some members stopped attending because they were no longer able because of disability, geographic location, or were reported by relatives or staff as having died.

Older members moved into retirement communities out of town, to areas of the country with warmer winters, or to be closer to adult children. Younger members departed for school or job relocations. None of these were remarkable.

What did set the experience of this congregation apart was the effect of the departure of Pastor Mark, whose preaching and vision had transformed the church. Even our small sample captured this effect—with over a quarter of respondents describing their departure as directly related to the loss of the head pastor. Nearly as significant were other types of relational losses. Two former members described leaving because of divorce or relational breakup (not wanting to attend where a former spouse or girlfriend was attending, or feeling embarrassed because their marriage failed in a very family-oriented church). Conversely, another had married and, because his spouse was not interested in participating, had started to attend so sporadically he was no longer listed as a member. Another said she and her husband had become involved with the church because of the Christian School, and once their children had graduated, they moved on to other things.

St. Andrews: Geography, Intergenerational Connections, and Self-Selection in Joining

Nearly all of the members who were no longer attending St. Andrews at the end of our study had stopped attending because of a geographic move or because the church itself had moved its location, putting it just out of range for some to regularly attend services. We know from other research on Orthodoxy in America[9] that most membership loss is related to second-generation immigrant children thinking of Orthodoxy as an aspect of the "Old Country" they are eager to put aside (or at least minimize) in their effort to assimilate to Anglo-American culture. Thus far at St. Andrews, that does not appear to be the case. The children and grandchildren of the small number of first generation immigrant families still generally attend, some even after starting college or getting jobs nearby. In addition, the membership overall is heavily weighted toward highly committed individuals who have conscientiously self-selected into Orthodoxy at St. Andrews. Given that the process of being received into the Church is lengthy, prospective members have ample opportunity to get to know both the local congregation and its beliefs. Only those who are comfortable with both eventually join and most maintain their level of involvement.

This is not to suggest that people didn't have their feelings hurt or decide to follow a non-Orthodox spouse elsewhere. Those were also, but much less frequently, mentioned as reasons why people moved to other congregations. One couple left after having a disagreement over how the church should be organized. One woman stopped attending after her spouse died, and two couples stopped attending during a time of acute marital difficulty. Overall, however, the membership at St. Andrews was more stable, with higher rates of retention through 2016 than either Valley Baptist or First Presbyterian. Still relatively small, the clergy continue to look for ways to help a diverse range of new members become involved in leadership and service, whether growing a community garden, working with youth, or coordinating informal retreats at regional monasteries.

Assessing Culture, Connections, and Institutional Strength

At the level of general explanations for membership attrition, our findings are consistent with those of previous research. Geographic mobility alone explains the largest number of congregational departures—something that is not surprising, given that we live in such a highly mobile society. Congregations also lose members for the simple reason that older members die or can no longer physically attend. Personal interests are also important: when programs or styles of worship or leadership change, members depart because they no longer feel comfortable or that their needs are being met. Changes in relationships are accompanied by changes in priorities: couples divorce; children become young adults and parents no longer feel the need to attend; or the threshold for recovering from a personal hurt may seem just too high. In one congregation (which we do not identify in order to additionally protect the anonymity of the victim), unwanted sexual advances toward a married member led to the eventual departure of the offender. In another, mental illness created conditions in which the person suffering was so confrontational that person was no longer able to attend. Under more ordinary circumstances, dating couples break up, or a person marries and the spouse is interested in attending elsewhere or nowhere, and others simply drift away. In each case, a relationship is broken, failed, or simply changed, and the connection to a particular congregation is no longer as salient as it once appeared.

What our analysis adds to this discussion is the ability to assess reasons for disaffiliation across types of congregation. Considering just those people who stopped attending because of personal hurts or doctrinal disagreement, Valley Baptist and St. Andrews experienced the least amount of membership loss—pointing to the importance of shared belief or religious subcultural strength in shaping congregational commitments. Few people stopped attending Valley Baptist or St. Andrews because their faith had changed—they left because of relational changes or changes in their address.

Our findings also suggest that strong religious subculture is not enough to maintain lasting connections to specific congregations. Religious subculture may matter, but so does institutional strength. Congregations with strong religious subcultures that are centered on individual leaders appear less resilient to change than are congregations that are both subculturally and institutionally strong. What First Presbyterian was able to offer in terms of stability during transitions in pastoral leadership, the independent Valley Baptist was unable to provide. At the same time, the strong religious subculture around personal transformation at Valley Baptist was not part of the congregational subculture at First Presbyterian, which also experienced some member attrition among those who tired of "the Bible as metaphor," as well as members at the other end of the continuum who were unpersuaded by the church's presentation of the Christian narrative and became Buddhists rather than Baptists. At St. Andrews, strong ethnic connections and self-selection of highly committed new members, along with the structure and stability of liturgical services themselves, create an environment in which membership appears to be more resilient to the kinds of personal and personality changes that lead people to leave.

Conclusion: Changing Persons, Relationships, and Congregations

Traditions new and old, leadership teams, schedule of services, and wide arrays of programs and opportunities for service are all intended to facilitate personal growth and deepen a sense that life, relationship, and identity are nurtured within local congregations. People who join these congregations change. Sometimes they change in modest ways through extending networks of friends. Sometimes change is more dramatic, as members work through habits of substance abuse or abusive relationships, become better parents, or more reliable and relatable partners or employees. And sometimes change is profoundly personal, as women and men reassess core values and deeply held beliefs.

Although our sample is small, we do find patterns and differences across congregations—both in terms of self-assessed change, reshaped relationships with family and friends, and changes that led some to no longer attend. At First Presbyterian and Valley Baptist, changes were both gendered and reflective of the predominant social class of the congregation. At both, women described becoming more consistent in their religious practice, whether getting to church or praying more often. At Valley Baptist, women also described attending church and praying more, and they went on to describe how the congregation helped them get on their feet financially and to feel more confident and independent. Men at the First Presbyterian church described growing to value volunteering and becoming more aware of God's grace, whereas men at Valley Baptist focused on being supported in their efforts to curb substance abuse and the significance of male friends in helping them obtain better jobs or become better fathers. Women and men at St. Andrews were similar in their thoughts about the importance of learning and cultivating personal change through prayer. Women and men who had come to St. Andrews from non-Orthodox backgrounds also described struggles, not always resolved, with family and friends who opposed or misunderstood their joining. In this transition, women described feeling more confident and peaceful, and men more secure, tender-hearted, and less alone.

More than twenty years ago, sociologists Reginald Bibby and Merlin Brinkerhoff wrote about "the circulation of the saints"[10] as a way to describe the turnover they observed in church membership. Our analysis confirms that the saints continue to circulate—albeit at different rates in different traditions and for somewhat different reasons. From the perspective of the clergy and other core leaders, it is overall numbers and the demographic characteristics of the membership that matter. Leaders must shape programs, budgets, and messages to the size and composition of specific congregations. In some ways, the specific identities of those thirty or three hundred are not especially relevant to the question of how many small groups should be formed or if there are adequate numbers of middle schoolers to warrant a separate youth group for preteens. Yet for those thirty or three hundred, the continuity of experience worshiping with familiar faces may be as salient, if not more so, than whether or not there are programs for their specific age group or interest area. The congregation at First Presbyterian, for example, experienced significant membership decline over the years, yet retained a core membership of 129—a church within the church. Although friends moved or died and clergy changed, sufficient numbers of "familiar others" allowed a sense of community in this neighborhood church to continue across the years. In contrast, Valley Baptist experienced a dramatic influx of new members, but it retained a smaller core of long-term members across the same time frame. Those who remain have seen half their congregation turn over— twice in fifteen years. As a result, long-term members at Valley Baptist are a small island in a sea of new faces, and they are likely to have a lot of experience training new leaders. The sanctuary is booming again with energy and enthusiasm, but it is nearly new in terms of who occupies the space. St. Andrews remains a relatively small congregation, but one that has experienced relatively less turnover and relatively more growth. Although the congregation is hardly recognizable compared to what it was fifteen years ago, a larger proportion of the 2002 membership continues to attend. As one long-term member described: "You hardly see anyone you know, but everyone you know is still there."

Regardless of whether congregations are growing or shrinking, the experience of worship is shaped by the continuity of the community. Religious subculture and institutional strength also matter. Their robustness is part of what draws people to particular congregations and supports personal change, and their failure or weakness is part of why some eventually leave.

8

Gender and Congregational Culture

WHY DO PEOPLE go to church? What is it that draws women and men to particular congregations? How does the embodiment of a tradition of faith in buildings and enacted in bodies draw them toward membership? What is the process through which they join? And in what ways does joining cause them to grow, give, and change as individuals and in relationships with others? Why is it, in other words, that religion won't just go away?

The Continuing Significance of Denomination

Despite living at a time when some make the case that denomination and religious doctrine no longer matter, congregational culture apparently still does. In fact, our analysis demonstrates that denomination, or broad historic tradition, continues to be embodied in the buildings and programs as well as the specific teachings and ethos of congregations. To be sure, specific congregational culture matters as well, as it is not Presbyterianism, or Baptist-ness, or the One Holy Catholic and Apostolic Orthodox Church with which women and men affiliate, but a specific Presbyterian congregation, an independent Baptist church, or a local Orthodox parish.

As I repeatedly tell my undergraduate students in Sociology of Religion, the simple friendliness and welcome of a congregation are important, as are the quality of the programs they offer. Yet remarking on churches as places that are friendly does nothing to help us understand why people go. After all, the people at the tennis club are friendly, too. What makes religious institutions unique is that they offer avenues for exploring and experiencing transcendence. Congregations offer distinctive moral, religious, and spiritual goods—whether space for quiet contemplation; an enjoyable hour of upbeat music and practical teaching; or participating in an ancient ritual that engages the senses as well as the heart and head.

Human beings need community; and churches, as a type of religious community, provide both ordinary goods (resources, people, and programs) and distinctive religious goods (moral frameworks and narratives around ultimate things) that are a significant part of the human experience. When we look at actual congregations, we find these goods integrated into the programs, buildings, and processes through which they add and orient new members. People join when they move into a community, when they need support after a loss, when their children are growing and they wonder how to teach them what it means to be a good person, when pausing to consider the great existential and ontological questions of life: What gives life meaning? What is the nature of personhood, gender, family, or work, in an always uncertain world?

The Embodiment of Faith in Buildings and Practice

The practices of these three congregations speak to personhood and the embeddedness of religious identities in enduring and persistent religious traditions. Whether the buildings, the space, the organization and movements of worship, or the dress, demeanor, and gestures of worshiping congregations, all embody and speak into the future distinctive sets of beliefs about what it means to be a person, connecting to others and to God.

Patterns of worship and uses of religious space at First Presbyterian Church draw on and extend into the future enduring beliefs about faith as an intellectually respectable and socially engaged enterprise. Rational, liberal, and pragmatic, First Presbyterian embraces an approach to faith in which the locus of authority is neither the church, nor the pastor, nor the text, but the educated and thoughtful individual. Although the pastors may argue that doctrine doesn't matter anymore, there are some doctrines that do, including good stewardship, self-determination, the intrinsic value of diversity, and the indeterminacy of absolute truths. Whereas Valley Baptist minimizes explicitly religious language, symbols, and forms in order to move people to a clear set of religiously defined relationship and goals, First Presbyterian Church uses explicitly religious language to defuse doctrinal absolutes. People who come to visit, and those who decide to stay and join, encounter a mode of high culture that can be appreciated without feeling overly narrow or demanding.

First Presbyterian creates space that invites contemplation more than expressive celebration. Although the congregation is relatively socially and economically privileged, privilege does not prevent people from experiencing the strains and pains of life. Work is more stable, but often (and increasingly) alienating, even for professionals. Family crises, personal loss, or scarcity and disruptions in time may be mitigated by the privileges of social class, but they are experienced subjectively as chaotic and grievous nonetheless. First Presbyterian, with its history of being a cornerstone and steward in the community, calls new and long-term members to pause, to be quieted, comforted, and encouraged to keep on living, and to do better by living a good and moral life. The ethos of the congregation celebrates the process of individual faith journeys without prescribing either the path or the destination in a loosely connected voluntary community. The process of looking for and doing good is the source of meaning, and its goal is connecting participants to a rich and enduring sense of history, personhood, and place.

For the congregation at Valley Baptist Church, practice, space, and movement also embody enduring tradition, as well as a clear set of propositions about what constitutes the nonnegotiable core of evangelical Christianity. Historically orthodox on issues of the Trinity and the incarnation, patterns of worship and ministry at Valley Baptist are intentionally minimally religious and streamlined. No smells, bells, hierarchy, or other paraphernalia to distract from the clear articulation of its core message: God loves you and, through Jesus, wants to give you a better life. The simplicity of the auditorium, the cleanness of the lines, the clear lighting and easy access create a space in which people who are nonchurchgoers can feel welcome and at ease. Rational and relational, the intentional un-Baptistness of Valley Baptist reflects the antiauthoritarian, experiential, and sentimental history of its evangelical Pietist heritage. The simple and entertaining format of the services mirrors the unimposing open structure of the worship center, where visitors and members hear good news. The music, the stories, and the humor provide scaffolding for feeling deeply the loving presence, provision, and acceptance of God within this community. Feelings are not trivial. They resonate and reflect the desire and experience of hope—hope for a better life and better relationships, through the experience of being born again and living a new life in Christ.

Entrepreneurial, hip, relaxed, and relevant, Valley Baptist Church conscientiously structures programs and Bible-based teaching to support the underlying goal of transforming individual lives for Christ. Recognizing that a substantial number of visitors and members of the congregation are working class, and that the leadership intentionally did not relocate the church even as jobs moved elsewhere and housing in the neighborhood deteriorated, the message of transformation and new life is profound. Particularly for those who are the leadership's primary audience, finding a place where you can walk in unashamed and be offered hope is an undeniable good. You don't have to have a job, a partner, or an education to be welcome. Come as you are. There is no high bar. Listen. Be encouraged. Embrace hope, and find in this positive environment a community, a story, and practical guidance for living a better life.

The embodiment of doctrine and its enactment in religious practice are also evident in patterns of worship at St. Andrews. Of these three strands of Christianity, Orthodoxy has the most clearly defined and carefully maintained set of doctrinal truths and practices. The odd way in which members describe it as ritualized yet personal; flexible and strict; beautiful and yet austere; rich and ascetic; demanding and compassionate; rational and emotive, simultaneously creates a religious space in which participants of any age, with any level of doctrinal sophistication, with any history of language or experience, can move toward and feel enriched by the presence of God in the Church.

The ambivalence, mystery, and flexibility of St. Andrews provide reprieve for Protestants whose experience has been rooted in the rationalism and individualism of the Reformed tradition. At the same time, the services at St. Andrew's highlight the reality of spiritual struggle and the anticipation of God breaking into the ordinary in much the same way as do charismatic Pietist and Pentecostal traditions. For conservative Protestants weary from the weight of solo scriptura, as well as liberal Protestants in search of aesthetic beauty and enduring history, Orthodoxy provides a lived alternative. On a religious map where truth is fragmented and temporary, the nonnegotiables of the creed are a refuge that is both ancient and postmodern. For authority it appeals not simply to a static text but to the ongoing embodiment of doctrine in practice and tradition. The building, the incense, the bells, the chanting, icons, candles, and communion connect worshipers to something significantly larger and more enduring than themselves. Shifting the locus of religious authority away from the individual, Orthodoxy invites participation in a common confession and lived tradition that offers to reenchant the world.

Cognitive Distance and Narratives of Joining

One significant pattern we found in narratives across congregations was that the greater the difference between the congregation people were visiting and their current or previous religious affiliation, the more extensive and detailed the narratives were of how they had come to be there visiting and considering joining. The bigger the distance, the bigger the story. Similarly, those who were considering a bigger move across traditions specified a greater number of approaches, ideas, programs, and other goods that attracted them to the new congregation. Women and men considering First Presbyterian were fairly brief in describing what they valued about that particular mainline congregation, just as currently Baptist and Orthodox women and men specified a short list of reasons for considering those churches. People transitioning from further afield on the religious map or those with more extensive narratives of religious seeking had a lot more to say about both their process and about the range of good things they saw within these churches.

One implication of this simple observation is that surveys of religious identity that ask about affiliation or count congregational membership may inadvertently truncate the degree to which religious identity itself is a thing in motion. Neither the concept of conversion nor the more recent language around religious switching captures the nuances of these stories of personal history and process. Even those who have been part of a particular tradition from birth are changing—connecting to greater or lesser degrees with their traditions and experiencing in an ongoing way what it means to be part of a particular iteration of Christianity in the United States.

Congregations as Arenas for Broadening Gender Experience

Gender shapes joining, though not in the directions or degree we might expect. At First Presbyterian, women and men were in agreement as to many of the relative goods they experienced, whether the husband-and-wife team, the reasoned sermons, the quality of the music and children's programs, the combination of traditional and contemporary elements, and ideas around the stewardship of resources, as well as democratic organization and doctrinal breadth. Many of these goods resonate with core Presbyterian sensibilities more generally, especially the values around community service, acceptability of diverse theological perspectives, emphasis on education, and classical and dignified architecture and music.

There was also substantial consensus about what attracted women and men to St. Andrews. There the gendered experience of members seems to differ least where it appears at the institutional level to matter most. Both women and men described being drawn by the beauty, the physicality and rhythm of the services, the embrace of mystery, ancient practice, resolution of personal theological questions and struggles, and sense of community. These facets of Orthodox experience were magnified for the growing number of new members not reared in Orthodox households—a trend that is reshaping Orthodoxy at both a local and national level. At St. Andrews, that sense of being in an ancient tradition that is working on ways to integrate diverse jurisdictions into a distinctive and unified Orthodox Church within the US context is both a challenge and part of the attraction for those considering membership.

We found less agreement in what women and men said attracted them to the congregation at Valley Baptist. To be sure, visitors were nearly unanimous in saying how much they appreciated the practical sermons and energetic worship music. However, these aspects of congregational culture are not unusual; they are part of Baptist culture more generally, as was the church's eventual decision to drop "Baptist" from its name in order to avoid the negative bias leaders believed was widespread among non-churchgoers and broaden its appeal to non-Baptist evangelicals. Nor did women and men at this conservative evangelical congregation describe the church's many gender-specific groups as drawing them to the church. Women did not talk much about the importance of the women's or children's ministries, or the small groups for moms; nor did men say much about the importance of being in a church whose tradition provided them with opportunities to lead.

Instead, what we found at Valley Baptist, as at our other two congregations, was that women were much more emphatic than men about the importance of doctrine in shaping the decision whether or not to join the church. In contrast, men at all three congregations talked about their appreciation for the warmth and acceptance of the people, the idea of being in community, and the opportunity for personal growth and transformation the church provided. They even talked, in slightly different ways, about how participating in these congregations offered them opportunity to feel safe, experience deeper connection to others, and to submit themselves to God. At Valley Baptist and at St. Andrews, men described the value they saw in how children were visible and integrated into the church, and they reinforced their underlying commitment to the church as an adopted family.[1] In each of these domains, men bring to these congregations aspects of their personhood that otherwise have limited opportunity to play. In a culture that remains deeply, if somewhat more subtly gender stratified and divided, religious institutions may be one of the few places in which men are free to feel, connect, nurture, and even yield.

For both women and men, then, connecting to congregations offers opportunity to experience additional dimensions of personhood that are broader than the current cultural gender script. Congregations provide robust narratives of transcendent truth that are experienced as empowering to women, as well as narratives of community, connection, and service for men. The fact that these themes appear in congregations located at very different points across the religious field underscores the salience of formal religious affiliation in the formation of adult personhood. This is not to suggest that congregations are the only or most significant groups in which adults have the opportunity to transcend themselves and grow. It is to say that the opportunity for transcendence uniquely experienced within congregations opens space for experiencing a broader and deeper self that for men, as well as women, is less available within the cultural constraints of gender, family, and work, yet remain a significant part of adult identity and experience.

Exploring the range of religious values and activities that women and men find meaningful across a range of traditions helps complicate the generalization that women are more religious than men. To be sure, women's membership in formal religious associations has been greater than men's, at least in the West, in Christianity, and in the twentieth and now twenty-first centuries. But as this analysis illustrates, the directions, dimensions, and degree of gender differences in values, goals, and participation are not always what we would expect. Rather than there being a cultural lag of secularization and modernity, where the gender gap in religiosity and participation is explained as a function of women's lagging employment, interest in expanding networks, and exposure to alternative/nonreligious frameworks of meaning, we find women drawn to contemplation, theology, and experience; and men drawn to the connections, acceptance, and opportunities for giving to others that congregations provide.

Implications for Future Research

Overall, our findings suggest that congregations provide a context in which women and men engage broader facets of their gender identity. Although we need to be careful not to overgeneralize from these three congregations to the denominations and traditions they represent, our findings on gender and joining, growing, and giving point to potentially fruitful areas of future research.

Most discussions of spiritual growth focus on the individual experience and cognitive processes involved; our analysis highlights the social context in which those concepts are formed, assessed, appropriated, and applied. Moreover, our findings highlight the variability of this core religious construct across Christian traditions, as well as significant variability in the level of consensus within small groups regarding what spiritual growth is and toward what ends it is intended. Given the recent interest in the study of spiritual capital, better assessments of the means and ends of spiritual growth as formed within congregations, embodied in its buildings, and enacted by its members should provide much needed analytical and theoretical perspectives on this salient and central facet of religious life.

Our analysis also has practical implications for practitioners of religion. Churches, as well as social scientists, can benefit from a better understanding of the ways in which congregations as communities grow, thrive, or fail in their efforts to provide the kind of moral vision, meaningful relationships, and programs they intend. Congregations might anticipate how to bridge relational losses following divorce, changing of church leadership, the death of a partner, or the changes that come with marriage. Recognizing that marriage can attenuate congregational connections as much as it strengthens them, could lead to better efforts to incorporate spouses and partners. Finally, given our analysis, congregations might do well to consider the extent to which their structure, worship, programs, and ministries mirror cultural ideals around gender, or provide and encourage a broader gender space for both women and men.

Congregational Culture, Gender, and Identity

Overall, then, we find that congregational culture matters. There are more to congregations than programs, aesthetics, and service delivery. There are relationships, meaning, and connection that are profoundly important to adult identity and sense of self. The embodiment and enacting of narratives and traditions that connect persons to the transcendent are central, nonnegotiable human goods that religious institutions are in a unique position to offer. In addition to aesthetic experience and practical programs, congregations are a locus of narratives of meaning, purpose, and morality. It is not surprising that relationships figure large in congregational culture, purpose, and growth. Personhood develops in community, and so does faith. But content and specificity of faith itself are also important. Doctrine (even if it is the belief that knowledge, belief, and practice are existential and individualized) as embodied in buildings and enacted in worship additionally gives meaning to and interprets the relationships that draw people into particular churches and sustains connections among them once there.

Across traditions and denominations, congregations offer the opportunity to address central questions about identity, belonging, meaning, and purpose. Although Americans may not be overtly tribal, exploring these questions in the company of like-minded others remains a significant part of the human experience. Perhaps in a postmodern America where identity is increasingly understood as malleable and transient, being rooted somewhere meaningful matters even more. It is no surprise then that congregations are described as families because they do what families do, and matter how family matters, providing an imperfect haven and connection for vulnerable persons, celebration of shared life, and food for the journey.

APPENDIX

Fieldwork in Three Congregations

In addition to reading some of the theology and history of these three traditions,[1] we conducted extensive fieldwork at each site, observing a range of services, programs, and new member/inquirer classes. Each site was visited an average of twice a month during regular worship services for two and a half years. Researchers participated in three or four sets of new member/inquirer classes and seminars, as well as youth group meetings, small groups, work projects, and special holiday programs at each site. We attended regular worship services, special feast days, holiday programs, baptisms, weddings (when the congregation as a whole was invited), adult Sunday School classes, small groups, potlucks, picnics, concerts, basketball and softball games, children's programs, women's conferences, and occasional leadership training events.

Fieldnotes from participant observations and sermon outlines were typed as soon as possible after each visit or event. Full transcripts of weekly sermons were made available by the mainline congregation, printed sermon outlines and sermon tapes were made available by the evangelical congregation, and scripture passages and explanations of saints' days and festivals were collected from weekly bulletins from the Orthodox congregation. Much of this information was also made available on each congregation's website. Between 2009 and 2012, each congregation had begun to make services remotely available through live-streaming or archived video or podcast.

PERSONAL INTERVIEWS WITH MEMBERS AND JOINERS

In addition to extensive congregational observations, the research team conducted in-depth personal interviews with (1) each pastor and their spouse; (2) a cross section of ten current members at each site (stratified by age and length of membership); and (3) a sample of regular visitors and inquirers who agreed to be interviewed again as they progressed through the new-member process (interviews with ninety-six prospective members overall). Prospective members were identified through lists of visitors generated weekly at each church, as well as informal conversations after Sunday services. This allowed us to talk with prospective members as early in the process as possible, rather than limit our interviews to those who decided to go on and participate in the church's formal membership classes or meetings.

Age of respondents ranged from twenty-one to eighty-five (with most being in their late twenties to early forties). All of the congregations were predominantly white European-American in terms of membership—figures that compare to national membership across the country (see Table A.1).

Sixty-three percent of the sample of prospective members at First Presbyterian Church were women, compared to 57 percent of congregational membership for Presbyterians in the United States. First Presbyterian was also slightly younger than the national denominational membership and, not surprisingly, more likely to have children in the home. First Presbyterian was also somewhat more middle income compared to the denomination as a whole, but it mirrored the income distribution for the county in which it is located. At the same time, a higher percentage had college and advanced degrees compared to the denomination overall. Just over half of the members at Valley Baptist Church were women, which is fairly similar to evangelical congregations across the country (55 percent versus 52 percent), while our sample of prospective members was slightly more skewed (64 percent women). Prospective members at Valley Baptist were also somewhat younger, more likely to have children, and better educated overall than are conservative Baptists nationally. Most of these characteristics are consistent with the efforts of this congregation to reach out to young adults and emphasize family-centered programs (including its Christian school). As with the mainline and evangelical congregations, the membership at St. Andrews included a greater proportion of individuals with college and graduate degrees than is the case for Orthodox Churches across the country. St. Andrews is more European-American than are Orthodox churches nationally, consistent with its location in the Pacific Northwest. It is also somewhat younger, has a larger proportion of families with four or more children, and is generally more middle income than Orthodox churches at the national level. Eighty percent of the congregation is married, compared to forty-eight percent of prospective members—suggesting something of the congregation's success in attracting students and young professionals who have moved to the area for work or education.

The substance of the personal interviews with both current and prospective members focused on respondents' history of religious involvement, current church attendance and interests, narrative regarding their first visits at each site and what appeals, attracts, seems right and good, as well as any questions, concerns, or drawbacks to further connection or commitment. Additional questions focused on concepts related to gender and family, ideas about the meaning of church affiliation, the

Table A.1 Members and Inquirers Characteristics Compared to Denomination

	Mainline (PCUSA)		Evangelical (CB)		Orthodox	
	First Presby	USA	Valley Baptist	USA	St. Andrews	USA
% Women						
Denomination		57		52		54
Congregation	62		55		54	
Potential new members	63		64		55	
% Married						
Denomination		62		60		58
Congregation	68		74		80	
Potential new members	63		50		48	
All Interviewees						
Family income (% earning)						
<30K	16	16	15	34	33	20
30–49.9K	23	19	30	25	27	24
50–74.9K	31	19	21	18	24	16
75–99.9K	19	18	24	10	10	13
100K+	12	28	10	13	6	28
Race (%)						
White	93	91	90	86	97	87
Black	0	4	0	5	0	6
Asian	7	2	0	1	0	2
Latino	0	2	10	3	0	1
Other	0	1	0	4	3	3
Age (%)						
18–29	10	8	36	14	34	18
30–49	54	31	39	38	30	38
50–64	13	30	14	26	30	27
65+	23	32	11	21	6	17
Education (%)						
Less than high school	0	18	3	17	0	6
High school graduate	1	27	13	43	7	26
Some college	18	24	26	22	18	22
BA/BS	33	19	14	13	35	28
Postgraduate	47	13	45	6	40	18

(continued)

Table A.1 (*Continued*)

	Mainline (PCUSA)		Evangelical (CB)		Orthodox	
	First Presby	USA	Valley Baptist	USA	St. Andrews	USA
No. of children (%)						
None	11	74	19	66	29	70
One	9	11	13	13	20	9
Two	54	10	30	13	13	14
Three	9	4	21	5	4	5
Four +	15	1	17	3	29	1

Data Sources: Pew Forum, Religion & Public Life, U.S. Religious Landscape Survey, 2009.

CB, Conservative Baptist; PCUSA, Presbyterian Church (USA).

http://religions.pewforum.org/pdf/report-religious-landscape-study-full.pdf

place of children in worship, and the consequences of congregational commitment for relationships with family and friends. Interviews were semistructured in order to provide similar questions across conversations with pastors, their spouses, members, and prospective members, as well as allow flexibility within interviews of the topics and areas of focus. The overall strategy was to create an informal interview in which respondents were invited to tell their own stories. Initial interview questions were pretested for ease and clarity, an introductory paragraph and informed consent section drafted, and revisions in both were made prior to beginning the fieldwork in order to ensure clarity, consistency, and integrity of the interview process.

Each prospective member was interviewed at least one other time (most often in person, but occasionally over the phone if that was his or her preference). Second and later interviews reiterated some of the same themes around the appeal of each congregation, deepening involvement, and perceived changes to other relationships. In these, we were particularly attentive to how motivations and perceptions (as well as vocabulary) changed as individuals became more closely integrated into congregational life. At the end of the third year, a telephone follow-up interview asked whether visitors were still attending, had joined or gone elsewhere, and what they thought about the formal membership process, as well as their experience as new members. With participants' permission, all personal interviews were recorded and later transcribed for systematic content analysis.

FOCUSING ON SPIRITUAL GROWTH

In 2006–2007, we returned to the field with an additional set of questions focused on ideas around spiritual growth. We went back to our three churches and posed a series of questions on the means and dimensions of spiritual growth. We chose focus groups for this phase of the research in order to observe how participants collectively generated a set of methods and meanings associated with spiritual growth, and how these approximated the broader culture, teachings, and practices of the congregations.

At this stage, we recontacted clergy at each church to inform them of the project, gain permission to conduct a follow-up study, and ask them to help identify a small group of members and regular attenders who might be interested in participating. We excluded occasional visitors in order to focus on those with adequate facility in the language and narratives of a particular tradition to articulate their understanding of the church's core messages. We also excluded those in leadership positions because of our interest in how concepts of spiritual growth are appropriated by ordinary believers rather than defined by church leadership or doctrinal statements. Our objective at this point was not to assess what the churches teach about spiritual growth, but how average attenders understand and claim to appropriate these ideas and practices.

Each focus group included between seven and eleven members and regular attenders. Groups met for approximately an hour and began with a short questionnaire that included questions on demographics (age, marital status, number and ages of any children, education, ethnicity; see Table A.2), as well as duration of attendance, what they liked most and least about being part of that congregation, and their sense of congregational culture, mission, and community.

Most important, we included three substantive open-ended questions asking respondents to define spiritual growth; enumerate some of the practices they

Table A.2 Focus Group Sample Characteristics

	First Presbyterian Church	Valley Baptist Church	St. Andrews Orthodox
Number	7	7	10
% Female	86	57	41
Age 20–35	1	2	1
Age 36–50	1	0	1
Age 51–70	2	3	6
Age 71+	3	2	2
Youngest	27	26	29
Oldest	81	86	71
% Married (no.)	57 (4)	86 (6)	70 (7)
% Divorced (no.)	28 (2)	14 (1)	20 (2)
% Euro-American (no.)	100 (7)	100 (7)	80 (8)

use to cultivate spiritual growth; and to describe what they thought were the specific objectives of growth. Those questions were used to guide the discussion that followed. With permission, each focus group discussion was recorded and transcribed for later analysis. Transcripts were read and reread, coding for themes that emerged around definitions, means, and ends of spiritual growth within these discussions. We were particularly attentive to breadth, diversity, and clarity of definitions across the respondents in each congregation. In addition, we were attentive to the ways in which any consensus around the topic of spiritual growth was described as contributing to a sense of congregational commitment, culture, and sense of mission. Here, as in our other sampling, it is important to note that we were purposive rather than random, and so our findings should not be interpreted as applying to these denomination as a whole, but read as a set of comparative case studies.

CONNECTING WITH THOSE WHO NO LONGER ATTEND

Finally, there is one thing that all organizations have in common: not all prospective members join and not all current members stay. Several studies make the case that within congregations, men are more likely to disaffiliate than are women and that higher levels of education are associated with disaffiliation.[2] People stop attending specific congregations for many reasons—because they die, move out of town, have a personal conflict with another member or leaders, or have work or family demands that make it difficult to remain involved. To explore these questions, we obtained directories of members for the years closest to the beginning and ending dates of the initial study from 2002 to 2009. We calculated the difference and proportionate change between the number of members listed in the original and later directories. Next, we highlighted the names of individuals who appeared in the first but not later directory and randomly selected a sample of twenty to thirty names from each to ask to be interviewed about the circumstances of their departure. Based on information provided by church pastors and staff, we omitted from that list anyone who had died (so we would not call a grieving partner or spouse) and obtained updated phone or other contact information for those who were known to have moved out of town. We then attempted to contact each respondent (calling each number a minimum of six times at various times of day) to ask for an interview. Given the demographics of our sample (both older adults who may have died or moved into retirement or nursing facilities, as well as younger adults who may have moved out of the area to marry or follow careers), we were not completely surprised to find a substantial proportion of phone numbers no longer working. In those cases, we were able to fill in some of the gaps by talking with key congregational members (the person or staff member who seems to know everyone)—and asked about those we had been unable to contact. The interview format we used with those no longer attending was an abbreviated version of the semistructured interview protocol used with members and prospective members, with additional items asking about the circumstances around their departure and whether they had since become affiliated with a different congregation.

Finally, we returned to each congregation in 2016 to speak with clergy and staff about changes in church programs, mission, and membership in the intervening years. We asked about how the congregations had navigated changes in staffing and leadership, as well as changing membership demographics. In addition, we cross-checked our sample and directory lists from 2009 with each congregation's current member list to assess longer term membership patterns of growth or decline. Our interest was in continuity, not just numbers, since being part of a congregation over the years that is the same size is not the same as being part of a congregation over the years that has the same people.

Notes

1. Kevin D. Dougherty, Byron R. Johnson, and Edward C. Polson, "Recovering the Lost: Remeasuring U.S. Religious Affiliation," *Journal for the Scientific Study of Religion* 46 (2007): 483–499; Paul Froese and Christopher Bader, *America's Four Gods: What We Say about God and What That Says about Us* (New York: Oxford University Press, 2010); Brian Steensland, Jerry Z. Park, Mark Regnerus, Lynn D. Robinson, W. Bradford Wilcox, and Robert D. Woodberry, "The Measure of American Religion: Toward Improving the State of the Art," *Social Forces* 79 (2000): 291–318. The thesis that America was becoming a secular society popularized by Peter Berger's *The Sacred Canopy* (Garden City, NY: Doubleday, 1967) has been modified to account for a number of recent trends in religiosity and religious affiliation in the United States. Evidence for secularization appears in the loss of political and public hegemony of the Protestant establishment— alternately celebrated or decried as by Richard John Neuhaus as the triumph of the *Naked Public Square* (Grand Rapids, MI: Eerdmans, 1984). Others have argued that secularization can be found in a shift away from institutional membership toward more privatized and individualistic religious expressions—the Sheilaism of Robert Bellah et al.'s *Habits of the Heart* (Berkeley: University of California Press, 1985). Despite the resurgence of conservative Protestantism and growth of non-Western religious congregations in the United States, the alienation from religious institutions and thinness of basic knowledge about religion characteristic of young adults suggest that connection to particular historic denominations may indeed be giving way to more amorphous, open-ended, and broadly defined religious identities. The growth of the "none's" in general social surveys is another indicator that identification with historic strands of religious tradition is becoming less a mainstay of US religious experience. See Elizabeth Drescher, *Choosing Our Religion: The Spiritual Lives of American's Nones* (New York: Oxford University Press, 2016).

2. Mark Chaves, *America Religion: Contemporary Trends* (Princeton, NJ: Princeton University Press, 2011); Vegard Skirbekk, Eric Kaufmann, and Anne Goujon, "Secularism, Fundamentalism, or Catholicism? The Religious Composition of the United States to 2043," *Journal for the Scientific Study of Religion* 49 (2010): 293–310.

3. Michelle Dillon, "Age, Generation, and Cohort in American Religion and Spirituality," in *Sage Handbook of the Sociology of Religion*, ed. James A. Beckford and N. J. Demerath III (Thousand Oaks, CA: Sage, 2007), 526–548; Mark D. Regnerus, Christian Smith, and Brad Smith, "Social Context in the Development of Adolescent Religiosity," *Applied Developmental Science* 8 (2004): 27–38.

4. Wade Clark Roof, *A Generation of Seekers: The Spiritual Journeys of the Baby Boomer Generation* (New York: Harper San Francisco, 1993); Wade Clark Roof, *Spiritual Marketplace* (Princeton, NJ: Princeton University Press, 2001); Christian Smith and Patricia Snell, *Souls in Transition: The Religious and Spiritual Lives of Emerging Adults* (New York: Oxford University Press, 2009).

5. Chris Ellison and J. S. Levin, "The Religion-Health Connection: Evidence, Theory, and Future Directions," *Health Education and Behavior* 25 (1998): 700–720; Chris Ellison and David Sherkat, "Religious Involvement and Subjective Well-Being," *Journal of Health and Social Behavior* 32 (1991): 80–100; L. J. Francis and P. Kaldor, "The Relationship Between Psychological Well-Being and Christian Faith and Practice in an Australian Population Sample," *Journal for the Scientific Study of Religion* (2002): 179–184; Neal Krause, "Religious Meaning and Subjective Well-Being in Late Life," *The Journals of Gerontology* 58 (2003): S160–S170; Neal Krause, Christopher Ellison, and Jack P. Marcum, "The Effects of Church-Based Emotional Support on Health," *Sociology of Religion* 63 (2002): 21–47.

6. Nancy Ammerman, *Pillars of Faith: American Congregations and Their Partners* (Berkeley: University of California Press, 2005); Nancy Ammerman, *Congregation and Community* (New Brunswick, NJ: Rutgers University Press, 1997); Penny Edgell Becker, *Congregations in Conflict* (New York: Cambridge University Press, 1999); Sally K. Gallagher, "Building Traditions: A Comparative Analysis of Space, Community and Theology in Three Christian Churches," *Review of Religious Research* 47 (2005): 70–85.

7. Christian Smith and Robert Faris, "Socioeconomic Inequality in the American Religious System: An Update and Assessment," *Journal for the Scientific Study of Religion* 44 (2005): 95–104; Richard F. Hamilton and William H. Form, "Categorical Usages and Complex Realities: Race Ethnicity and Religion in the United States," *Social Forces* 81 (2003): 693–714.

8. Brad Christerson, Korie L. Edwards, and Michael O. Emerson, *Against All Odds: The Struggle for Racial Integration in Religious Organizations* (New York: NYU Press, 2005); Kevin D. Dougherty, Gerado Marti, and Brandon C. Martinez, "Congregational Diversity and Attendance in a Mainline Protestant Denomination," *Journal for the Scientific Study of Religion* 54 (2015): 668–683;

Michael O. Emerson and Christian Smith, *Divided by Faith: Evangelical Religion and the Problem of Race in America* (New York: Oxford University Press, 2001); Jason Shelton and Michael O. Emerson, *Blacks and Whites in Christian America: How Racial Discrimination Shapes Religious Convictions* (New York: NYU Press, 2012).

9. Margaret Lamberts Bendroth, *Fundamentalism and Gender, 1875 to the Present* (New Haven, CT: Yale University Press 1996); Nancy Hardesty, *Women Called to Witness: Evangelical Feminism in the Nineteenth Century*, 2nd ed. (Knoxville: University of Tennessee Press, 1999); Robert T. Handy, *Christian America: Protestant Hopes and Historical Realities* (New York: Oxford University Press, 1984); Marta Trzebiatowska and Steve Bruce, *Why Are Women More Religious Than Men?* (New York: Oxford University Press, 2012).

10. Nancy Cott, *The Bonds of Womanhood: "Woman's Sphere" in New England, 1780–1835* (New Haven, CT: Yale University Press, 1977); Handy, *Christian America*, 1984; Barbara Welter, *Dimity Convictions: The American Woman in the Nineteenth Century* (Athens: Ohio University Press, 1976).

11. Susan Juster, *Disorderly Women: Sexual Politics and Evangelicalism in Revolutionary New England* (Ithaca, NY: Cornell University Press, 1994).

12. During these revivals, tensions flared between churches and ministers that encouraged lay ministry and the experience of conversion and those that did not. While their Puritan grandparents had long held to the necessity of personal conversion, that experience had largely been understood as the result of a long process of study, corporate worship, contemplation, and prayer–preparatory exercises that were not the means of grace, but simply the disciplines through which one placed oneself in a position where one might be the recipient of grace. Revival telescoped this process into an unpredictable, often ecstatic encounter with God in which conviction, repentance, regeneration, and salvation took place in a moment of new birth. For a fuller presentation of this history, see John Bartkowski, "The Changing of the Gods: The Gender and Family Discourse of American Evangelicalism in Historical Perspective," *History of the Family: An International Quarterly* 3 (1998): 95–115; Philip J. Greven, *The Protestant Temperament: Patterns of Child-Rearing, Religious Experience, and the Self in Early America* (New York: Knopf, 1977); Juster, *Disorderly Women*.

13. Pew Research Center Forum on Religion & Public Life, *U.S. Religious Landscape Survey* 2014, http://www.pewforum.org/religious-landscape-study/religious-tradition (accessed October 4, 2016); Linda Woodhead, "Gendering Secularization Theory," *Social Compass* 55 (2008): 187–193.

14. Michelle Dillon and Paul Wink, *In the Course of a Lifetime: Tracing Religious Belief, Practice, and Change* (Berkeley: University of California Press, 2007).

15. Matt Bradshaw and Christopher G. Ellison, "The Nature-Nurture Debate Is Over, and Both Sides Lost! Implications for Understanding Gender Differences in Religiosity," *Journal for the Scientific Study of Religion* 48 (2009): 241–251; Jessica L. Collett and Omar Lizardo, "A Power-Control Theory of Gender and

Religiosity," *Journal for the Scientific Study of Religion* 48 (2009): 213–231; John P. Hoffman, "Gender, Risk, and Religiousness: Can Power Control Provide the Theory?" *Journal for the Scientific Study of Religion* 48 (2009): 232–240; Alan S. Miller and Rodney Stark, "Gender and Religiousness: Can Socialization Explanations Be Saved?" *American Journal of Sociology* 107 (2002): 1399–1423; Rodney Stark, "Physiology and Faith: Addressing the 'Universal' Gender Difference in Religious Commitment," *Journal for the Scientific Study of Religion* 41 (2002): 495–507; Trzebiatowska and Bruce, *Why Are Women More Religious Than Men?*

16. Marie Cornwall, "Reifying Sex Differences Isn't the Answer: Gendering Processes, Risk, and Religiosity," *Journal for the Scientific Study of Religion* 48 (2009): 252–255; Sally K. Gallagher, "Are Women More Religious Than Men?: Gendered Narratives of Affiliation, Service, and Participation" (paper presented at the annual meeting of the Society for the Scientific Study of Religion, Boston, MA, November 7–10, 2013).

17. Landon Schnabel, "How Religious Are American Women and Men? Gender Differences and Similarities," *Journal for the Scientific Study of Religion* 54 (2015): 616–622; D. Paul Sullins, "Gender and Religion: Deconstructing Universality, Constructing Complexity," *American Journal of Sociology* 112 (2006): 838–880.

18. John Bartkowski, *Remaking the Godly Marriage: Gender Negotiation in Evangelical Families* (New Brunswick, NJ: Rutgers University Press, 2001); John Bartkowski, *The Promise Keepers: Servants, Soldiers, and Godly Men* (New Brunswick, NJ: Rutgers University Press, 2003); Sally K. Gallagher, *Evangelical Identity and Gendered Family Life* (New Brunswick, NJ: Rutgers University Press, 2003); John Bartkowski and Lynn M. Hempel, "Sex and Gender Traditionalism among Conservative Protestants: Does the Difference Make a Difference?" *Journal for the Scientific Study of Religion* 48 (2009): 805–816; W. Bradford Wilcox, *Soft Patriarchs, New Men: How Christianity Shapes Fathers and Husbands* (Chicago: University of Chicago Press, 2004).

19. Nancy Ammerman, *Sacred Stories, Spiritual Tribes: Finding Religion in Everyday Life* (New York: Oxford University Press, 2014); Nancy Ammerman, ed., *Everyday Religion: Observing Modern Religious Life* (New York: Oxford University Press, 2007); David Hall, *Lived Religion in America: Toward a History of Practice* (Princeton, NJ: Princeton University Press, 1997); Meredith B. McGuire, *Lived Religion: Faith and Practice in Everyday Life* (New York: Oxford University Press, 2008).

20. John Lofland and Rodney Stark, "Becoming a World-Saver," *American Sociological Review* 30 (1965): 862–875; Roof, *Spiritual Marketplace*, 1999; Rodney Stark and Roger Finke, *Acts of Faith: Explaining the Human Side of Religion* (London: University of California Press, Ltd, 2000); Robert Wuthnow, *After*

Heaven: Spirituality in America since the 1950s (Berkeley: University of California Press, 1998).

21. Christian Smith, *Moral, Believing Animals: An Essay on Human Personhood and Culture* (New York: Oxford University Press, 2003); Christian Smith, *American Evangelicalism: Embattled and Thriving* (Chicago: University of Chicago Press, 1998).

22. Meredith B. McGuire, "Embodied Practices: Negotiation and Resistance," in *Everyday Religion: Observing Modern Religious Lives*, ed. Nancy Ammerman (New York: Oxford University Press, 2007), 187–200.

23. James Bielo, *Emerging Evangelicals: Faith, Modernity and the Desire for Authenticity* (New York: New York University Press, 2011); Dan Kimball, *The Emerging Church: Vintage Christianity for New Generations* (Grand Rapids, MI: Zondervan, 2003); Brian McLaren, *The Church on the Other Side: Doing Ministry in the Postmodern Matrix* (Grand Rapids, MI: Zondervan, 1998); Brian McLaren, *The Story We Find Ourselves In: Further Adventures of a New Kind of Christian* (San Francisco: Jossey-Bass, 2003); Scot McKnight, "Five Streams of the Emerging Church," *Christianity Today* 51, January 19, 2007, http://www.christianitytoday.com/ct/2007/February/11.35.html (accessed October 4, 2016); Dave Tomlinson, *The Post-Evangelical* (Grand Rapids, MI: Zondervan, 2003).

24. Robert Brenneman and Brian J. Miller, "When Bricks Matter: Four Arguments for the Sociological Study of Religious Buildings," *Sociology of Religion* 77 (2016):82–101; E. Frances King, *Material Religion and Popular Culture* (New York and London: Routledge, 2009); Meredith B. McGuire, *Religion and the Body: Rematerializing the Human Body in the Social Sciences of Religion* (New Haven, CT: Yale University Press, 1990); McGuire, *Lived Religion*; Colleen McDannell, *Material Christianity: Religion and Popular Culture in America* (New Haven, CT: Yale University Press, 1995).

25. Brenneman and Miller, "When Bricks Matter"; Gallagher, "Building Traditions"; Jeanne Halgren Kilde, *When Church Became Theatre* (New York: Oxford University Press, 2002); Michael S. Rose, *Ugly as Sin* (Manchester, NH: Sophia Institute Press, 2001).

26. Michael E. DeSanctis, *Building from Belief* (Collegeville, MN: Liturgical Press, 2002); Richard Kieckhefer, *Theology in Stone* (New York: Oxford University Press, 2004): Rose, *Ugly as Sin*, 2001; James F. White, *Protestant Worship and Church Architecture* (Eugene, OR: Wipf & Stock, 2003).

27. Kilde, *When Church Became Theatre*.

28. Berger, *The Sacred Canopy*.

29. Bellah, et al, *Habits of the Heart*.

30. Roof, *A Generation of Seekers*.

31. Smith, *American Evangelicalism*; Christian Smith, *Christian America? What Evangelicals Really Want* (Berkeley: University of California Press, 2000).

32. Lawrence R. Iannaccone and Sean F. Everton, "Never on Sunny Days: Lessons from Weekly Attendance Counts," *Journal for the Scientific Study of Religion* 43 (2004): 191–207; Jeremy N. Thomas and Daniel V. A. Olson, "Testing the Strictness Thesis and Competing Theories of Congregational Growth," *Journal for the Scientific Study of Religion* 49 (2010): 619–639.

33. Richard Flory and Donald E. Miller, *Finding Faith: The Spiritual Quest of the Post-Boomer Generation* (New Brunswick, NJ: Rutgers University Press, 2008); Peter E. Gillquist, *Becoming Orthodox: A Journey to the Ancient Christian Faith*, rev. ed. (Ben Lomond, CA: Conciliar Press, 1999): Frederica Mathews-Green, *At the Corner of East and Now* (New York: Tarcher/Putnam, 1999); Amy Slagle, *The Eastern Church in the Spiritual Marketplace: American Conversions to Orthodox Christianity* (DeKalb, IL: Northern Illinois University Press, 2011); Daniel Winchester, "Converting to Continuity: Temporality and Self in Eastern Orthodox Conversion Narratives," *Journal for the Scientific Study of Religion* 54 (2015): 439–460; Rico Vitz, ed., *Turning East: Contemporary Philosophers and the Ancient Christian Faith* (Yonkers, NY: St. Vladimir's Seminary Press, 2012).

34. Chaves, *American Religion*; Skirbekk et al., "Secularism."

35. Roger Finke and Laurence Iannoccone, "Supply-Side Explanations for Religious Change," *Annals of the American Academy of Political and Social Science* 527 (1993): 27–40; Roger Finke and Rodney Stark, "Religious Choice and Competition," *American Sociological Review* 63 (1998): 761–766; Roger Finke and Rodney Stark, *The Churching of America, 1776–2005: Winners and Losers in our Religious Economy*, 2nd ed. (New Brunswick, NJ: Rutgers University Press, 2005); Stark and Finke, *Acts of Faith*.

36. Smith, *American Evangelicalism*.

37. Willem Kox, Wim Meeus, and Harm't Hart, "Religious Conversion of Adolescents: Testing the Lofland and Stark Model of Religious Conversion," *Sociological Analysis* 52 (1991): 227–240; John Lofland, *Doomsday Cult* (New York: Irvington, 1977); John Lofland and Norman Skonovd, "Conversion Motifs," *Journal for the Scientific Study of Religion* 20 (1981): 373–385; Lofland and Stark, "Becoming a World-Saver."

38. Pew, *U.S. Religious Landscape Survey*.

39. Stark and Finke, *Acts of Faith*; David Yamane, "Initiation Rites in the Contemporary Catholic Church: What Difference Do They Make," *Review of Religious Research* 54 (2012): 401–420.

40. Matthew Loveland, "Religious Switching: Preference Development, Maintenance, and Change," *Journal for the Scientific Study of Religion* 42 (2003): 147–157; Marc Musick and John Wilson, "Religious Switching for Marriage Reasons," *Sociology of Religion* 56 (1995): 257–270.

41. Lora Lawton and Regina Bures, "Parental Divorce and the 'Switching' of Religious Identity," *Journal for the Scientific Study of Religion* 40 (2001): 99–111.

42. Ross Stolzenberg, Mary Blair-Loy, and Linda Waite, "Age and Family Life Cycle Effects on Church Membership," *American Sociological Review* 60 (1995): 84–103.

43. Darren E. Sherkat, "Leaving the Faith: Testing Theories of Religious Switching Using Survival Models," *Social Science Research* 20 (1991): 171–187.

44. Dean R. Hodge and Jackson W. Carroll, "Determinants of Commitment and Participation in Suburban Protestant Churches," *Journal for the Scientific Study of Religion* (June 1978): 107–128; Frank Newport, "The Religious Switcher in the United States," *American Sociological Review* (August 1979): 528–552; Wade Clark Roof and Christopher Kirk Hadaway, "Denominational Switching in the Seventies: Going beyond Stark and Glock," *Journal for the Scientific Study of Religion* 18 (1979): 363–377.

45. Chaves, *American Religion*.

46. Stromberg, Peter, *Language and Self-Transformation: A Study of the Christian Conversion Narrative* (New York: Cambridge University Press, 1993).

47. Winchester, "Converting to Continuity," 2015.

48. The number of Americans who identify with historic Protestant denominations has been declining for over forty years (Chaves, *American Religion*). If current attitudes among American young adults remain stable (Smith and Denton, *Soul Searching*; Smith and Snell, *Souls in Transition*), we would expect that trend to continue as more and more Americans begin identifying as nondenominational, "just Christian" (a designation that includes many evangelicals), unaffiliated (spiritual but not religious), or "other." Part of that trend is a weakening of the connection between ethnic identity and denomination, with being British and Methodist, or Scottish and Presbyterian, or Scandinavian and Lutheran. Americans may be connected to specific congregations, but they are less likely to identify with a denominational label (Dougherty, Johnson, and Polson, "Recovering the Loss"). The increase in the numbers of Americans identifying as "nondenominational" Protestant may also be a side effect of the recent shift among conservative Protestant churches to rename their churches in order to appeal to a broader constituency. In an effort to attract new members from among those who are likely to be either turned off or simply confused by the lables "Baptist" or "Assemblies of God," these churches may be contributing to the loss of specific denominational identity while remaining, as we will see, consistently Baptist in faith and in practice located firmly within the broader evangelical movement.

49. Stark and Finke, *Acts of Faith*.

50. Smith, *American Evangelicalism*.

51. John Binns, *An Introduction to the Orthodox Church* (New York: Cambridge University Press, 2002); John H. Erickson, *Orthodox Christians in America* (New York: Oxford University Press, 1999; Alexei Krindatch, "Orthodox (Eastern Christian) Churches in the United States at the Beginning of a New

Millennium," *Journal for the Scientific Study of Religion* 41 (2002): 533–563; Winchester, "Converting to Continuity."

52. Nancy Ammerman, "Golden Rule Christianity: Lived Religion in the American Mainstream," in *Lived Religion in America: Toward A History of Practice,* ed. David Hall (Princeton, NJ: Princeton University Press, 1997), 196–216; Margaret Lamberts Bendroth, *Growing Up Protestant* (New Brunswick, NJ: Rutgers University Press, 2002); Finke and Stark, The *Churching of America.*

CHAPTER 2

1. Kilde, *When Church Became Theatre.*
2. Stephen Ellingson, *The Megachurch and the Mainline: Remaking Religious Tradition in the Twenty-First Century* (Chicago: University of Chicago Press, 2007); R. Stephen Warner, *New Wine in Old Wineskins* (Berkeley: University of California Press, 1988).
3. John Gibson, "Jesus we Celebrate your Victory" (Thankyou Music, 1987), 26–28.
4. Brenton Brown and Brian Doerksen, "Hallelujah (Your love is Amazing)" [c]2000 Vineyard Songs (UK/Eire).
5. Mathews-Green, *At the Corner of East and Now.*
6. Kilde, *When Church Became Theatre.*

CHAPTER 3

1. *Book of Common Worship.* Prepared by The Theology and Worship Ministry Unit for the Presbyterian Church (USA) and the Cumberland Presbyterian Church (Louisville, KY: Westminster/John Knox Press, 1993).
2. *Book of Common Worship,* 455.

CHAPTER 4

1. Gallagher, *Evangelical Identity,* 2003; Sally K. Gallagher, "Where Are the Antifeminist Evangelicals? Evangelical Identity, Subcultural Location, and Attitudes Towards Feminism," *Gender & Society 18* (2004): 451–472.

CHAPTER 5

1. Roger Finke, "Spiritual Capital: Definitions, Applications, and New Frontiers," (2003), http://www.metanexus.net/archive/spiritualcapitalresearchprogram/pdf/finke.pdf (accessed October 17, 2016); Stark and Finke, *Acts of Faith.*
2. Stark and Finke, *Acts of Faith.*
3. M. Peyrot and F. M. Sweeney, "Derminants of Parishioner Satisfaction among Practicing Catholics," *Sociology of Religion* 61 (2000): 209–221.

4. A. Michael Maclean, Lawrence J. Walker, and M. Kyle Matsuba, "Transcendence and the Moral Self: Identity Integration, Religion and Moral Life," *Journal for the Scientific Study of Religion* 43 (2004): 429–437; Elizabeth Weiss Ozorak, "Love of God and Neighbor: Religion and Volunteer Service among College Students," *Review of Religious Research* 44 (2004): 285–299; Smith, *Moral, Believing Animals.*

5. David Yamane and Sarah MacMillen, with Kelly Culver, *Real Stories of Christian Initiation: Lessons for and from the RCIA* (Collegeville, MN: Liturgical Press, 2006).

6. James K. Wellman, "Religion Without a Net: Strictness in the Religious Practices of West Coast Urban Liberal Christian Congregations," *Review of Religious Research* 44 (2002): 184–199; James K. Wellman, *Evangelical vs Liberal: The Clash of Christian Cultures in the Pacific Northwest* (New York: Oxford University Press, 2008).

7. Some of the ideas in this chapter were first explored in Sally K. Gallagher and Chelsea Newton, "Defining Spiritual Growth: Congregations, Community & Connectedness," *Sociology of Religion* 70 (2009): 232–261.

8. Stark and Finke, *Acts of Faith.*

CHAPTER 6

1. Steven Nock, *Marriage in Men's Lives* (New York: Oxford University Press, 1998); Wilcox, *Soft Patriarchs,* 2004; W. Bradford Wilcox and Nicholas H. Wolfinger, *Soul Mates: Religion, Sex, Love and Marriage among African Americans and Latinos* (New York: Oxford University Press, 2016).

2. Smith, *American Evangelicalism*; Corwin Smidt, *American Evangelicals Today* (Lanham, MD: Rowman & Littlefield, 2013).

CHAPTER 7

1. Henri Gooren, *Religious Conversion and Disaffiliation: Tracing Patterns of Change in Faith Practices* (New York: Palgrave Macmillan, 2010); Henri Gooren, "Reassessing Approaches to Conversion," *Journal for the Scientific Study of Religion* 46 (2007): 337–353; Sharon Sandomirsky and John Wilson, "Patterns of Disaffiliation: Religious Mobility among Men and Women," *Social Forces* 68 (1990): 1211–1229; Smith, *American Evangelicalism*; Nicholas Vargas, "Retrospective Accounts of Religious Disaffiliation in the United States: Stressors, Skepticism, and Political Factors," *Sociology of Religion* 73 (2012): 200–223.

2. Berger, *The Sacred Canopy.*

3. Cristel Manning, *Losing our Religion: How Unaffiliated Parents Are Raising Their Children* (New York: New York University Press, 2015); Roof, *Spiritual Marketplace*; David Sikkink, "Social Predictors of Retention in and Switching from the Religious Faith of Family of Origin," *Review of Religious Research* 45 (2003):188–206; Smith and Snell, *Souls in Transition*; Wuthnow, *After Heaven.*

4. Dillon and Wink, *In the Course.*
5. Vargas, "Retrospective Accounts"; Wellman, "Religion Without a Net."
6. Smith, *American Evangelicalism*; Smith and Denton, *Soul Searching.*
7. Between 2002 and 2009 membership in the denomination declined 15 percent, compared with a 10 percent decline at First Presbyterian. Between 2009 and 2014, denominational membership declined by 24 percent, whereas the membership of First Presbyterian declined 34 percent (Pew, *U.S. Religious Landscape Survey*).
8. The median congregation in the United States has 70 regular attenders (50 of whom are adults), whereas the average adult churchgoer is in a congregation with an average of 310 participants (reflecting the fact that most churchgoers go to relatively large churches, but that most churches are quite small). See Mark Chaves and Alison Eagle, *Religious Congregations in 21st Century America: A Report from the National Congregations Study* (Department of Sociology, Duke University, 2015). Available at http://www.soc.duke.edu/natcong/Docs/NCSIII_report_final.pdf.
9. Krindatch, "Orthodox Churches."
10. Reginald W. Bibby and Merlin B. Brinkerhoff, "Circulation of the Saints, 1966–1900: New Data, New Reflections," *Journal for the Scientific Study of Religion* 33 (1994): 273–280.

CHAPTER 8

1. For a more indepth assessment of the ways in which children are integrated into these congregations, see Sally K. Gallagher, "Children as Religious Resources," *Journal for the Scientific Study of Religion* 46 (2007): 169–183.

APPENDIX

1. Bendroth, *Growing Up Protestant*; Marsden, *Understanding Fundamentalism and Evangelicalism* (Grand Rapids, MI: Eerdmans, 1991); Thomas Hopko, *The Orthodox Faith, Volume 4: Spirituality* (New York: Orthodox Church in America Religious Education Department, 1984); Wade Clark Roof and William McKinney, *American Mainline Religion: Its Changing Shape and Future* (New Brunswick, NJ: Rutgers University Press, 1987); Alexander Schmemann, *For the Life of the World* (Crestwood, NY: Saint Vladimir's Seminary Press, 1998); Bruce Shelley, *A History of Conservative Baptists*, 3rd ed. (Wheaton, IL: Conservative Baptist Press, 1981); Corwin E. Smidt, *American Evangelicals Today* (Lanham, MD: Rowman & Littlefield, 2013); Smith, *American Evangelicalism*; Timothy Ware, *The Orthodox Church*, 3rd ed. (New York: Penguin, 2015); Timothy Ware, *The Orthodox Way*, rev. ed. (Crestwood, NY: St.Vladimir's Seminary Press, 1995); Kallistos Ware, *The Inner Kingdom* (Crestwood, NY: Saint Vladimir's Seminary Press, 2000);

David Harrington Watt, *A Transforming Faith: Explorations of Twentieth-Century American Evangelicalism* (New Brunswick, NJ: Rutgers University Press, 1991).

2. C. Kirk Hadaway, "Identifying American Apostates: A Cluster Analysis," *Journal for the Scientific Study of Religion* 28 (1989): 201–215; C. Kirk Hadaway and Wade Clark Roof, "Apostasy in American Churches: Evidence from National Survey Data," in *Falling From the Faith: Causes and Consequences of Religious Apostasy*, edited by David Bromley (Newbury Park, CA: Sage Publications, 1988), 29–46; Darren E. Sherkat and John Wilson, "Preferences, Constraints, and Choices in Religious Markets: An Examination of Religious Switching and Apostasy," *Social Forces* 75 (1995):993–1026; John Wilson and Darren E. Sherkat. "Returning to the Fold," *Journal for the Scientific Study of Religion* 33 (1994): 148–161; Vargas, 2012.

References

Ammerman, Nancy. 1997. *Congregation and Community*. New Brunswick, NJ: Rutgers University Press.

Ammerman, Nancy. 1997. "Golden Rule Christianity: Lived Religion in the American Mainstream." In *Lived Religion in America: Toward a History of Practice*, edited by David Hall, 196–216. Princeton, NJ: Princeton University Press.

Ammerman, Nancy. 2005. *Pillars of Faith: American Congregations and Their Partners*. Berkeley, CA: University of California Press.

Ammerman, Nancy, ed. 2007. *Everyday Religion: Observing Modern Religious Lives*. New York: Oxford University Press.

Ammerman, Nancy. 2014. *Sacred Stories, Spiritual Tribes: Finding Religion in Everyday Life*. New York: Oxford University Press.

Bartkowski, John. 1998. "The Changing of the Gods: The Gender and Family Discourse of American Evangelicalism in Historical Perspective." *History of the Family: An International Quarterly* 3:95–115.

Bartkowski, John. 2001. *Remaking the Godly Marriage: Gender Negotiation in Evangelical Families*. New Brunswick, NJ: Rutgers University Press.

Bartkowski, John. 2003. *The Promise Keepers: Servants, Soldiers, and Godly Men*. New Brunswick, NJ: Rutgers University Press.

Bartkowski, John, and Lynn M. Hempel. 2009. "Sex and Gender Traditionalism among Conservative Protestants: Does the Difference Make a Difference?" *Journal for the Scientific Study of Religion* 48:805–816.

Becker, Penny Edgell. 1999. *Congregations in Conflict*. New York: Cambridge University Press.

Bellah, Robert N., Richard Madsen, Richard, William M. Sullivan, Ann Swidler, and Steve M. Tipton. 1985. *Habits of the Heart: Individualism and Commitment in American Life*. Berkeley: University of California Press.

Bendroth, Margaret Lamberts. 1996. *Fundamentalism and Gender, 1875 to the Present*. New Haven, CT: Yale University Press.

Bendroth, Margaret Lamberts. 2002. *Growing Up Protestant.* New Brunswick, NJ: Rutgers University Press

Berger, Peter. 1967. *The Sacred Canopy.* Garden City, NY: Doubleday.

Bibby, Reginald W., and Merlin B. Brinkerhoff. 1994. "Circulation of the Saints, 1966–1990: New Data, New Reflections." *Journal for the Scientific Study of Religion* 33: 273–280.

Bielo, James S. 2011. *Emerging Evangelicals: Faith, Modernity and the Desire for Authenticity.* New York: New York University Press.

Binns, John. 2002. *An Introduction to the Orthodox Church.* New York: Cambridge University Press.

Book of Common Worship. 1993. Prepared by the Theology and Worship Ministry Unit for the Presbyterian Church (USA) and the Cumberland Presbyterian Church. Louisville, Kentucky: Westminster/John Knox Press.

Bradshaw, Matt, and Christopher G. Ellison. 2009. "The Nature-Nurture Debate Is Over, and Both Sides Lost! Implications for Understanding Gender Differences in Religiosity." *Journal for the Scientific Study of Religion* 48: 241–251.

Brenneman, Robert, and Brian J. Miller. 2016. "When Bricks Matter: Four Arguments for the Sociological Study of Religious Buildings," *Sociology of Religion* 77:82–101.

Brown, Brenton, and Doerksen, Brian. "Hallelujah (Your love is Amazing)" [c]2000 Vineyard Songs (UK/Eire).

Chaves, Mark. 2011. *American Religion: Contemporary Trends.* Princeton, NJ: Princeton University Press.

Chaves, Mark, and Alison J. Eagle. 2015. *Religious Congregations in 21st Century America: A Report from the National Congregations Study.* Department of Sociology, Duke University, Durham, NC. http://www.soc.duke.edu/natcong/Docs/NCSIII_report_final.pdf (accessed November 14, 2016).

Christerson, Brad, Korie L. Edwards, and Michael O. Emerson. 2005. *Against All Odds: The Struggle for Racial Integration in Religious Organizations.* New York: NYU Press.

Collett, Jessica L., and Omar Lizardo. 2009. "A Power-Control Theory of Gender and Religiosity." *Journal for the Scientific Study of Religion* 48:213–231.

Cornwall, Marie. 2009. "Reifying Sex Differences Isn't the Answer: Gendering Processes, Risk, and Religiosity." *Journal for the Scientific Study of Religion* 48: 252–255.

Cott, Nancy. 1977. *The Bonds of Womanhood: "Woman's Sphere" in New England, 1780–1835.* New Haven, CT: Yale University Press.

DeSanctis, Michael E. 2002. *Building from Belief.* Collegeville, MN: Liturgical Press.

Dillon, Michelle. 2007. "Age, Generation, and Cohort in American Religion and Spirituality." In *Sage Handbook of the Sociology of Religion,* edited by James A. Beckford and N. J. Demerath III, 526–548. Thousand Oaks, CA: Sage.

Dillon, Michele, and Paul Wink. 2007. *In the Course of a Lifetime: Tracing Religious Belief, Practice, and Change.* Berkeley: University of California Press.

Dougherty, Kevin D., Gerado Marti, and Brandon C. Martinez. 2015. "Congregational Diversity and Attendance in a Mainline Protestant Denomination." *Journal for the Scientific Study of Religion* 54:668–683.

Dougherty, Kevin D., Byron R. Johnson, and Edward C. Polson. 2007. "Recovering the Lost: Remeasuring U.S. Religious Affiliation." *Journal for the Scientific Study of Religion* 46:483–499.

Drescher, Elizabeth. 2016. *Choosing Our Religion: The Spiritual Lives of American's Nones.* New York: Oxford University Press.

Ellingson, Stephen. 2007. *The Megachurch and the Mainline: Remaking Religious Tradition in the Twenty-First Century.* Chicago: University of Chicago Press.

Ellison, Chris, and J. S. Levin. 1998. "The Religion-Health Connection: Evidence, Theory and Future Directions." *Health Education and Behavior* 25:700–720.

Ellison, Chris, and David Sherkat. 1991. "Religious Involvement and Subjective Well-Being." *Journal of Health and Social Behavior* 32:80–100.

Emerson, Michael O., and Christian Smith. 2001. *Divided by Faith: Evangelical Religion and the Problem of Race in America.* New York: Oxford University Press.

Erickson, John H. 1999. *Orthodox Christians in America.* New York: Oxford University Press.

Finke, Roger. 2003. "Spiritual Capital: Definitions, Applications, and New Frontiers." http://www.metanexus.net/archive/spiritualcapitalresearchprogram/pdf/finke.pdf (accessed October 17, 2016).

Finke, Roger, and Laurence Iannoccone. 1993. "Supply-Side Explanations for Religious Change." *Annals of the American Academy of Political and Social Science* 527:27–40.

Finke, Roger, and Rodny Stark. 1998. "Religious Choice and Competition." *American Sociological Review* 63:761–766.

Finke, Roger, and Rodney Stark. 2005. *The Churching of America, 1776–2005: Winners and Losers in Our Religious Economy* (2nd ed.). New Brunswick, NJ: Rutgers University Press.

Flory, Richard, and Donald E. Miller. 2008. *Finding Faith: The Spiritual Quest of the Post-Boomer Generation.* New Brunswick, NJ: Rutgers University Press.

Francis, L. J., and P. Kaldor. 2002. "The Relationship Between Psychological Well-Being and Christian Faith and Practice in an Australian Population Sample." *Journal for the Scientific Study of Religion* 41:179–184.

Froese, Paul, and Christopher Bader. 2010. *America's Four Gods: What We Say about God and What That Says about Us.* New York: Oxford University Press.

Gallagher, Sally K. 2003. *Evangelical Identity and Gendered Family Life.* New Brunswick, NJ: Rutgers University Press.

Gallagher, Sally K. 2004. "Where Are the Anti-Feminist Evangelicals? Evangelical Identity, Subcultural Location and Attitudes Toward Feminism." *Gender & Society* 18:451–472.

Gallagher, Sally K. 2005. "Building Traditions: A Comparative Analysis of Space, Community and Theology in Three Christian Churches." *Review of Religious Research* 47:70–85.

Gallagher, Sally K. 2007. "Children as Religious Resources." *Journal for the Scientific Study of Religion* 46: 169–183.

Gallagher, Sally K. 2013. "Are Women More Religious Than Men? Gendered Narratives of Affiliation, Service, and Participation." Paper presented at the annual meeting of the Society for the Scientific Study of Religion, Boston, November 7–10.

Gallagher, Sally K., and Chelsey Newton. 2009. "Defining Spiritual Growth: Congregations, Community & Connectedness." *Sociology of Religion* 70: 232–261.

Gibson, John. 1987. "Jesus we Celebrate your Victory." Thankyou Music, 26–28.

Gillquist, Peter E. 1999. *Becoming Orthodox: A Journey to the Ancient Christian Faith.* Rev. ed. Ben Lomond, CA: Conciliar Press.

Gooren, Henri. 2007. "Reassessing Approaches to Conversion." *Journal for the Scientific Study of Religion* 46:337–353.

Gooren, Henri. 2010. *Religious Conversion and Disaffiliation: Tracing Patterns of Change in Faith Practices.* New York: Palgrave Macmillan.

Greven, Philip J. 1977. *The Protestant Temperament: Patterns of Child-Rearing, Religious Experience, and the Self in Early America.* New York: Knopf.

Hadaway, C. Kirk. 1989. "Identifying American Apostates: A Cluster Analysis." *Journal for the Scientific Study of Religion* 28:201–215.

Hadaway, C. Kirk, and Wade Clark Roof. 1988. "Apostasy in American Churches: Evidence from National Survey Data." In *Falling From the Faith: Causes and Consequences of Religious Apostasy*, edited by David Bromley, 29–46. Newbury Park, CA: Sage.

Hall, David. 1997. *Lived Religion in America: Toward a History of Practice.* Princeton, NJ: Princeton University Press.

Hamilton, Richard F., and William H. Form. 2003. "Categorical Usages and Complex Realities: Race Ethnicity and Religion in the United States." *Social Forces* 81:693–714.

Handy, Robert T. 1984. *Christian America: Protestant Hopes and Historical Realities.* New York: Oxford University Press.

Hardesty, Nancy. 1999. *Women Called to Witness: Evangelical Feminism in the Nineteenth Century.* 2nd ed. Knoxville: University of Tennessee Press.

Hodge, Dean R., and Jackson W. Carroll. 1978. "Determinants of Commitment and Participation in Suburban Protestant Churches." *Journal for the Scientific Study of Religion* (June), 107–128.

Hoffman, John P. 2009. "Gender, Risk, and Religiousness: Can Power Control Provide the Theory?" *Journal for the Scientific Study of Religion* 48:232–240.

Hopko, Thomas. 1984. *The Orthodox Faith, Volume 4: Spirituality.* New York: Orthodox Church in America Religious Education Department.

Iannaccone, Lawrence R., and Sean F. Everton. 2004. "Never on Sunny Days: Lessons from Weekly Attendance Counts," *Journal for the Scientific Study of Religion* 43:191–207.

Juster, Susan. 1994. *Disorderly Women: Sexual Politics and Evangelicalism in Revolutionary New England*. Ithaca, NY: Cornell University Press.

Kieckhefer, Richard. 2004. *Theology in Stone*. New York: Oxford University Press.

Kilde, Jeanne Halgren. 2002. *When Church Became Theatre*. New York: Oxford University Press.

Kimball, Dan. 2003. *The Emerging Church: Vintage Christianity for New Generations*. Grand Rapids, MI: Zondervan.

King, E. Frances. 2009. *Material Religion and Popular Culture*. New York and London: Routledge.

Kox, Willem, Wim Meeus, and Harm't Hart. 1991. "Religious Conversion of Adolescents: Testing the Lofland and Stark Model of Religious Conversion." *Sociological Analysis* 52:227–240.

Krause, Neal. 2003. "Religious Meaning and Subjective Well-Being in Late Life." *The Journals of Gerontology* 58:S160–S170.

Krause, Neal, Christopher Ellison, and Jack P. Marcum. 2002. "The Effects of Church-based Emotional Support on Health." *Sociology of Religion* 63:21–47.

Krindatch, Alexei. 2002. "Orthodox (Eastern Christian) Churches in the United States at the Beginning of a New Millennium." *Journal for the Scientific Study of Religion* 41:533–563.

Lawton, Lora, and Regina Bures. 2001. "Parental Divorce and the 'Switching' of Religious Identity." *Journal for the Scientific Study of Religion* 40:99–111.

Lofland, John. 1977. *Doomsday Cult*. New York: Irvington.

Lofland, John, and Rodney Stark. 1965. "Becoming a World-Saver." *American Sociological Review* 30:862–875.

Lofland, John, and Norman Skonovd. 1981. "Conversion Motifs." *Journal for the Scientific Study of Religion* 4:373–385.

Loveland, Matthew. 2003. "Religious Switching: Preference Development, Maintenance, and Change." *Journal for the Scientific Study of Religion* 42:147–157.

Maclean, Michael A., Lawrence J. Walker, and M. Kyle Matsuba. 2004. "Transcendence and the Moral Self: Identity Integration, Religion and Moral Life." *Journal for the Scientific Study of Religion* 43:429–437.

Manning, Cristel. 2015. *Losing Our Religion: How Unaffiliated Parents Are Raising Their Children*. New York: New York University Press.

Marsden, George. 1991. *Understanding Fundamentalism and Evangelicalism*. Grand Rapids, MI: Eerdmans.

Mathews-Green, Frederica. 1999. *At the Corner of East and Now*. New York: Tarcher/Putnam.

McDannell, Colleen. 1995. *Material Christianity: Religion and Popular Culture in America*. New Haven, CT: Yale University Press.

McGuire, Meredith B. 1990. *Religion and the Body: Rematerializing the Human Body in the Social Sciences of Religion*. New Haven, CT: Yale University Press.

McGuire, Meredith B. 2007. "Embodied Practices: Negotiation and Resistance." In *Everyday Religion: Observing Modern Religious Lives*, edited by Nancy Ammerman, 187–200. New York: Oxford University Press.

McGuire, Meredith. 2008. *Lived Religion: Faith and Practice in Everyday Life*. New York: Oxford University Press.

McKnight, Scot. "Five Streams of the Emerging Church." *Christianity Today* 51, January 19, 2007. http://www.christianitytoday.com/ct/2007/February/11.35.html (accessed October 4, 2016).

McLaren, Brian. 1998. *The Church on the Other Side: Doing Ministry in the Postmodern Matrix*. Grand Rapids, MI: Zondervan.

McLaren, Brian. 2003. *The Story We Find Ourselves In: Further Adventures of a New Kind of Christian*. San Francisco: Jossey-Bass.

Miller, Alan S., and Rodney Stark. 2002. "Gender and Religiousness: Can Socialization Explanations Be Saved?" *American Journal of Sociology* 107:1399–1423;

Musick, Marc, and John Wilson. 1995. "Religious Switching for Marriage Reasons." *Sociology of Religion* 56:257–270.

Neuhaus, Richard John. 1984. *The Naked Public Square*. Grand Rapids, MI: Eerdmans.

Newport, Frank. 1979. "The Religious Switcher in the United States." *American Sociological Review* 4:528–552.

Nock, Steven. 1998. *Marriage in Men's Lives*. New York: Oxford University Press.

Ozorak, Elizabeth Weiss. 2004. "Love of God and Neighbor: Religion and Volunteer Service among College Students." *Review of Religious Research* 44:285–299.

Peyrot, M., Sweeney, F. M. 2000. "Determinants of Parishioner Satisfaction among Practicing Catholics." *Sociology of Religion* 61:209–221.

Pew Research Center Forum on Religion & Public Life. 2014. *U.S. Religious Landscape Survey*. http://www.pewforum.org/religious-landscape-study (accessed October 4, 2016).

Regnerus, Mark D., Christian Smith, and Brad Smith. 2004. "Social Context in the Development of Adolescent Religiosity." *Applied Developmental Science* 8:27–38.

Roof, Wade Clark. 1993. *A Generation of Seekers: The Spiritual Journeys of the Baby Boomer Generation*. New York: Harper SanFrancisco.

Roof, Wade Clark. 2001. *Spiritual Marketplace*. Princeton, NJ: Princeton University Press.

Roof, Wade Clark, and Christopher Kirk Hadaway. 1979. "Denominational Switching in the Seventies: Going Beyond Stark and Glock." *Journal for the Scientific Study of Religion* 18:363–377.

Roof, Wade Clark, and William McKinney. 1987. *American Mainline Religion: Its Changing Shape and Future*. New Brunswick, NJ: Rutgers University Press.

Rose, Michael S. 2001. *Ugly as Sin*. Manchester, NH: Sophia Institute Press.

Sandomirsky, Sharon, and John Wilson. 1990. "Patterns of Disaffiliation: Religious Mobility among Men and Women." *Social Forces* 68: 1211–1229.

Schmemann, Alexander. 1998. *For the Life of the World*. Crestwood, NY: Saint Vladimir's Seminary Press.

Schnabel, Landon. 2015. "How Religious Are American Women and Men? Gender Differences and Similarities." *Journal for the Scientific Study of Religion* 54:616–622.

Shelley, Bruce. 1981. *A History of Conservative Baptists*. 3rd ed. Wheaton, IL: Conservative Baptist Press.

Shelton, Jason, and Michael O. Emerson. 2012. *Blacks and Whites in Christian America: How Racial Discrimination Shapes Religious Convictions*. New York: NYU Press.

Sherkat, Darren E. 1991. "Leaving the Faith: Testing Theories of Religious Switching Using Survival Models." *Social Science Research* 20:171–187.

Sherkat, Darren E., and John Wilson. 1995. "Preferences, Constraints, and Choices in Religious Markets: An Examination of Religious Switching and Apostasy." *Social Forces* 75:993–1026.

Sikkink, David. 2003. "Social Predictors of Retention in and Switching from the Religious Faith of Family of Origin." *Review of Religious Research* 45:188–206.

Skirbekk, Vegard, Eric Kaufmann, and Anne Goujon. 2010. "Secularism, Fundamentalism, or Catholicism? The Religious Composition of the United States to 2043." *Journal for the Scientific Study of Religion* 49:293–310.

Slagle, Amy. 2011. *The Eastern Church in the Spiritual Marketplace: American Conversions to Orthodox Christianity*. DeKalb, IL: Northern Illinois University Press.

Smidt, Corwin. 2013. *American Evangelicals Today*. Lanham, MD: Rowman & Littlefield.

Smith, Christian. 1998. *American Evangelicalism: Embattled and Thriving*. Chicago: University of Chicago Press.

Smith, Christian. 2000. *Christian America? What Evangelicals Really Want*. Berkeley: University of California Press.

Smith, Christian. 2003. *Moral, Believing Animals: An Essay on Human Personhood and Culture*. New York: Oxford University Press.

Smith, Christian, with Melinda Lundquist Denton. 2005. *Soul Searching: The Religious and Spiritual Lives of American Teenagers*. New York: Oxford University Press.

Smith, Christian, with Patricia Snell. 2009. *Souls in Transition: The Religious and Spiritual Lives of Emerging Adults*. New York: Oxford University Press.

Smith, Christian, and Robert Faris. 2005. "Socioeconomic Inequality in the American Religious System: An Update and Assessment." *Journal for the Scientific Study of Religion* 44:95–104.

Stark, Rodney. 2002. "Physiology and Faith: Addressing the 'Universal' Gender Difference in Religious Commitment." *Journal for the Scientific Study of Religion* 41:495–507.

Stark, Rodney, and Roger Finke. 2000. *Acts of Faith: Explaining the Human Side of Religion*. London: University of California Press.

Steensland, Brian, Jerry Z. Park, Mark Regnerus, Lynn D. Robinson, W. Bradford Wilcox, and Robert D. Woodberry 2000. "The Measure of American Religion: Toward Improving the State of the Art." *Social Forces* 79:291–318.

Stolzenberg, Ross, Mary Blair-Loy, and Linda Waite. 1995. "Age and Family Life Cycle Effects on Church Membership." *American Sociological Review* 60:84–103.

Stromberg, Peter. 1993. *Language and Self-Transformation: A Study of the Christian Conversion Narrative.* New York: Cambridge University Press.

Sullins, D. Paul. 2006. "Gender and Religion: Deconstructing Universality, Constructing Complexity." *American Journal of Sociology* 112:838–880.

Thomas, Jeremy N., and Daniel V. A. Olson. 2010. "Testing the Strictness Thesis and Competing Theories of Congregational Growth." *Journal for the Scientific Study of Religion* 49:619–639.

Tomlinson, Dave. 2003. *The Post-Evangelical.* Grand Rapids, MI: Zondervan.

Trzebiatowska, Marta, and Steve Bruce. 2012. *Why Are Women More Religious Than Men?* New York: Oxford University Press.

Vargas, Nicholas. 2012. "Retrospective Accounts of Religious Disaffiliation in the United States: Stressors, Skepticism, and Political Factors." *Sociology of Religion* 73:200–223.

Vitz, Rico, ed. 2012. *Turning East: Contemporary Philosophers and the Ancient Christian Faith.* Yonkers, NY: St. Vladimir's Seminary Press.

Ware, Kallistos Ware. 1995. *The Orthodox Way.* Rev. ed. Crestwood, NY: St. Vladimir's Seminary Press.

Ware, Kallistos. 2000. *The Inner Kingdom.* Crestwood, NY: St. Vladimir's Seminary Press.

Ware, Timothy. 2015. *The Orthodox Church.* 3rd ed. New York: Penguin.

Warner, R. Stephen. 1988. *New Wine in Old Wineskins.* Berkeley: University of California Press.

Warren, Rick. 2002. *The Purpose Driven Life.* Grand Rapids, MI: Zondervan.

Watt, David Harrington. 1991. *A Transforming Faith: Explorations of Twentieth-Century American Evangelicalism.* New Brunswick, NJ: Rutgers University Press.

Wellman, James K. 2002. "Religion Without a Net: Strictness in the Religious Practices of West Coast Urban Liberal Christian Congregations." *Review of Religious Research* 44:184–199.

Wellman, James K. 2008. *Evangelical vs Liberal: The Clash of Christian Cultures in the Pacific Northwest.* New York: Oxford University Press.

Welter, Barbara. 1976. *Dimity Convictions: The American Woman in the Nineteenth Century.* Athens: Ohio University Press.

White, James F. 2003. *Protestant Worship and Church Architecture.* Eugene, OR.: Wipf & Stock.

Wilcox, W. Bradford. 2004. *Soft Patriarchs, New Men: How Christianity Shapes Fathers and Husbands.* Chicago: University of Chicago Press.

Wilcox, W. Bradford, and Nicholas H. Wolfinger. 2016. *Soul Mates: Religion, Sex, Love and Marriage among African Americans and Latinos*. New York: Oxford University Press.

Wilson, John, and Darren E. Sherkat. 1994. "Returning to the Fold." *Journal for the Scientific Study of Religion* 33:148–161.

Winchester, Daniel. 2015 "Converting to Continuity: Temporality and Self in Eastern Orthodox Conversion Narratives." *Journal for the Scientific Study of Religion* 54:439–460.

Woodhead, Linda. 2008. "Gendering Secularization Theory." *Social Compass* 55:187–193.

Wuthnow, Robert. 1998. *After Heaven: Spirituality in America since the 1950s*. Berkeley: University of California Press.

Yamane, David 2012. "Initiation Rites in the Contemporary Catholic Church: What Difference Do They Make?" *Review of Religious Research* 54:401–420.

Yamane, David, and Sarah MacMillen, with Kelly Culver. 2006. *Real Stories of Christian Initiation: Lessons for and from the RCIA*. Collegeville, MN: Liturgical Press.

Index

37190208R00149

Made in the USA
San Bernardino, CA
28 May 2019